LUKE CAGE

EVERYMAN

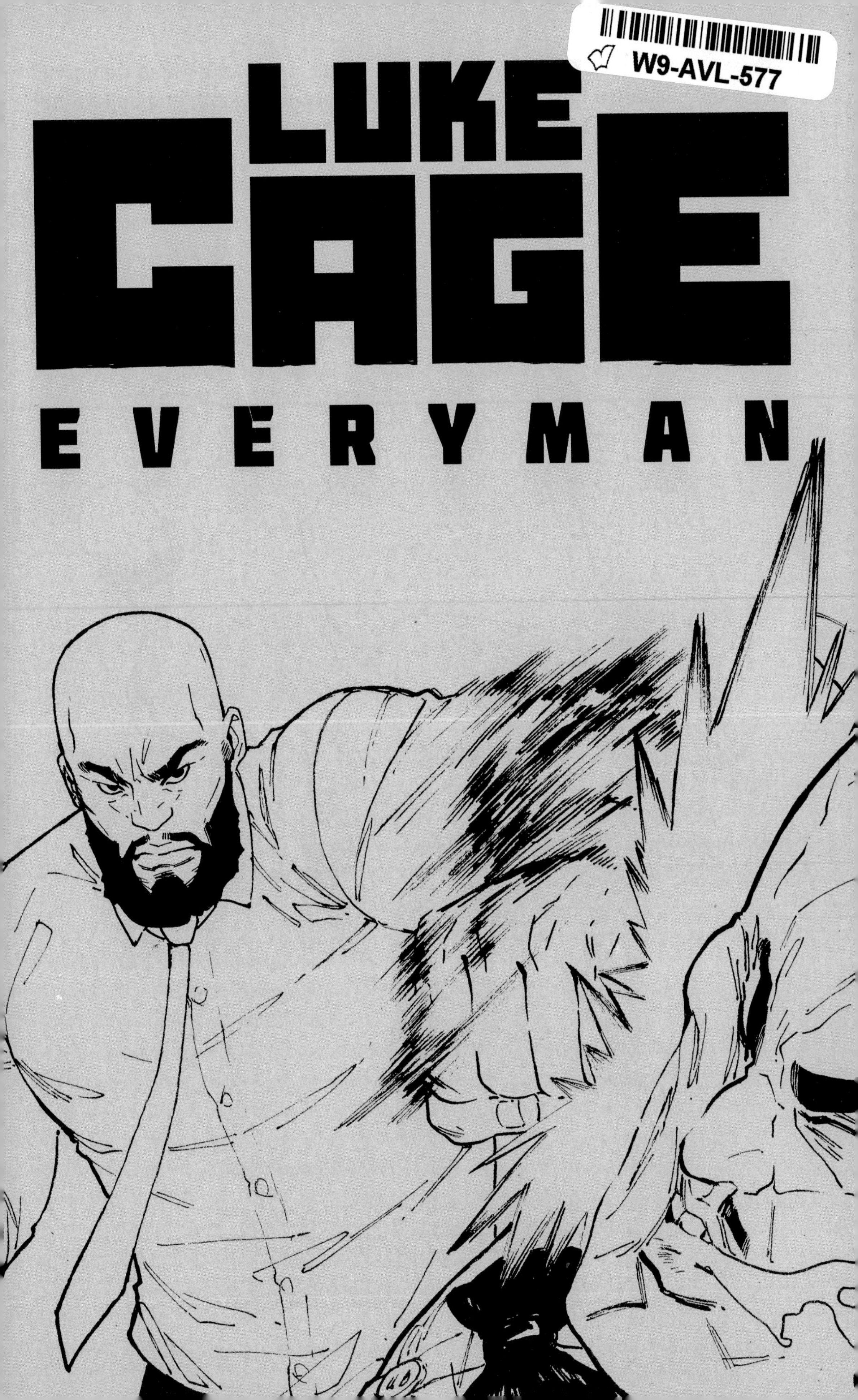

While imprisoned for a crime he did not commit, LUKE CAGE was subjected to medical experiments that gave him superhuman strength and bulletproof skin. Once free, he used his abilities to become a Hero for Hire, protecting people who had nowhere else to turn. His mission takes him all over the world, but he always finds his way back to his family and friends in Harlem.

LUKE CAGE: EVERYMAN. First printing 2018. ISBN 978-1-302-91291-8. Published by MARVEL WORLDWIDE, INC., a subsidiary of MARVEL ENTERTAINMENT, LLC. OFFICE OF PUBLICATION: 135 West 50th Street, New York, NY 10020. Copyright © 2018 MARVEL No similarity between any of the names, characters, persons, and/or institutions in this magazine with those of any living or dead person or institution is intended, and any such similarity which may exist is purely coincidental. **Printed in the U.S.A.** DAN BUCKLEY, President, Marvel Entertainment; JOHN NEE, Publisher; JOE QUESADA, Chief Creative Officer; TOM BREVOORT, SVP of Publishing; DAVID BOGART, SVP of Business Affairs & Operations, Publishing & Partnership; DAVID GABRIEL, SVP of Sales & Marketing, Publishing; JEFF YOUNGQUIST, VP of Production & Special Projects; DAN CARR, Executive Director of Publishing Technology; ALEX MORALES, Director of Publishing Operations; DAN EDINGTON, Managing Editor; SUSAN CRESPI, Production Manager; STAN LEE, Chairman Emeritus. For information regarding advertising in Marvel Comics or on Marvel.com, please contact Vit DeBellis, Custom Solutions & Integrated Advertising Manager, at vdebellis@marvel.com. For Marvel subscription inquiries, please call 888-511-5480. **Manufactured between 9/21/2018 and 10/23/2018 by LSC COMMUNICATIONS INC., KENDALLVILLE, IN, USA.**

10 9 8 7 6 5 4 3 2 1

LUKE CAGE
EVERYMAN

ANTHONY DEL COL
WRITER

JAHNOY LINDSAY
ARTIST

IAN HERRING
COLOR ARTIST

VC's CLAYTON COWLES
LETTERER

DECLAN SHALVEY & JORDIE BELLAIRE
COVER ART

ALANNA SMITH WITH **JAKE THOMAS & MARK BASSO**
EDITORS

TOM BREVOORT
EXECUTIVE EDITOR

COLLECTION EDITOR JENNIFER GRÜNWALD
ASSISTANT EDITOR CAITLIN O'CONNELL
ASSOCIATE MANAGING EDITOR KATERI WOODY
EDITOR, SPECIAL PROJECTS MARK D. BEAZLEY
VP PRODUCTION & SPECIAL PROJECTS JEFF YOUNGQUIST
SVP PRINT, SALES & MARKETING DAVID GABRIEL

BOOK DESIGNERS ADAM DEL RE WITH CARLOS LAO

EDITOR IN CHIEF C.B. CEBULSKI
CHIEF CREATIVE OFFICER JOE QUESADA
PRESIDENT DAN BUCKLEY
EXECUTIVE PRODUCER ALAN FINE

EVERYMAN

CHAPTER 1

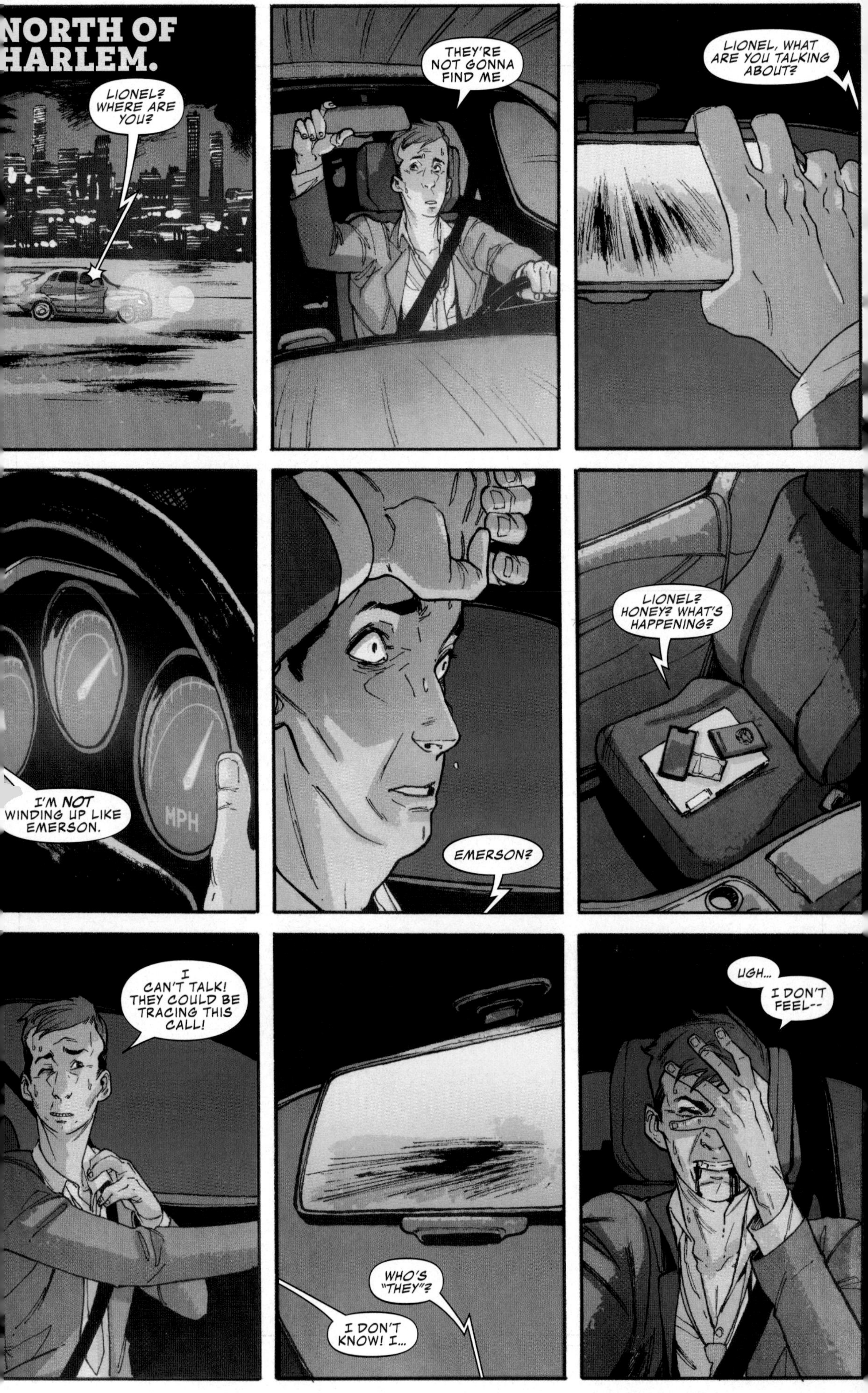
NORTH OF HARLEM.
LIONEL? WHERE ARE YOU?
THEY'RE NOT GONNA FIND ME.
LIONEL, WHAT ARE YOU TALKING ABOUT?
I'M NOT WINDING UP LIKE EMERSON.
EMERSON?
LIONEL? HONEY? WHAT'S HAPPENING?
I CAN'T TALK! THEY COULD BE TRACING THIS CALL!
WHO'S "THEY"?
I DON'T KNOW! I...
UGH...
I DON'T FEEL--

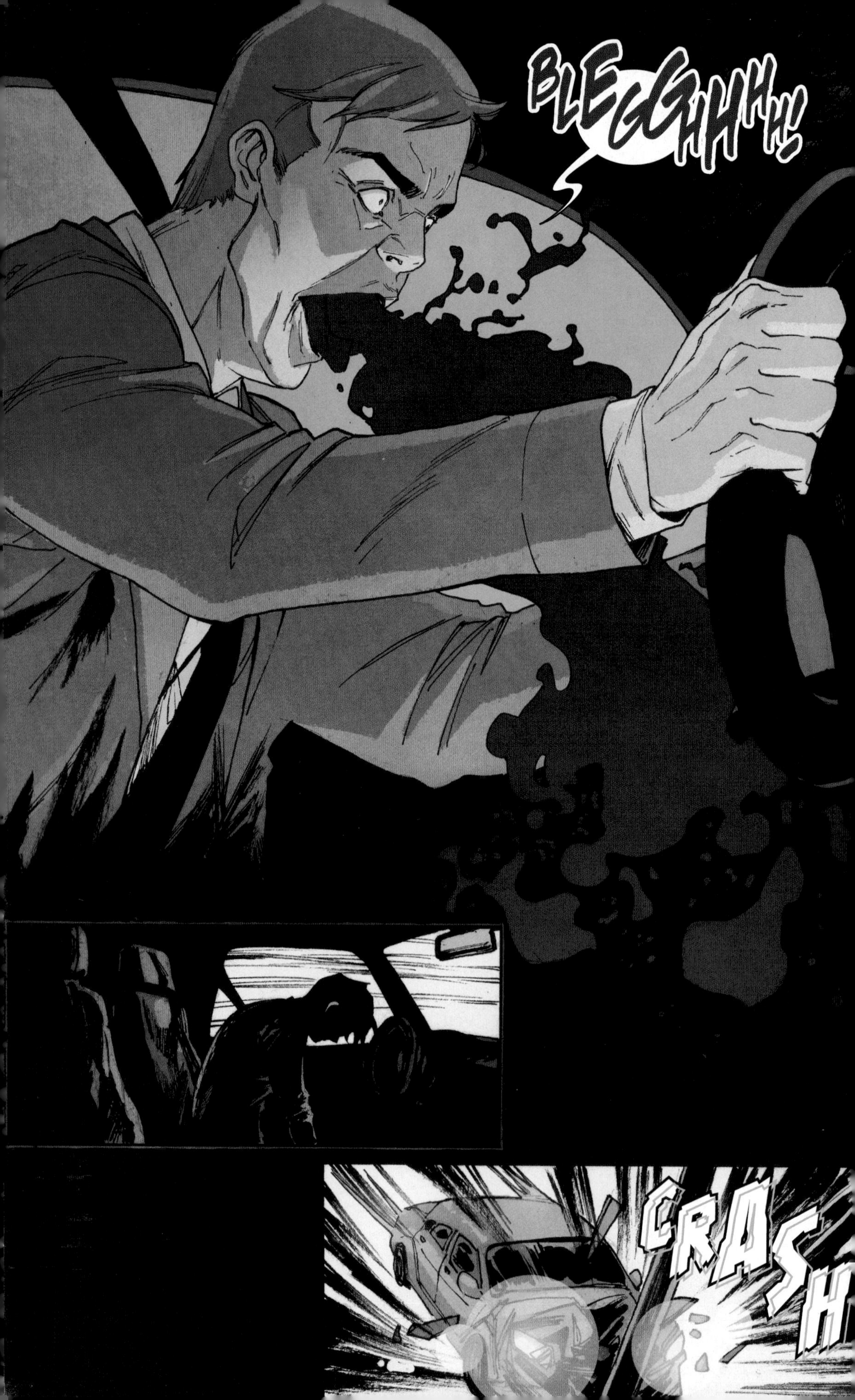
BLEGGHHHH!
CRASH

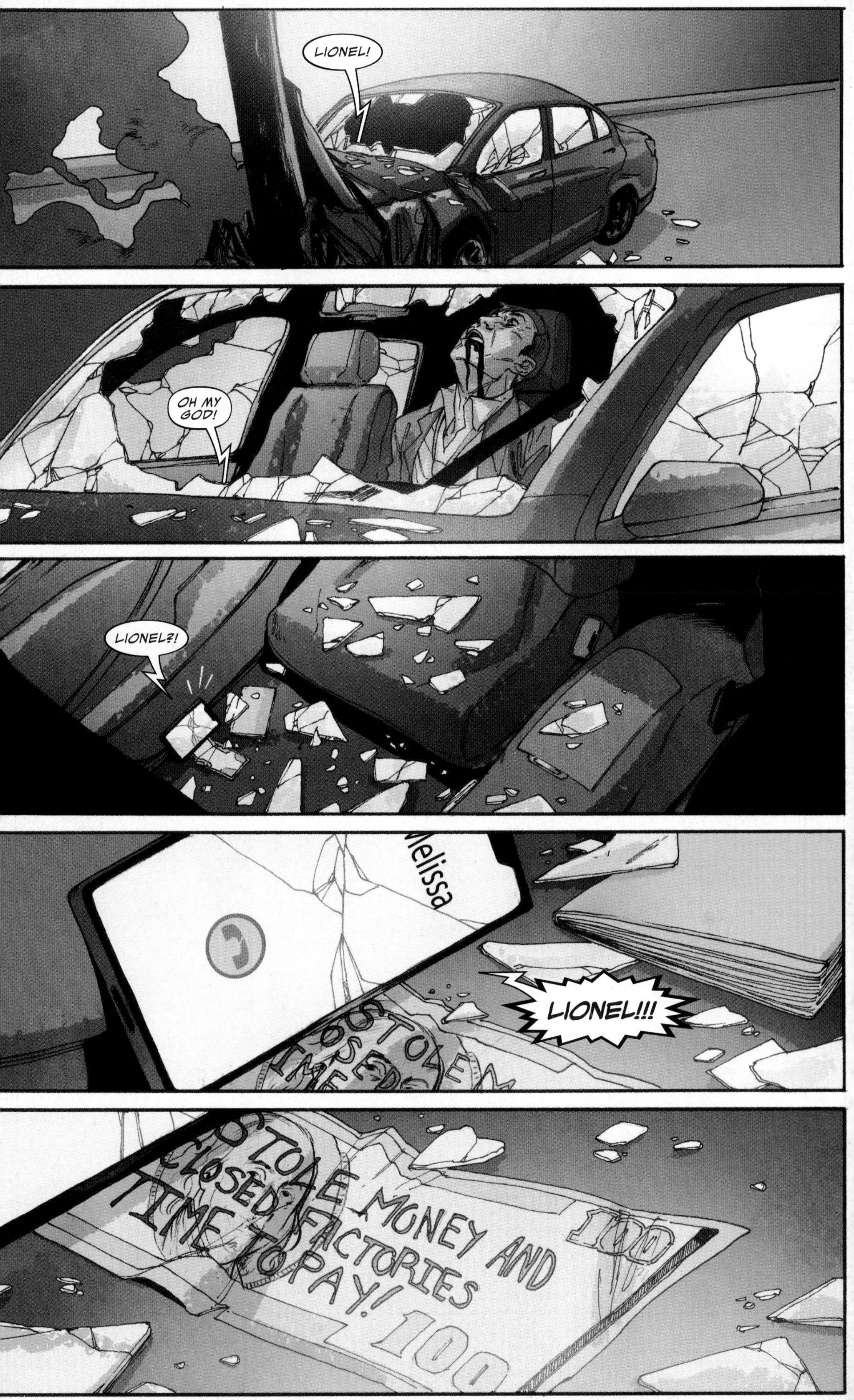
LIONEL!
OH MY GOD!
LIONEL?!
Melissa
LIONEL!!!
STOLE MONEY AND
CLOSED FACTORIES
TIME TO PAY!
100
100

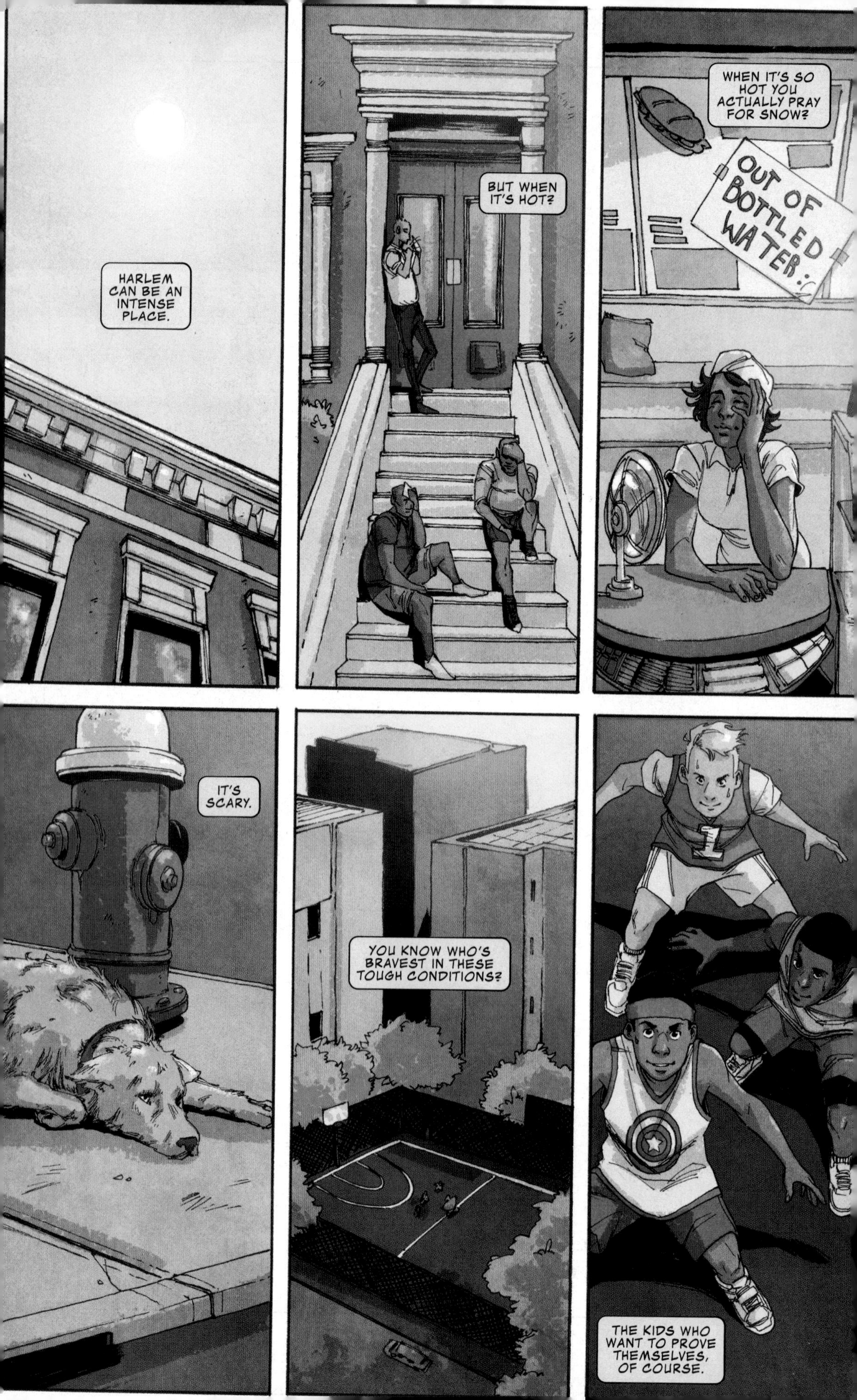
HARLEM CAN BE AN INTENSE PLACE.
BUT WHEN IT'S HOT?
WHEN IT'S SO HOT YOU ACTUALLY PRAY FOR SNOW?
OUT OF BOTTLED WATER :(
IT'S SCARY.
YOU KNOW WHO'S BRAVEST IN THESE TOUGH CONDITIONS?
THE KIDS WHO WANT TO PROVE THEMSELVES, OF COURSE.

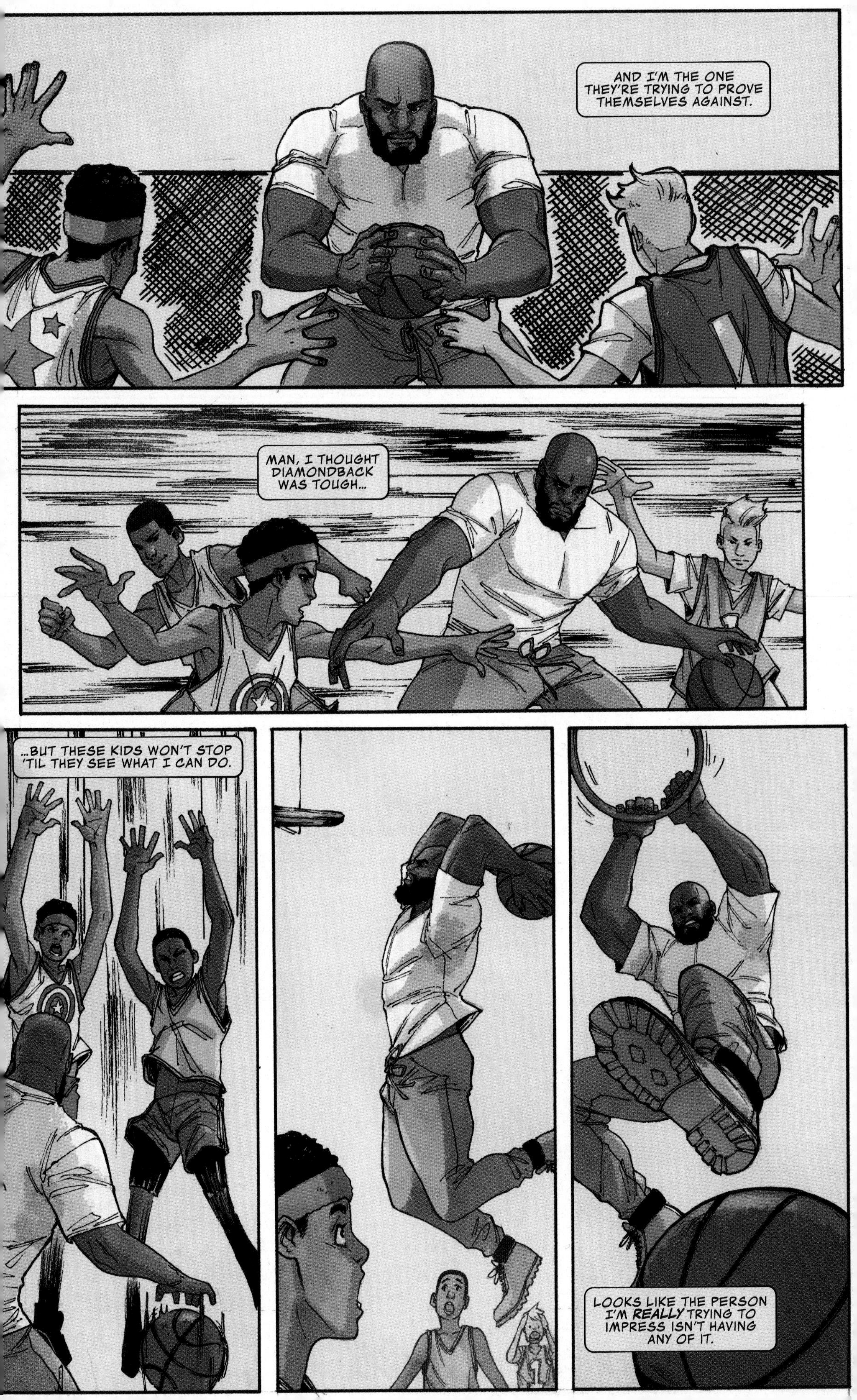
AND I'M THE ONE THEY'RE TRYING TO PROVE THEMSELVES AGAINST.
MAN, I THOUGHT DIAMONDBACK WAS TOUGH...
...BUT THESE KIDS WON'T STOP 'TIL THEY SEE WHAT I CAN DO.
LOOKS LIKE THE PERSON I'M *REALLY* TRYING TO IMPRESS ISN'T HAVING ANY OF IT.

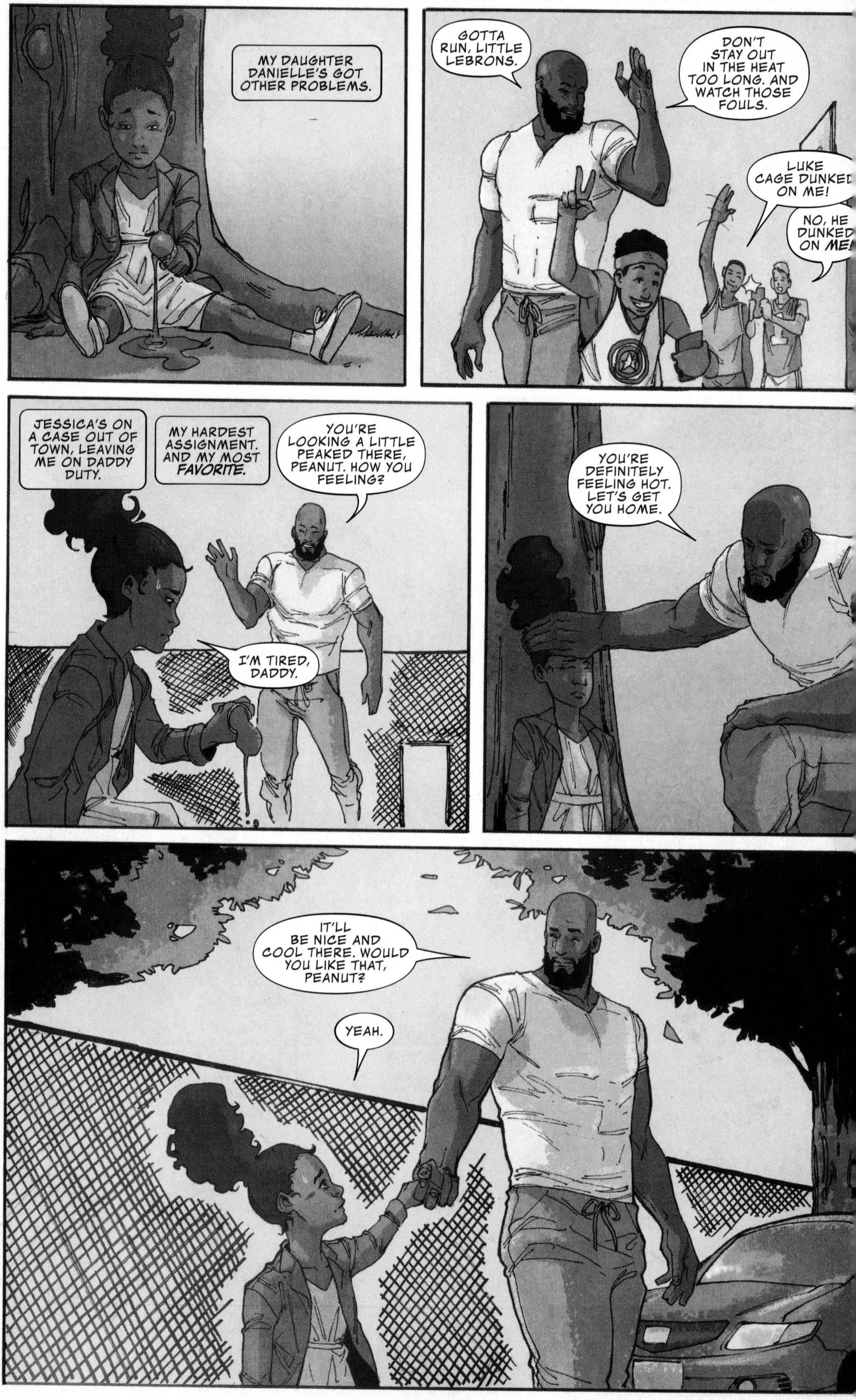
MY DAUGHTER DANIELLE'S GOT OTHER PROBLEMS.
GOTTA RUN, LITTLE LEBRONS.
DON'T STAY OUT IN THE HEAT TOO LONG. AND WATCH THOSE FOULS.
LUKE CAGE DUNKED ON ME!
NO, HE DUNKED ON ME!
JESSICA'S ON A CASE OUT OF TOWN, LEAVING ME ON DADDY DUTY.
MY HARDEST ASSIGNMENT. AND MY MOST FAVORITE.
YOU'RE LOOKING A LITTLE PEAKED THERE, PEANUT. HOW YOU FEELING?
I'M TIRED, DADDY.
YOU'RE DEFINITELY FEELING HOT. LET'S GET YOU HOME.
IT'LL BE NICE AND COOL THERE. WOULD YOU LIKE THAT, PEANUT?
YEAH.

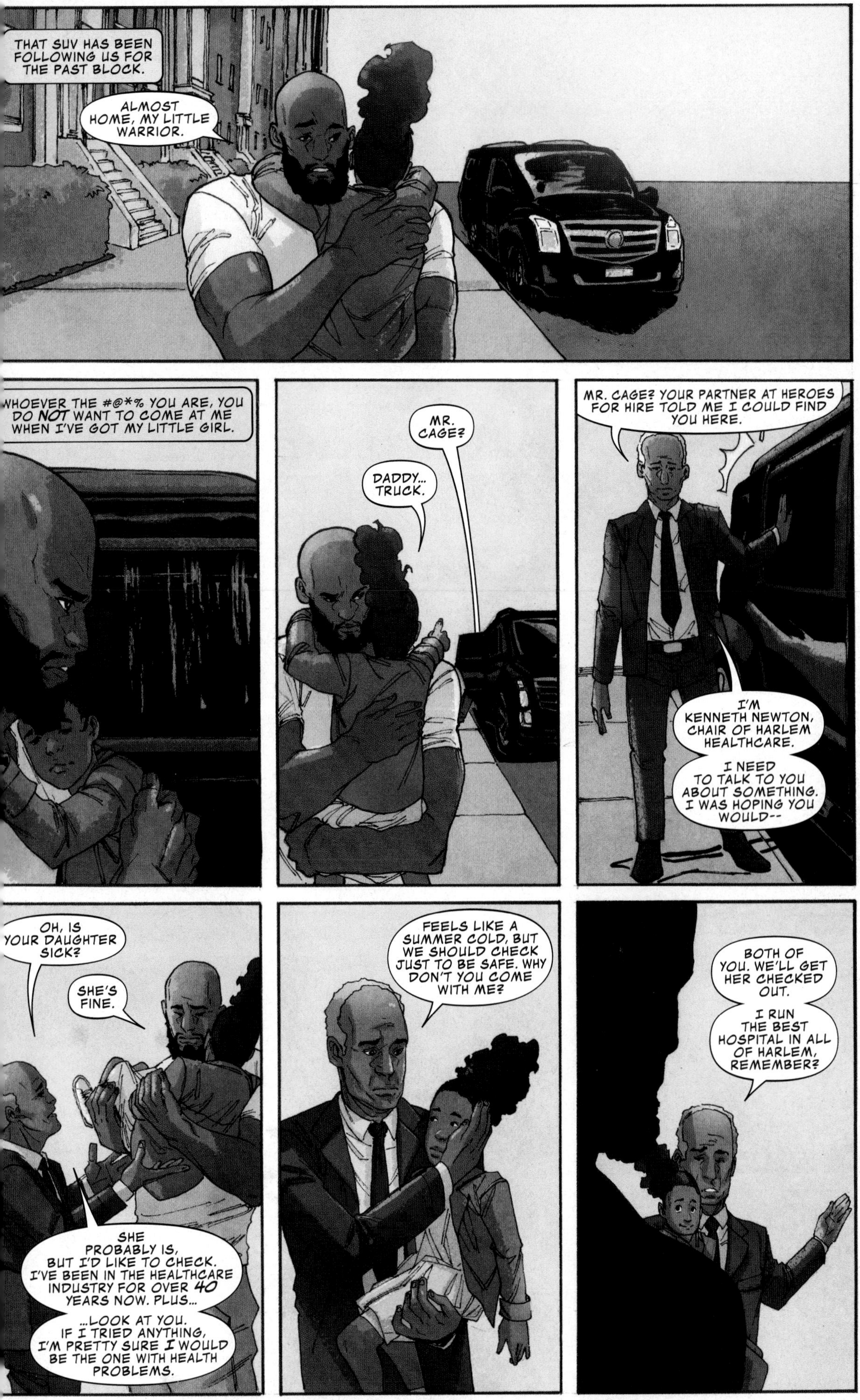
THAT SUV HAS BEEN FOLLOWING US FOR THE PAST BLOCK.
ALMOST HOME, MY LITTLE WARRIOR.
WHOEVER THE #@*% YOU ARE, YOU DO NOT WANT TO COME AT ME WHEN I'VE GOT MY LITTLE GIRL.
MR. CAGE?
DADDY... TRUCK.
MR. CAGE? YOUR PARTNER AT HEROES FOR HIRE TOLD ME I COULD FIND YOU HERE.
I'M KENNETH NEWTON, CHAIR OF HARLEM HEALTHCARE.
I NEED TO TALK TO YOU ABOUT SOMETHING. I WAS HOPING YOU WOULD--
OH, IS YOUR DAUGHTER SICK?
SHE'S FINE.
SHE PROBABLY IS, BUT I'D LIKE TO CHECK. I'VE BEEN IN THE HEALTHCARE INDUSTRY FOR OVER 40 YEARS NOW. PLUS...
...LOOK AT YOU. IF I TRIED ANYTHING, I'M PRETTY SURE I WOULD BE THE ONE WITH HEALTH PROBLEMS.
FEELS LIKE A SUMMER COLD, BUT WE SHOULD CHECK JUST TO BE SAFE. WHY DON'T YOU COME WITH ME?
BOTH OF YOU. WE'LL GET HER CHECKED OUT.
I RUN THE BEST HOSPITAL IN ALL OF HARLEM, REMEMBER?

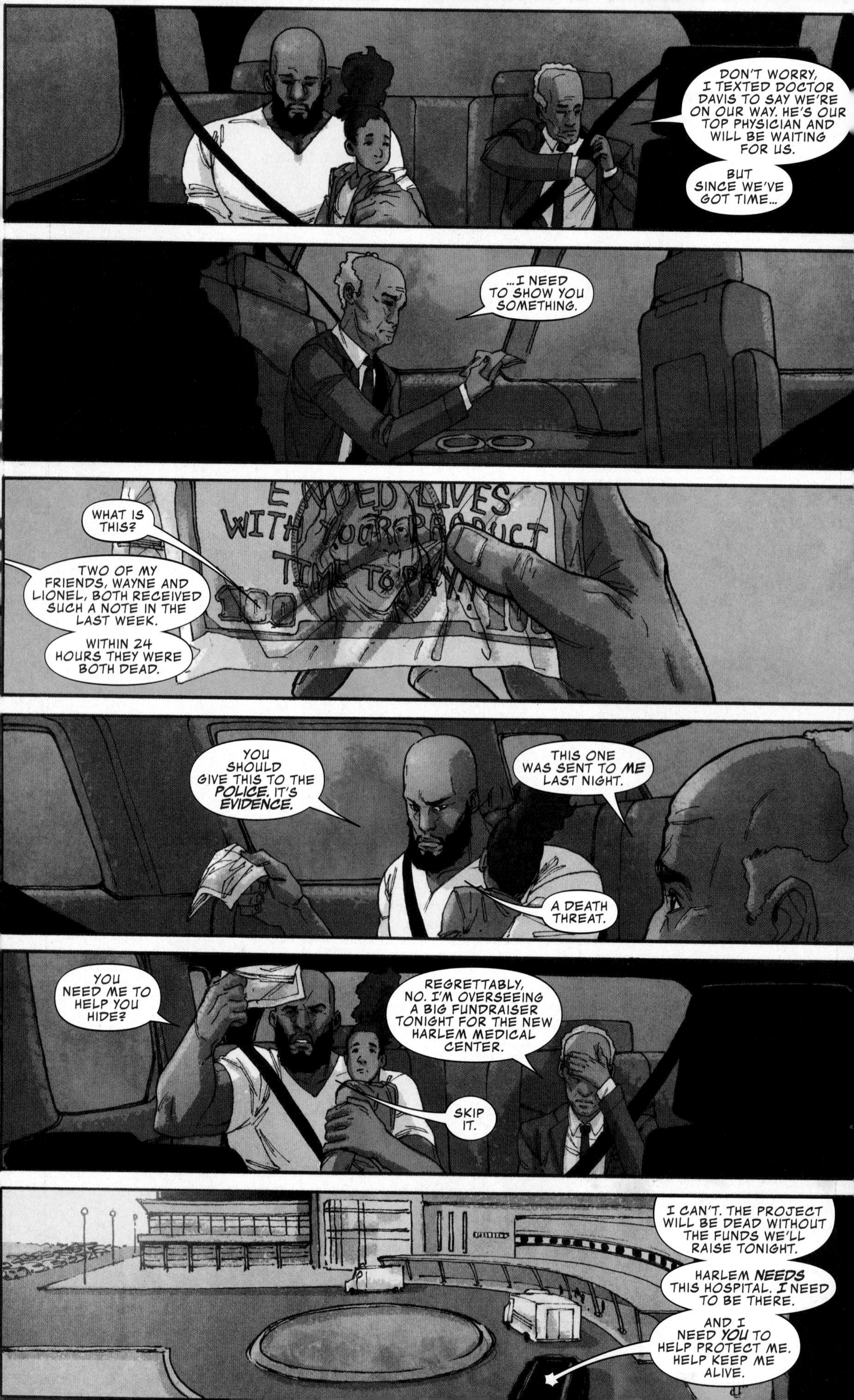
DON'T WORRY, I TEXTED DOCTOR DAVIS TO SAY WE'RE ON OUR WAY. HE'S OUR TOP PHYSICIAN AND WILL BE WAITING FOR US.
BUT SINCE WE'VE GOT TIME...
...I NEED TO SHOW YOU SOMETHING.
WHAT IS THIS?
TWO OF MY FRIENDS, WAYNE AND LIONEL, BOTH RECEIVED SUCH A NOTE IN THE LAST WEEK.
WITHIN 24 HOURS THEY WERE BOTH DEAD.
YOU SHOULD GIVE THIS TO THE POLICE. IT'S EVIDENCE.
THIS ONE WAS SENT TO ME LAST NIGHT.
A DEATH THREAT.
YOU NEED ME TO HELP YOU HIDE?
REGRETTABLY, NO. I'M OVERSEEING A BIG FUNDRAISER TONIGHT FOR THE NEW HARLEM MEDICAL CENTER.
SKIP IT.
I CAN'T. THE PROJECT WILL BE DEAD WITHOUT THE FUNDS WE'LL RAISE TONIGHT.
HARLEM NEEDS THIS HOSPITAL. I NEED TO BE THERE.
AND I NEED YOU TO HELP PROTECT ME. HELP KEEP ME ALIVE.

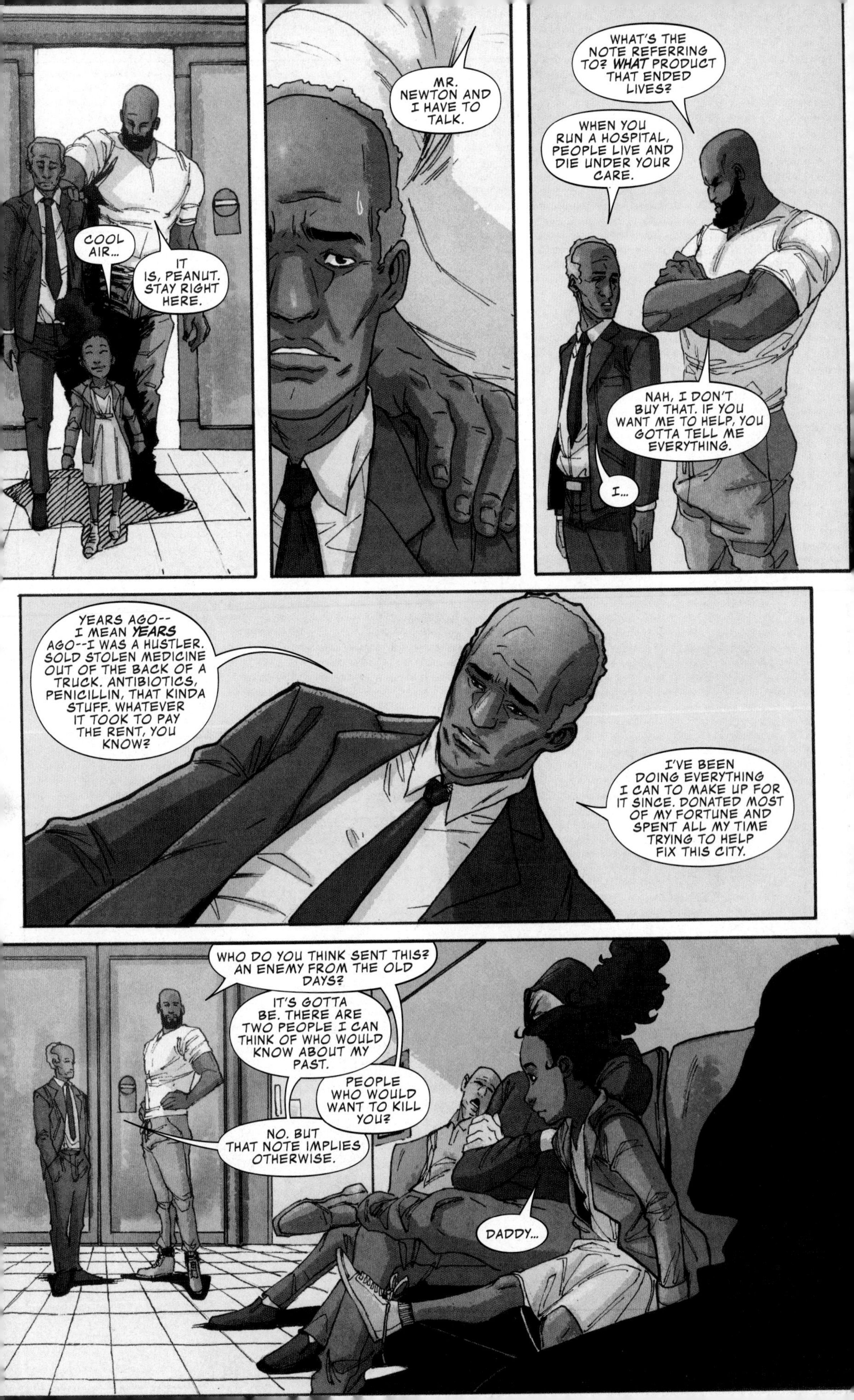
COOL AIR...
IT IS, PEANUT. STAY RIGHT HERE.
MR. NEWTON AND I HAVE TO TALK.
WHAT'S THE NOTE REFERRING TO? WHAT PRODUCT THAT ENDED LIVES?
WHEN YOU RUN A HOSPITAL, PEOPLE LIVE AND DIE UNDER YOUR CARE.
NAH, I DON'T BUY THAT. IF YOU WANT ME TO HELP, YOU GOTTA TELL ME EVERYTHING.
I...
YEARS AGO-- I MEAN YEARS AGO--I WAS A HUSTLER. SOLD STOLEN MEDICINE OUT OF THE BACK OF A TRUCK. ANTIBIOTICS, PENICILLIN, THAT KINDA STUFF. WHATEVER IT TOOK TO PAY THE RENT, YOU KNOW?
I'VE BEEN DOING EVERYTHING I CAN TO MAKE UP FOR IT SINCE. DONATED MOST OF MY FORTUNE AND SPENT ALL MY TIME TRYING TO HELP FIX THIS CITY.
WHO DO YOU THINK SENT THIS? AN ENEMY FROM THE OLD DAYS?
IT'S GOTTA BE. THERE ARE TWO PEOPLE I CAN THINK OF WHO WOULD KNOW ABOUT MY PAST.
PEOPLE WHO WOULD WANT TO KILL YOU?
NO. BUT THAT NOTE IMPLIES OTHERWISE.
DADDY...

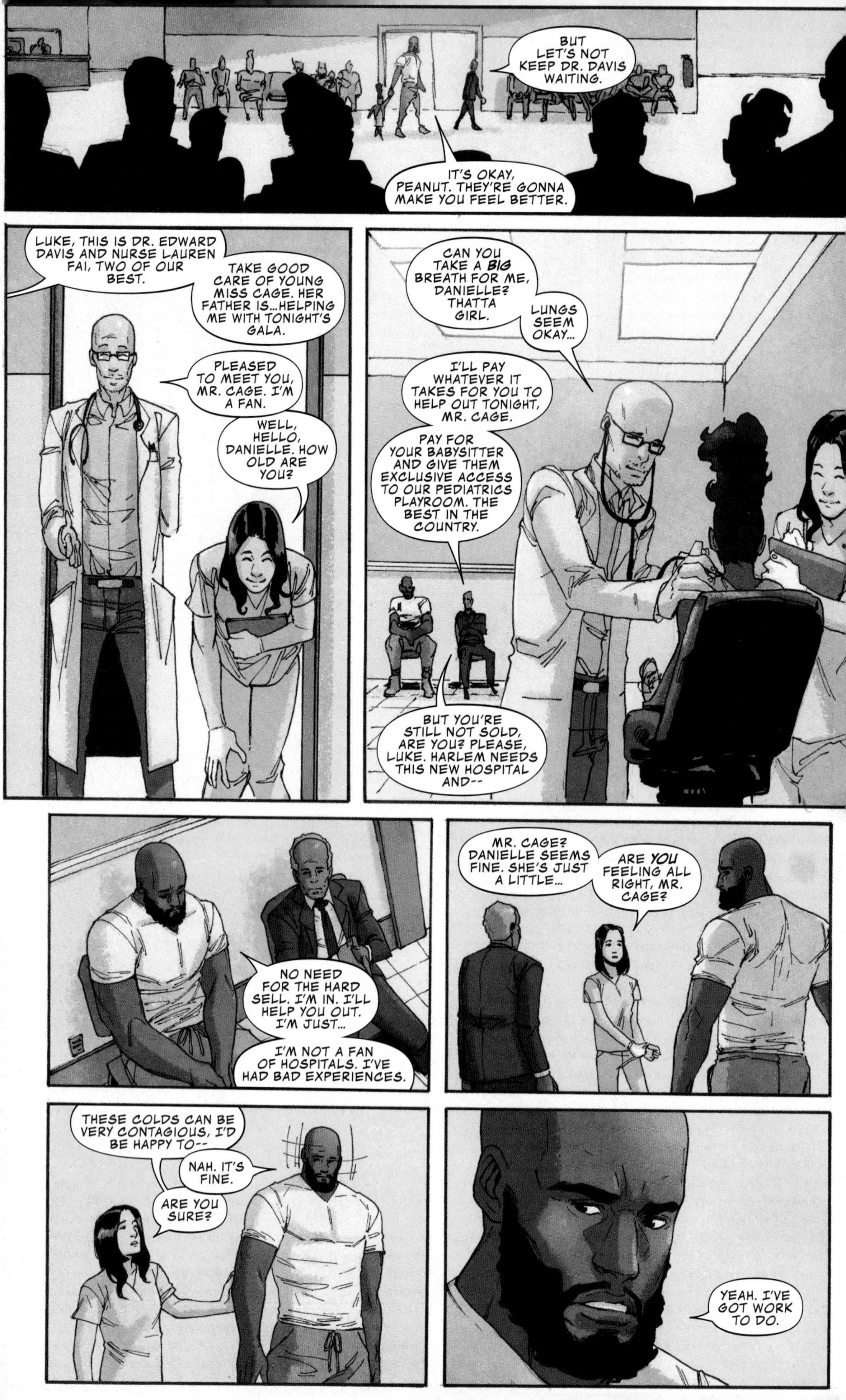

BUT LET'S NOT KEEP DR. DAVIS WAITING.
IT'S OKAY, PEANUT. THEY'RE GONNA MAKE YOU FEEL BETTER.
LUKE, THIS IS DR. EDWARD DAVIS AND NURSE LAUREN FAI, TWO OF OUR BEST.
TAKE GOOD CARE OF YOUNG MISS CAGE. HER FATHER IS...HELPING ME WITH TONIGHT'S GALA.
PLEASED TO MEET YOU, MR. CAGE. I'M A FAN.
WELL, HELLO, DANIELLE. HOW OLD ARE YOU?
CAN YOU TAKE A BIG BREATH FOR ME, DANIELLE? THATTA GIRL.
LUNGS SEEM OKAY...
I'LL PAY WHATEVER IT TAKES FOR YOU TO HELP OUT TONIGHT, MR. CAGE.
PAY FOR YOUR BABYSITTER AND GIVE THEM EXCLUSIVE ACCESS TO OUR PEDIATRICS PLAYROOM. THE BEST IN THE COUNTRY.
BUT YOU'RE STILL NOT SOLD, ARE YOU? PLEASE, LUKE. HARLEM NEEDS THIS NEW HOSPITAL AND--
NO NEED FOR THE HARD SELL. I'M IN. I'LL HELP YOU OUT. I'M JUST...
I'M NOT A FAN OF HOSPITALS. I'VE HAD BAD EXPERIENCES.
MR. CAGE? DANIELLE SEEMS FINE. SHE'S JUST A LITTLE...
ARE YOU FEELING ALL RIGHT, MR. CAGE?
THESE COLDS CAN BE VERY CONTAGIOUS, I'D BE HAPPY TO--
NAH. IT'S FINE.
ARE YOU SURE?
YEAH. I'VE GOT WORK TO DO.

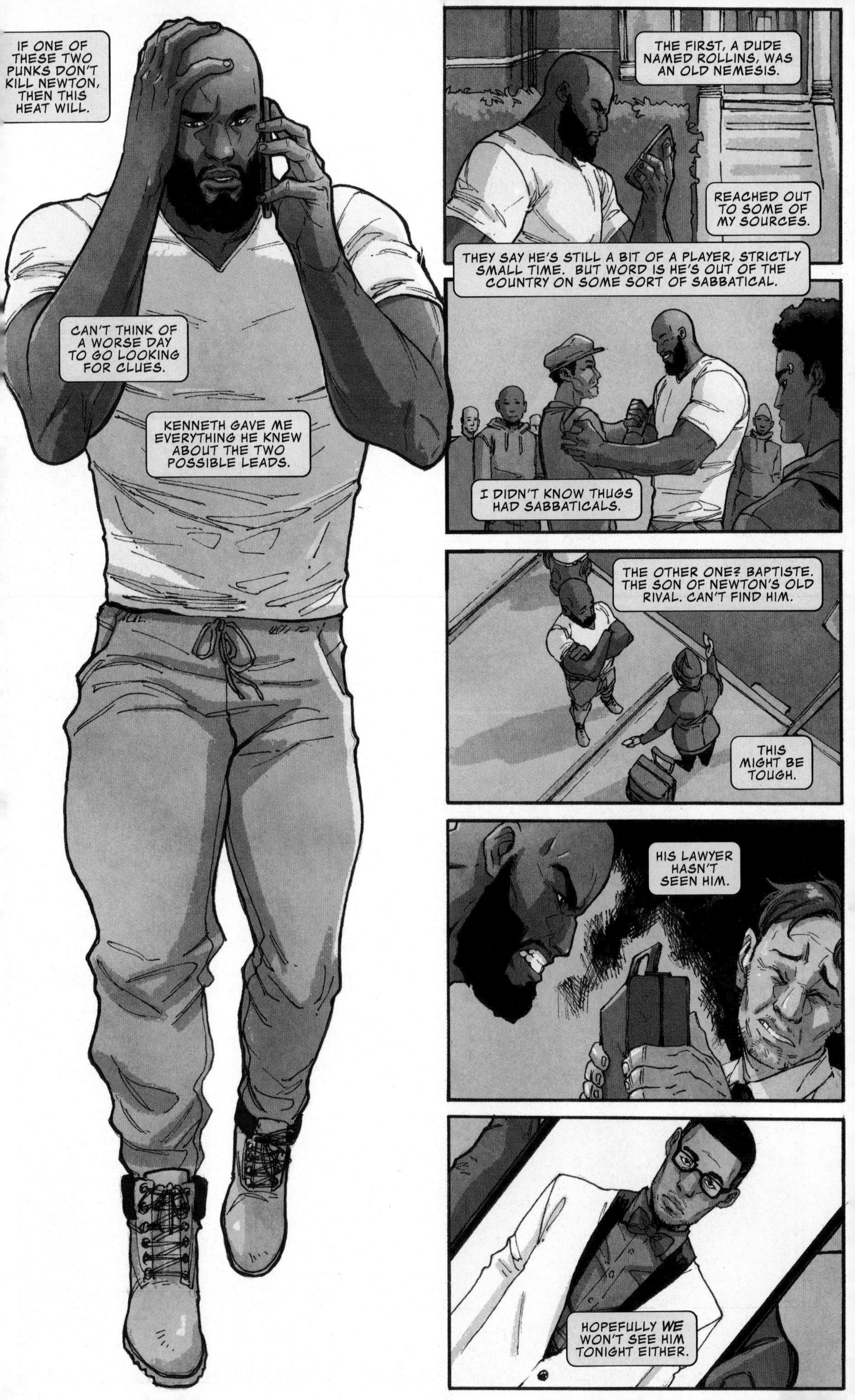
IF ONE OF THESE TWO PUNKS DON'T KILL NEWTON, THEN THIS HEAT WILL.
CAN'T THINK OF A WORSE DAY TO GO LOOKING FOR CLUES.
KENNETH GAVE ME EVERYTHING HE KNEW ABOUT THE TWO POSSIBLE LEADS.
THE FIRST, A DUDE NAMED ROLLINS, WAS AN OLD NEMESIS.
REACHED OUT TO SOME OF MY SOURCES.
THEY SAY HE'S STILL A BIT OF A PLAYER, STRICTLY SMALL TIME. BUT WORD IS HE'S OUT OF THE COUNTRY ON SOME SORT OF SABBATICAL.
I DIDN'T KNOW THUGS HAD SABBATICALS.
THE OTHER ONE? BAPTISTE. THE SON OF NEWTON'S OLD RIVAL. CAN'T FIND HIM.
THIS MIGHT BE TOUGH.
HIS LAWYER HASN'T SEEN HIM.
HOPEFULLY WE WON'T SEE HIM TONIGHT EITHER.

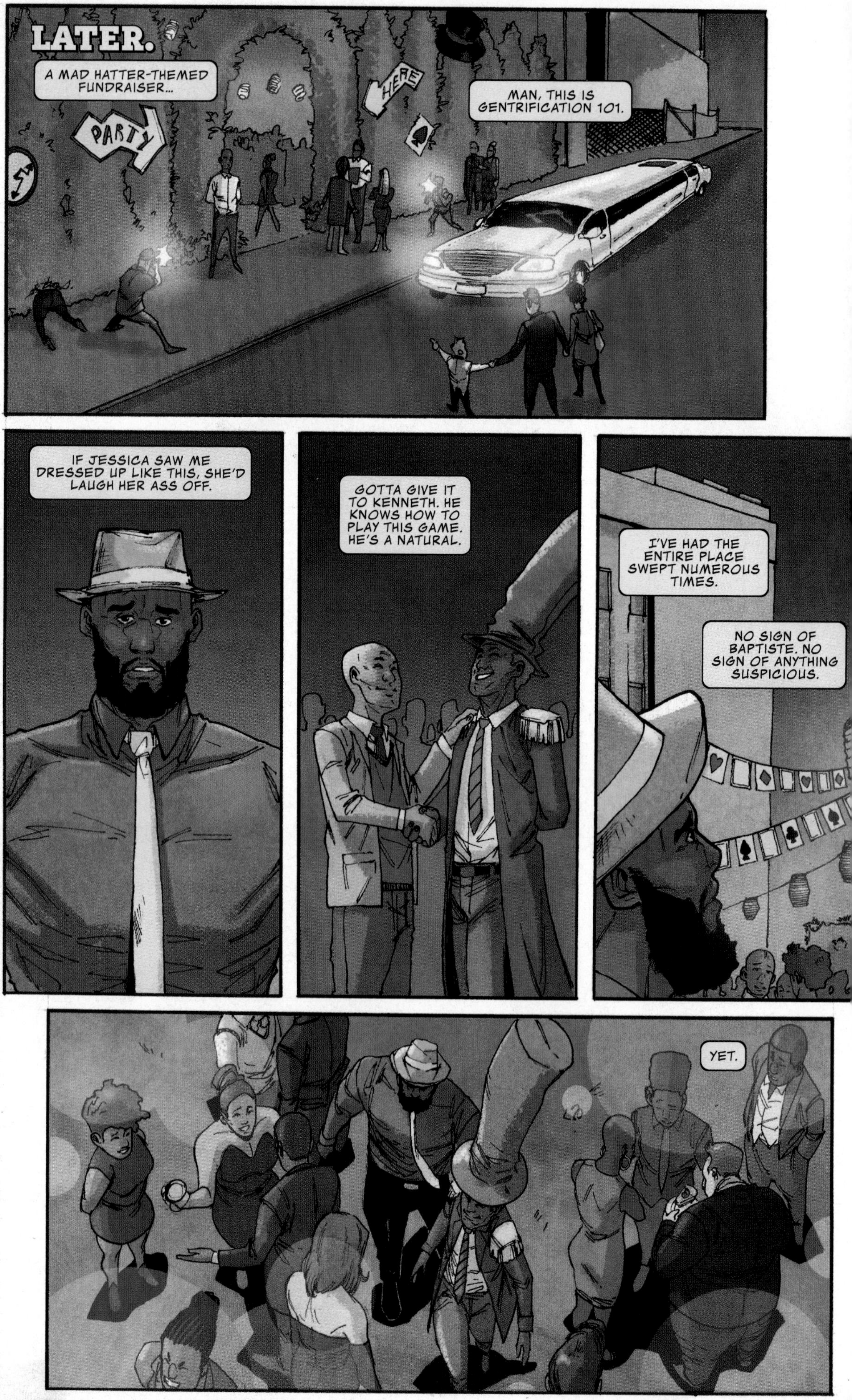
LATER.
A MAD HATTER-THEMED FUNDRAISER...
PARTY
HERE
MAN, THIS IS GENTRIFICATION 101.
IF JESSICA SAW ME DRESSED UP LIKE THIS, SHE'D LAUGH HER ASS OFF.
GOTTA GIVE IT TO KENNETH. HE KNOWS HOW TO PLAY THIS GAME. HE'S A NATURAL.
I'VE HAD THE ENTIRE PLACE SWEPT NUMEROUS TIMES.
NO SIGN OF BAPTISTE. NO SIGN OF ANYTHING SUSPICIOUS.
YET.

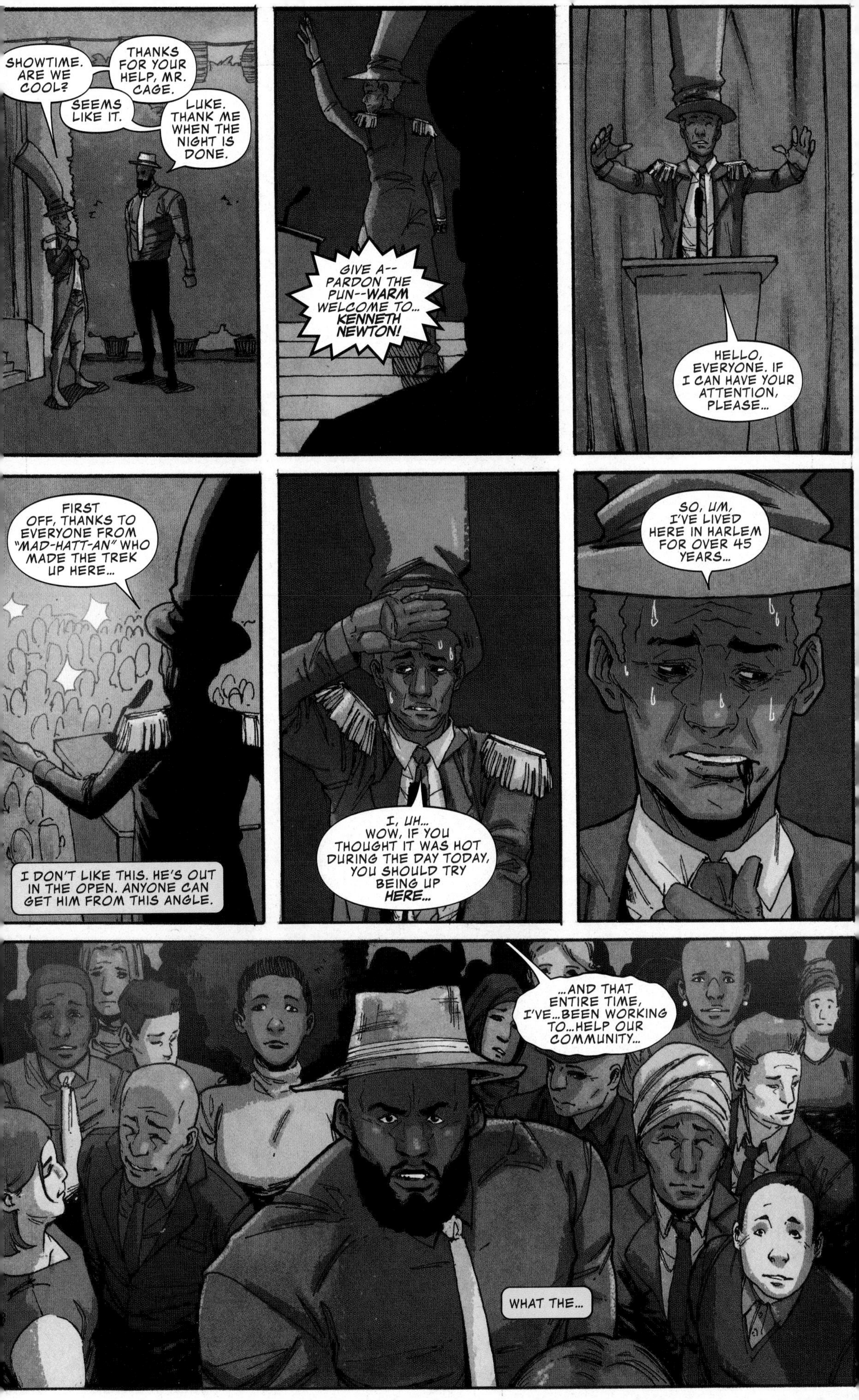
SHOWTIME. ARE WE COOL?
THANKS FOR YOUR HELP, MR. CAGE.
SEEMS LIKE IT.
LUKE. THANK ME WHEN THE NIGHT IS DONE.
GIVE A-- PARDON THE PUN--WARM WELCOME TO... KENNETH NEWTON!
HELLO, EVERYONE. IF I CAN HAVE YOUR ATTENTION, PLEASE...
FIRST OFF, THANKS TO EVERYONE FROM "MAD-HATT-AN" WHO MADE THE TREK UP HERE...
I DON'T LIKE THIS. HE'S OUT IN THE OPEN. ANYONE CAN GET HIM FROM THIS ANGLE.
I, UH... WOW, IF YOU THOUGHT IT WAS HOT DURING THE DAY TODAY, YOU SHOULD TRY BEING UP HERE...
SO, UM, I'VE LIVED HERE IN HARLEM FOR OVER 45 YEARS...
...AND THAT ENTIRE TIME, I'VE...BEEN WORKING TO...HELP OUR COMMUNITY...
WHAT THE...

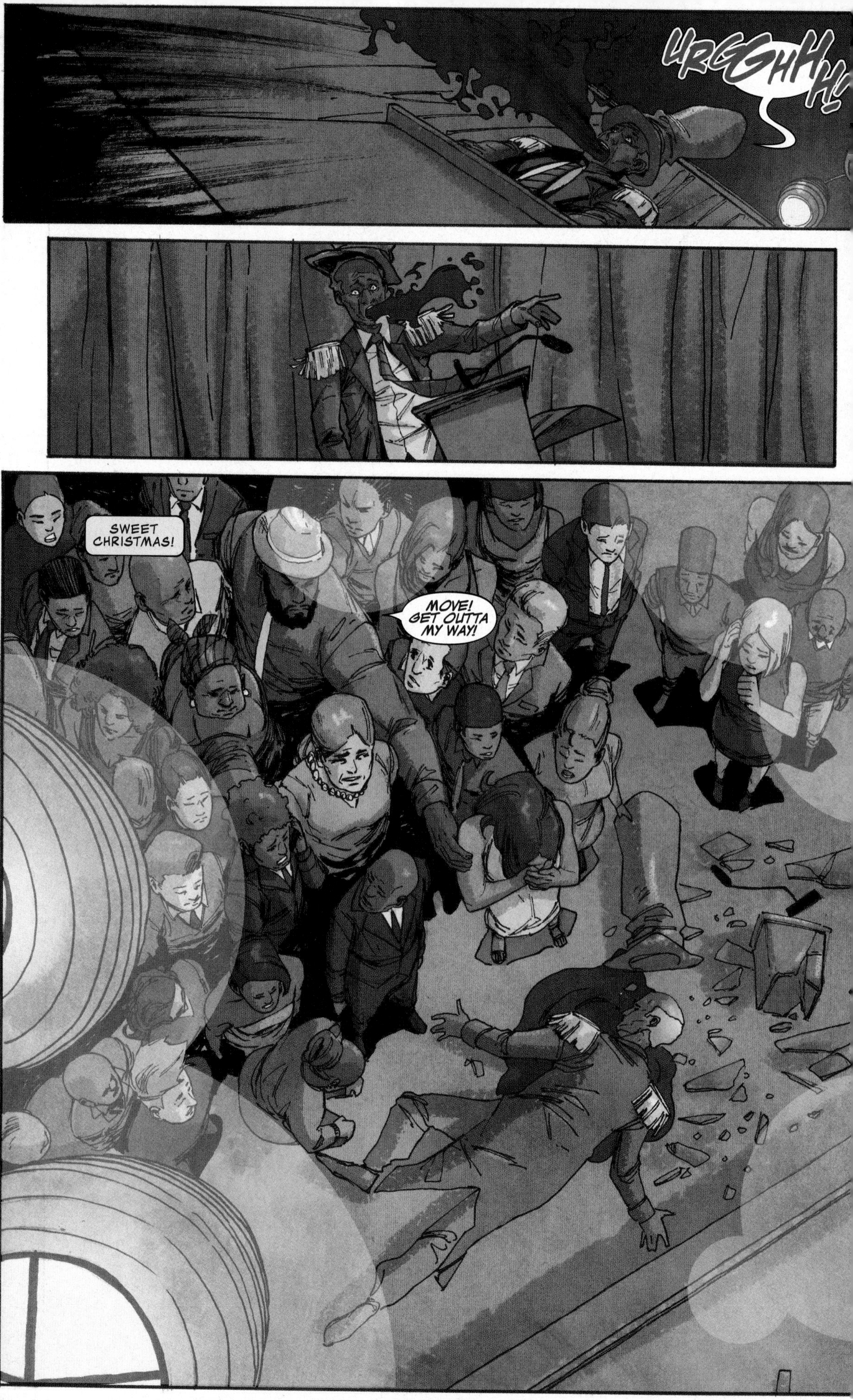
URGGHHH!
SWEET CHRISTMAS!
MOVE! GET OUTTA MY WAY!

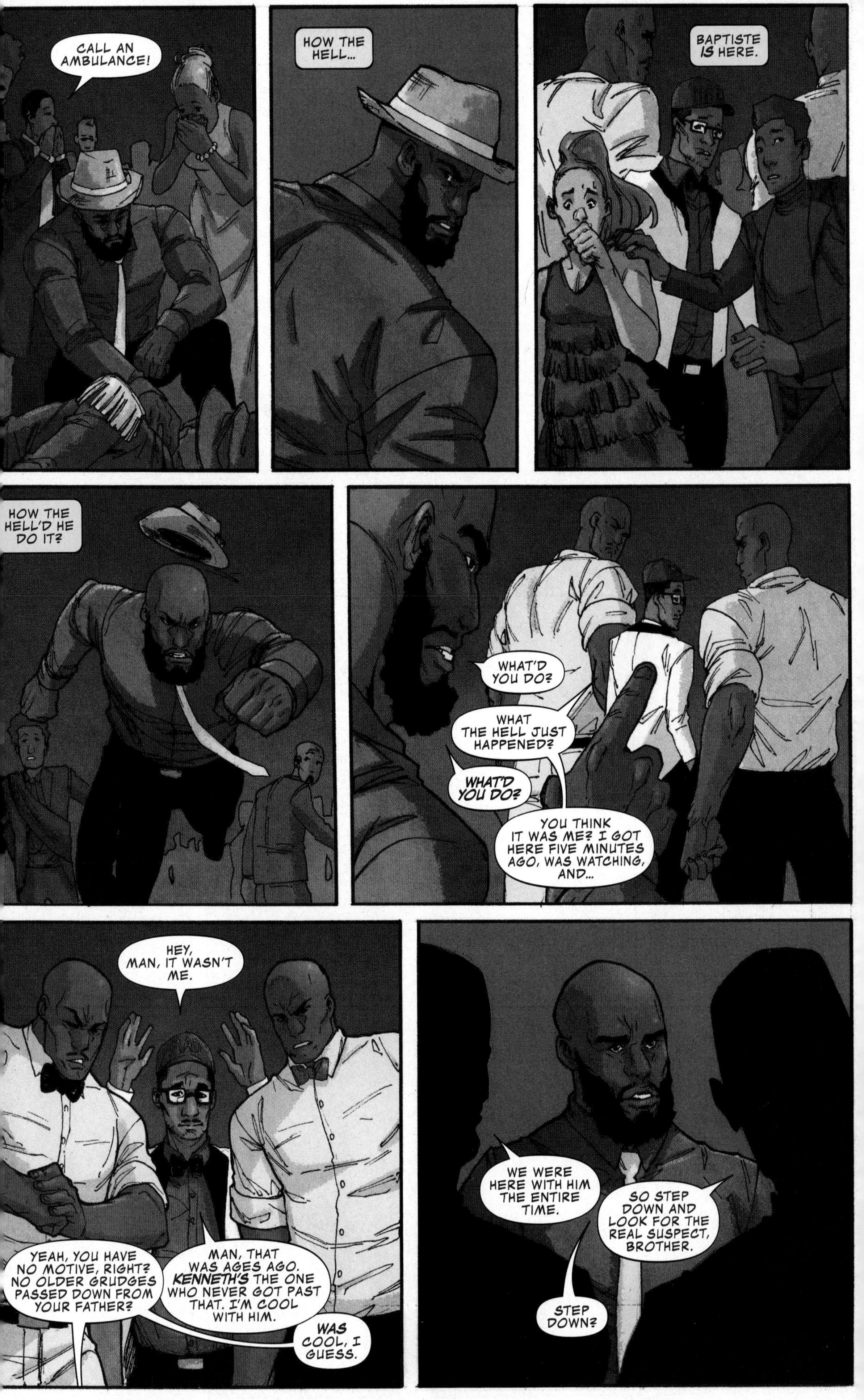
CALL AN AMBULANCE!
HOW THE HELL...
BAPTISTE IS HERE.
HOW THE HELL'D HE DO IT?
WHAT'D YOU DO?
WHAT THE HELL JUST HAPPENED?
WHAT'D YOU DO?
YOU THINK IT WAS ME? I GOT HERE FIVE MINUTES AGO, WAS WATCHING, AND...
HEY, MAN, IT WASN'T ME.
YEAH, YOU HAVE NO MOTIVE, RIGHT? NO OLDER GRUDGES PASSED DOWN FROM YOUR FATHER?
MAN, THAT WAS AGES AGO. KENNETH'S THE ONE WHO NEVER GOT PAST THAT. I'M COOL WITH HIM.
WAS COOL, I GUESS.
WE WERE HERE WITH HIM THE ENTIRE TIME.
SO STEP DOWN AND LOOK FOR THE REAL SUSPECT, BROTHER.
STEP DOWN?

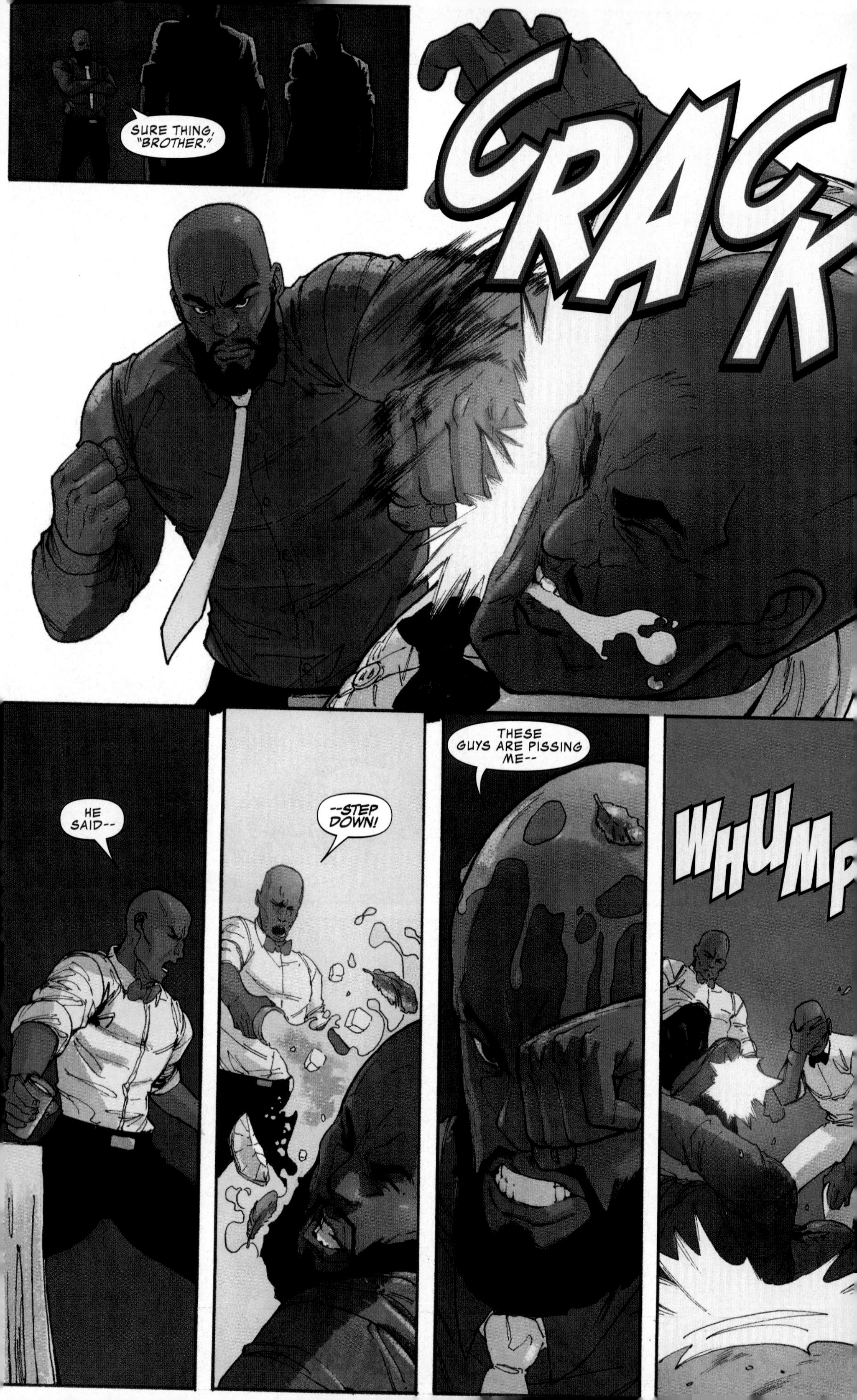
SURE THING, "BROTHER."
CRACK
HE SAID--
--STEP DOWN!
THESE GUYS ARE PISSING ME--
WHUMP

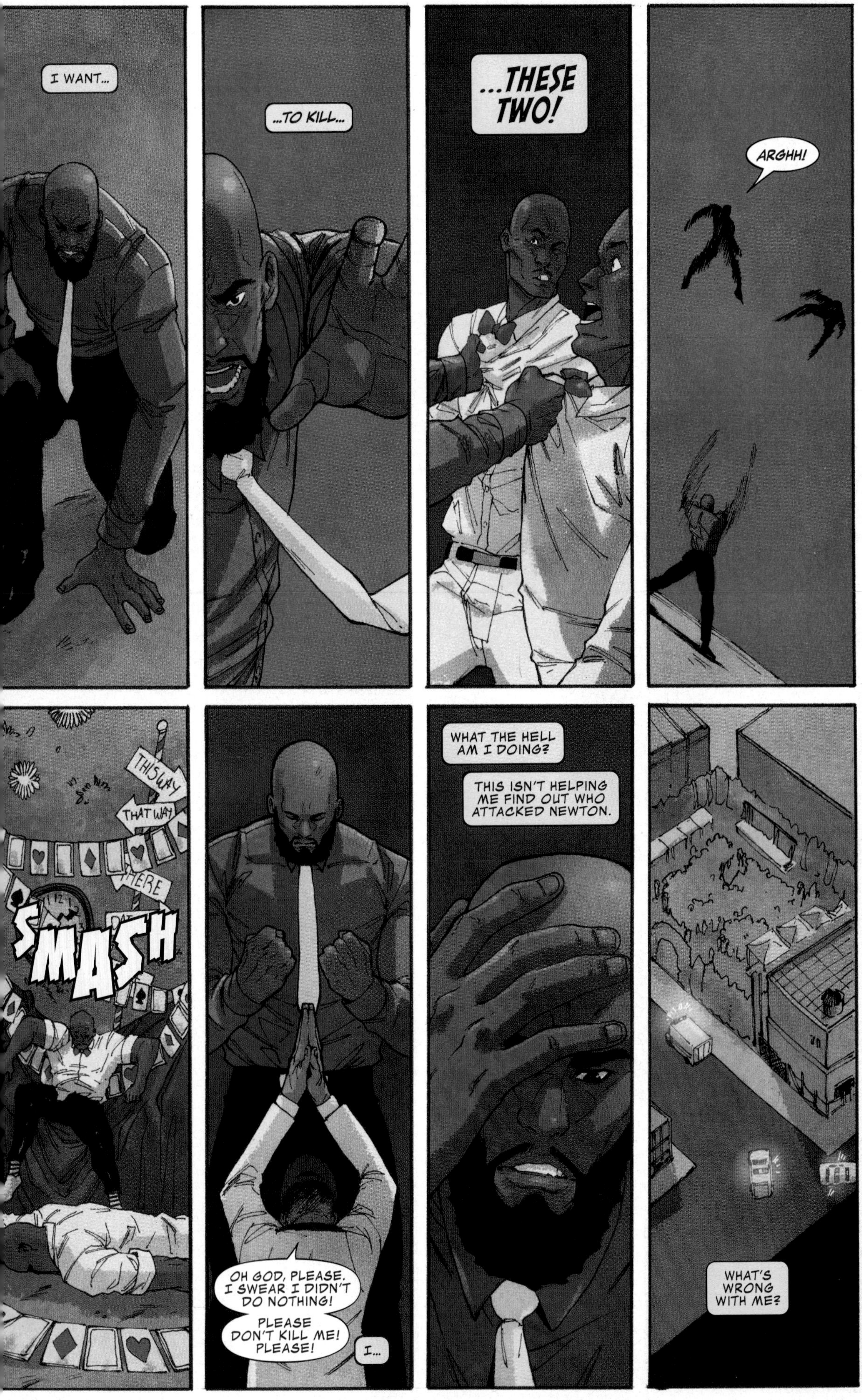
I WANT...
...TO KILL...
...THESE TWO!
ARGHH!
THIS WAY
THAT WAY
HERE
SMASH
OH GOD, PLEASE. I SWEAR I DIDN'T DO NOTHING!
PLEASE DON'T KILL ME! PLEASE!
I...
WHAT THE HELL AM I DOING?
THIS ISN'T HELPING ME FIND OUT WHO ATTACKED NEWTON.
WHAT'S WRONG WITH ME?

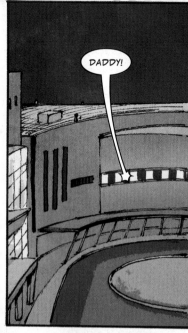

DADDY!

DADDY, YOU'RE BACK!

OF COURSE I AM. IT'S SO GOOD TO SEE YOU...

...

OH MY GOD. I CAN'T REMEMBER IT.

MY OWN DAUGHTER'S NAME.

DOC, I NEED YOUR HELP. YOU NEED TO CHECK ME OUT.

WHAT IS IT?

I THINK...

...I MAY HAVE WHAT KENNETH NEWTON HAD.

AM I GONNA EXPLODE RIGHT HERE?

IN FRONT OF DANIELLE?

AT LEAST I REMEMBER HER NAME NOW.

MR. CAGE...

THANKS FOR EXPEDITING ME AND DOING ALL THOSE TESTS AND SCANS, DOC.

DO I...DO I HAVE WHAT HE HAD?

WE'RE STILL TRYING TO FIGURE OUT *WHAT* HAPPENED TO KENNETH. LOOKS LIKE HE HAD A WHOLE CORNUCOPIA OF CONDITIONS. NEVER SEEN ANYTHING LIKE IT.

BUT IN LOOKING AT YOUR TESTS...

...YOU DON'T SEEM TO HAVE *ANY* OF HIS CONDITIONS.

THANK GOD. I DIDN'T WANT DANIELLE...

I JUST GOT A LITTLE SPOOKED. I NEED TO GET BACK TO WORK. FIGURE OUT WHO KILLED KENNETH. THAT DEATH WAS ANYTHING BUT NATURAL.

BEFORE YOU GO, MR. CAGE...I KNOW IT'S A STUPID QUESTION, BUT I NEED TO ASK IT.

YOU'VE BEEN IN A LOT OF FIGHTS, RIGHT? LOTS OF IMPACT ON YOUR BODY?

MORE IMPACT ON OTHERS, BUT SOME ON ME, YEAH.

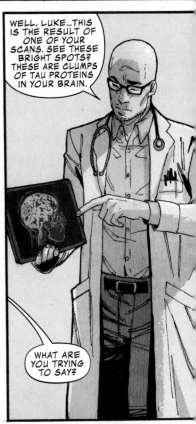

WELL, LUKE...THIS IS THE RESULT OF ONE OF YOUR SCANS. SEE THESE BRIGHT SPOTS? THESE ARE CLUMPS OF TAU PROTEINS IN YOUR BRAIN.

WHAT ARE YOU TRYING TO SAY?

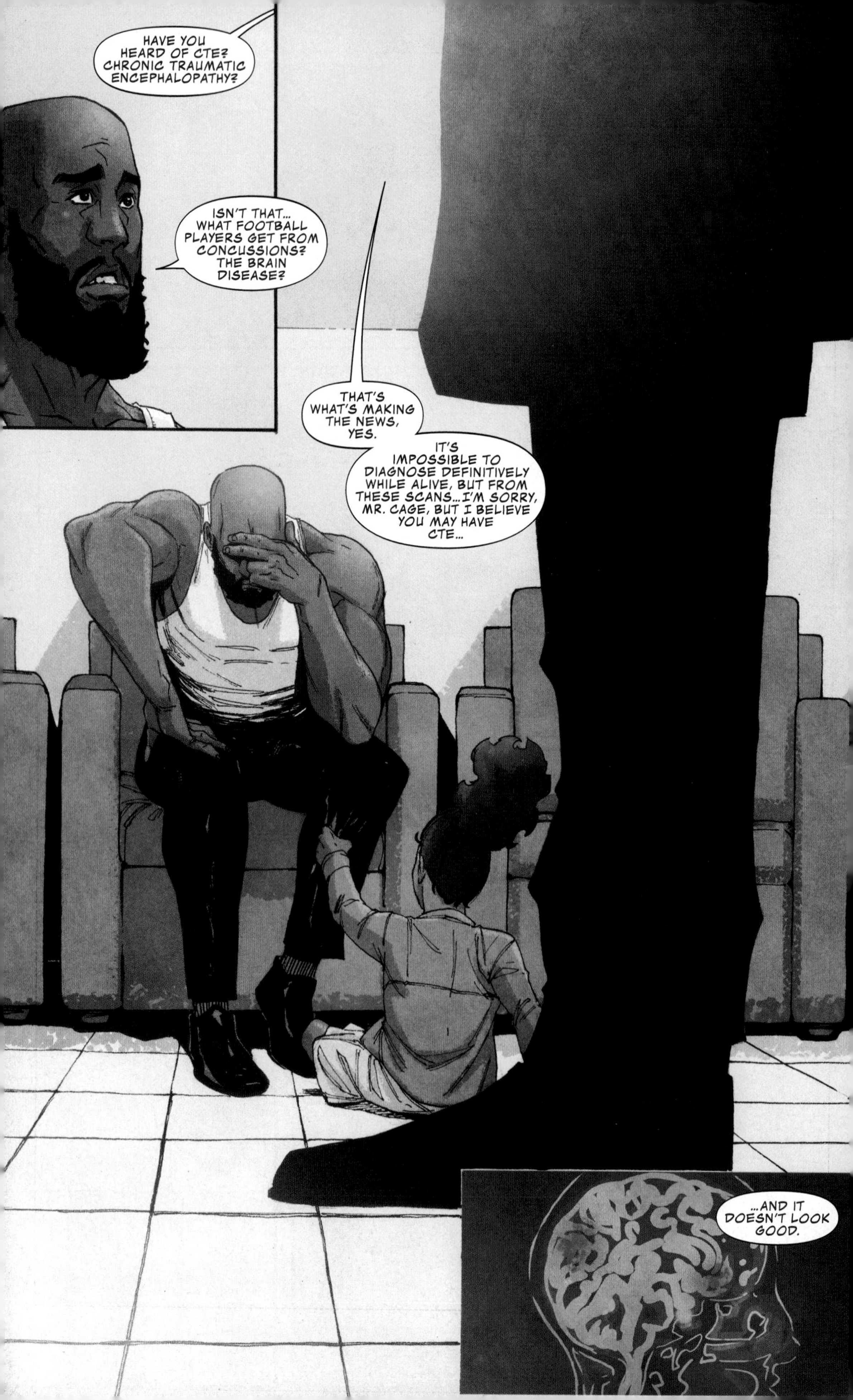
HAVE YOU HEARD OF CTE? CHRONIC TRAUMATIC ENCEPHALOPATHY?
ISN'T THAT... WHAT FOOTBALL PLAYERS GET FROM CONCUSSIONS? THE BRAIN DISEASE?
THAT'S WHAT'S MAKING THE NEWS, YES.
IT'S IMPOSSIBLE TO DIAGNOSE DEFINITIVELY WHILE ALIVE, BUT FROM THESE SCANS...I'M SORRY, MR. CAGE, BUT I BELIEVE YOU MAY HAVE CTE...
...AND IT DOESN'T LOOK GOOD.

EVERYMAN:
CHAPTER 2

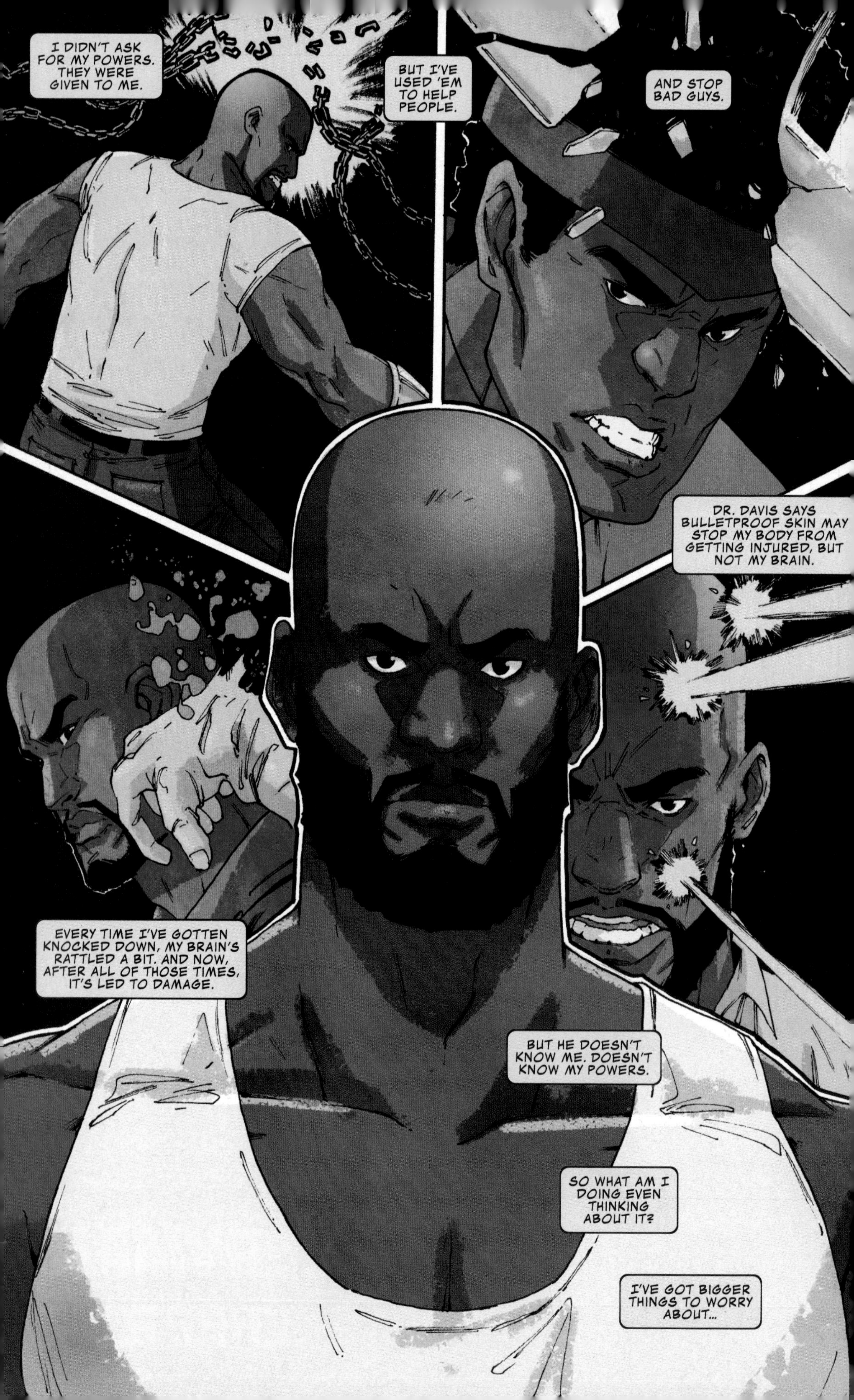
I DIDN'T ASK FOR MY POWERS. THEY WERE GIVEN TO ME.
BUT I'VE USED 'EM TO HELP PEOPLE.
AND STOP BAD GUYS.
DR. DAVIS SAYS BULLETPROOF SKIN MAY STOP MY BODY FROM GETTING INJURED, BUT NOT MY BRAIN.
EVERY TIME I'VE GOTTEN KNOCKED DOWN, MY BRAIN'S RATTLED A BIT. AND NOW, AFTER ALL OF THOSE TIMES, IT'S LED TO DAMAGE.
BUT HE DOESN'T KNOW ME. DOESN'T KNOW MY POWERS.
SO WHAT AM I DOING EVEN THINKING ABOUT IT?
I'VE GOT BIGGER THINGS TO WORRY ABOUT...

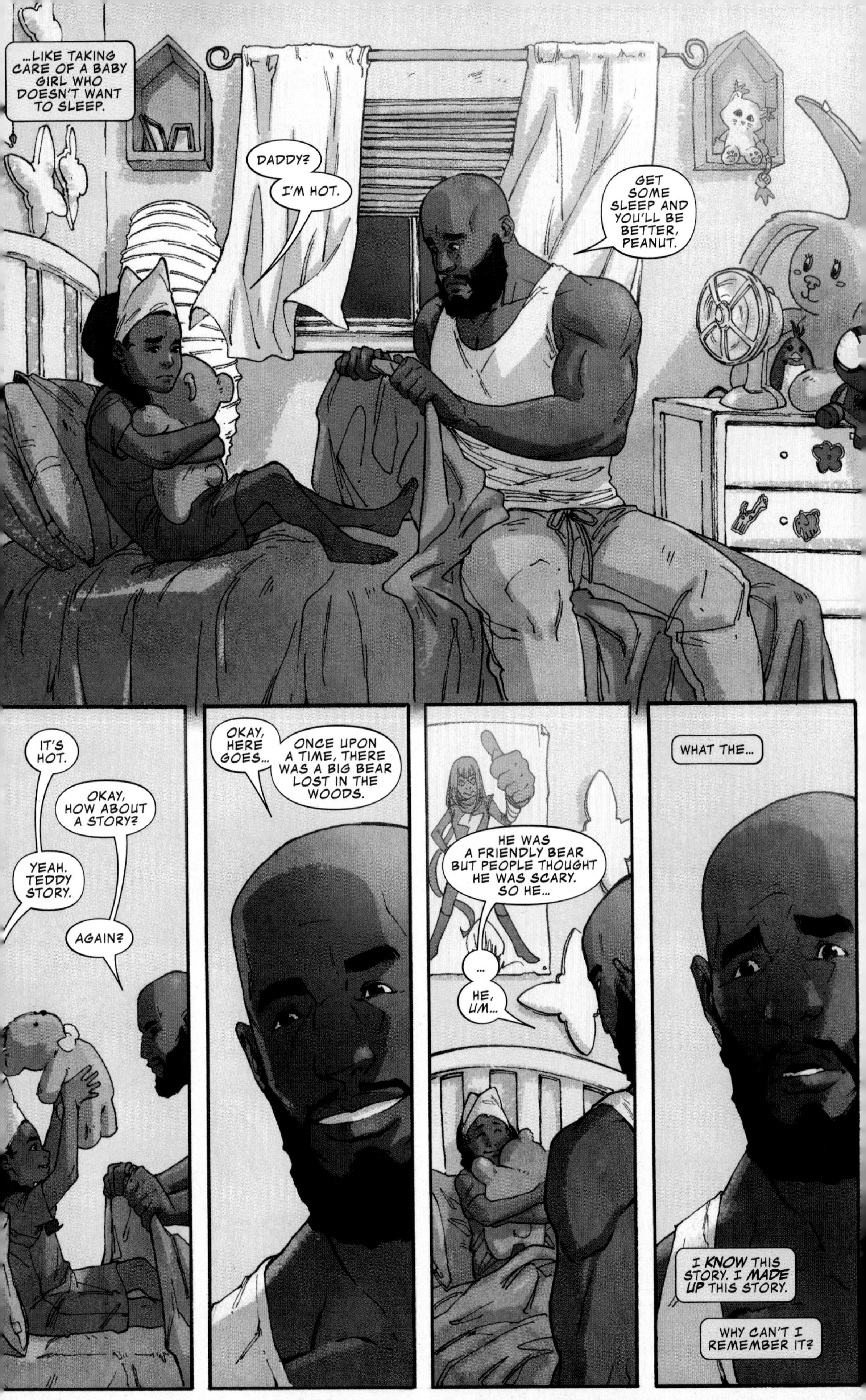
...LIKE TAKING CARE OF A BABY GIRL WHO DOESN'T WANT TO SLEEP.
DADDY?
I'M HOT.
GET SOME SLEEP AND YOU'LL BE BETTER, PEANUT.
IT'S HOT.
OKAY, HOW ABOUT A STORY?
YEAH. TEDDY STORY.
AGAIN?
OKAY, HERE GOES...
ONCE UPON A TIME, THERE WAS A BIG BEAR LOST IN THE WOODS.
HE WAS A FRIENDLY BEAR BUT PEOPLE THOUGHT HE WAS SCARY. SO HE...
...
HE, UM...
WHAT THE...
I **KNOW** THIS STORY. I **MADE UP** THIS STORY.
WHY CAN'T I REMEMBER IT?

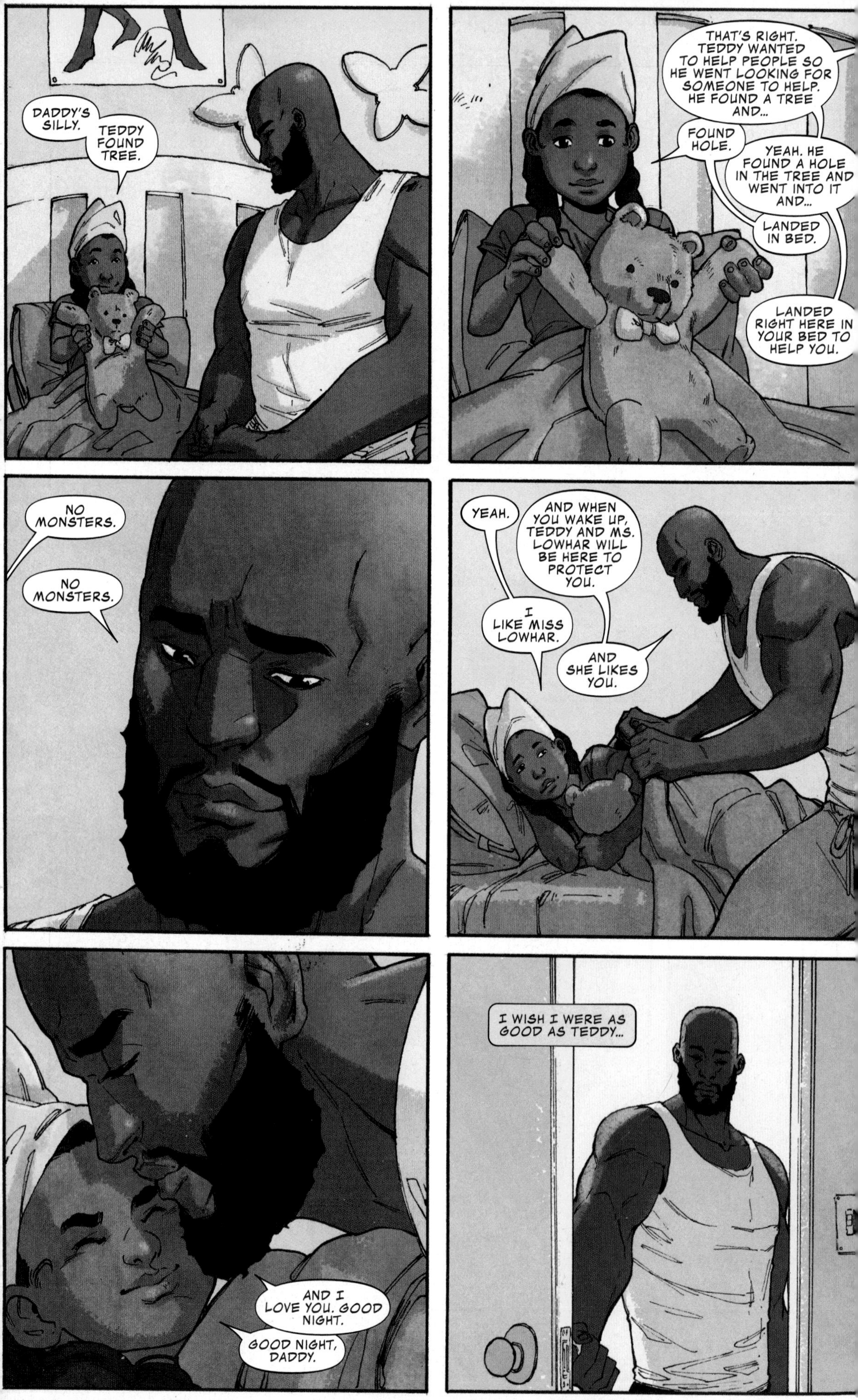
DADDY'S SILLY.
TEDDY FOUND TREE.
THAT'S RIGHT. TEDDY WANTED TO HELP PEOPLE SO HE WENT LOOKING FOR SOMEONE TO HELP. HE FOUND A TREE AND...
FOUND HOLE.
YEAH. HE FOUND A HOLE IN THE TREE AND WENT INTO IT AND...
LANDED IN BED.
LANDED RIGHT HERE IN YOUR BED TO HELP YOU.
NO MONSTERS.
NO MONSTERS.
YEAH.
AND WHEN YOU WAKE UP, TEDDY AND MS. LOWHAR WILL BE HERE TO PROTECT YOU.
I LIKE MISS LOWHAR.
AND SHE LIKES YOU.
AND I LOVE YOU. GOOD NIGHT.
GOOD NIGHT, DADDY.
I WISH I WERE AS GOOD AS TEDDY...

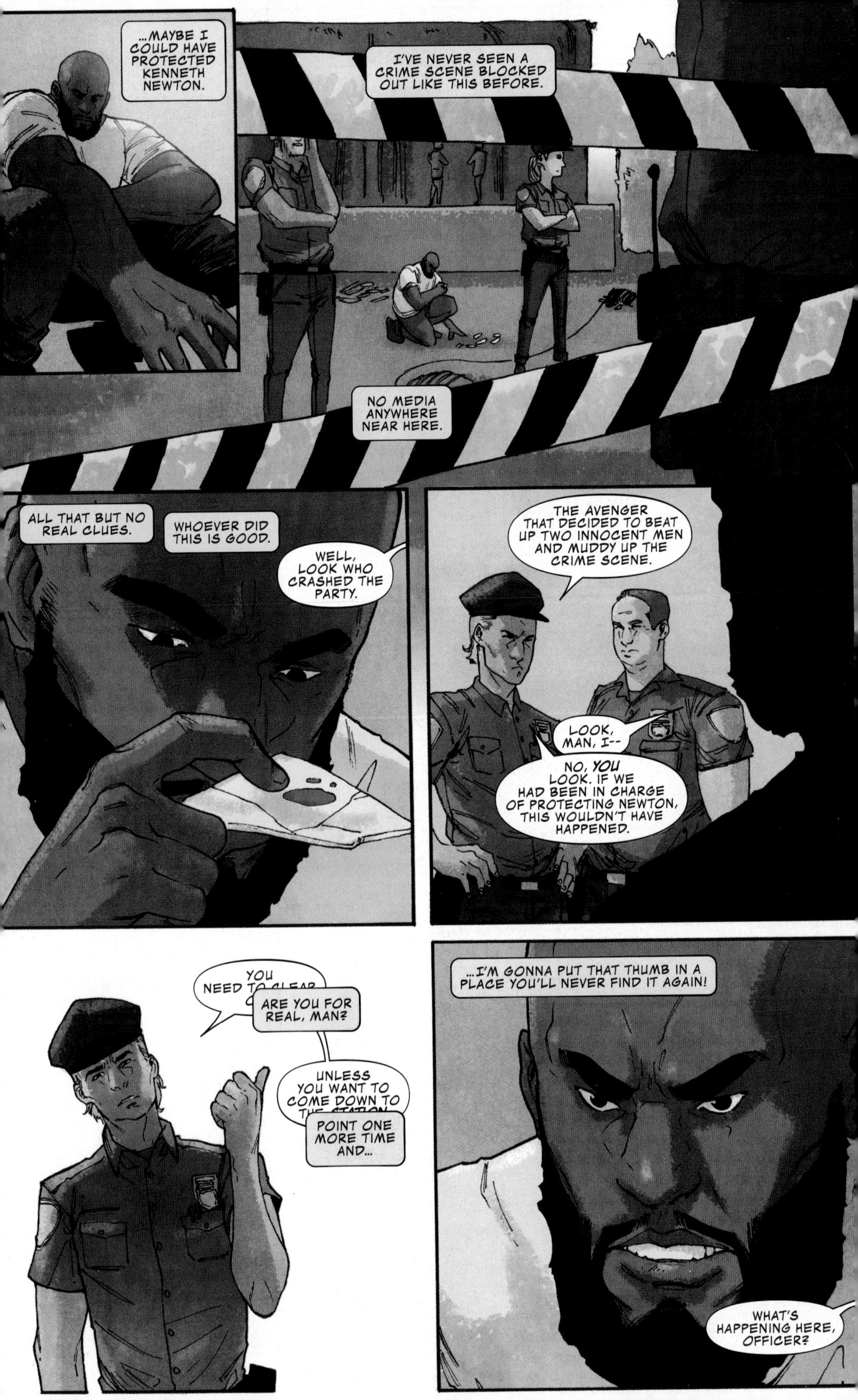
...MAYBE I COULD HAVE PROTECTED KENNETH NEWTON.
I'VE NEVER SEEN A CRIME SCENE BLOCKED OUT LIKE THIS BEFORE.
NO MEDIA ANYWHERE NEAR HERE.
ALL THAT BUT NO REAL CLUES.
WHOEVER DID THIS IS GOOD.
WELL, LOOK WHO CRASHED THE PARTY.
THE AVENGER THAT DECIDED TO BEAT UP TWO INNOCENT MEN AND MUDDY UP THE CRIME SCENE.
LOOK, MAN, I--
NO, *YOU* LOOK. IF WE HAD BEEN IN CHARGE OF PROTECTING NEWTON, THIS WOULDN'T HAVE HAPPENED.
YOU NEED TO
ARE YOU FOR REAL, MAN?
UNLESS YOU WANT TO COME DOWN TO
POINT ONE MORE TIME AND...
...I'M GONNA PUT THAT THUMB IN A PLACE YOU'LL NEVER FIND IT AGAIN!
WHAT'S HAPPENING HERE, OFFICER?

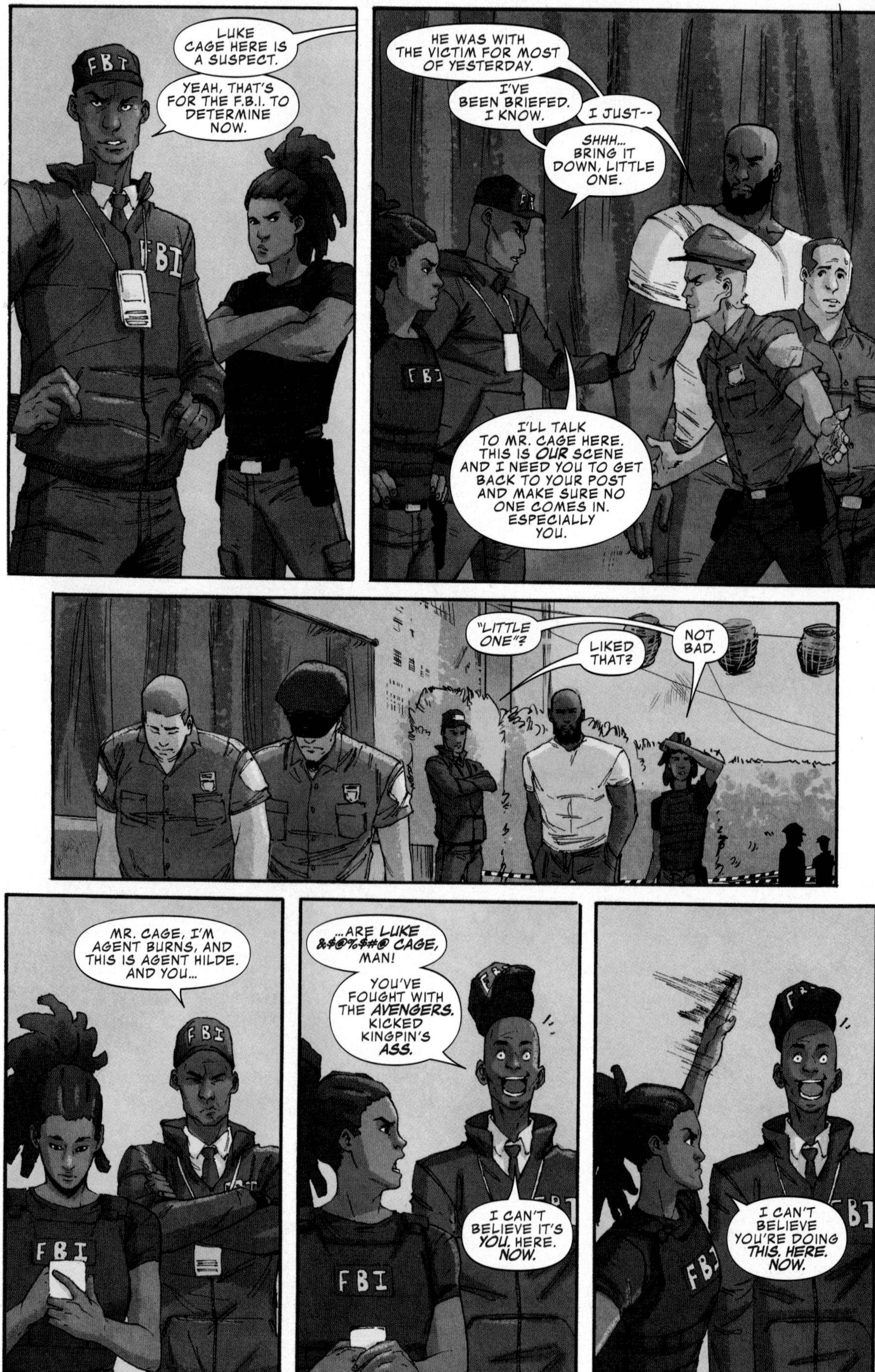
LUKE CAGE HERE IS A SUSPECT.
YEAH, THAT'S FOR THE F.B.I. TO DETERMINE NOW.
HE WAS WITH THE VICTIM FOR MOST OF YESTERDAY.
I'VE BEEN BRIEFED. I KNOW.
I JUST--
SHHH... BRING IT DOWN, LITTLE ONE.
I'LL TALK TO MR. CAGE HERE. THIS IS OUR SCENE AND I NEED YOU TO GET BACK TO YOUR POST AND MAKE SURE NO ONE COMES IN. ESPECIALLY YOU.
"LITTLE ONE"?
LIKED THAT?
NOT BAD.
MR. CAGE, I'M AGENT BURNS, AND THIS IS AGENT HILDE. AND YOU...
...ARE LUKE &$@%$#@ CAGE, MAN!
YOU'VE FOUGHT WITH THE AVENGERS. KICKED KINGPIN'S ASS.
I CAN'T BELIEVE IT'S YOU. HERE. NOW.
I CAN'T BELIEVE YOU'RE DOING THIS. HERE. NOW.

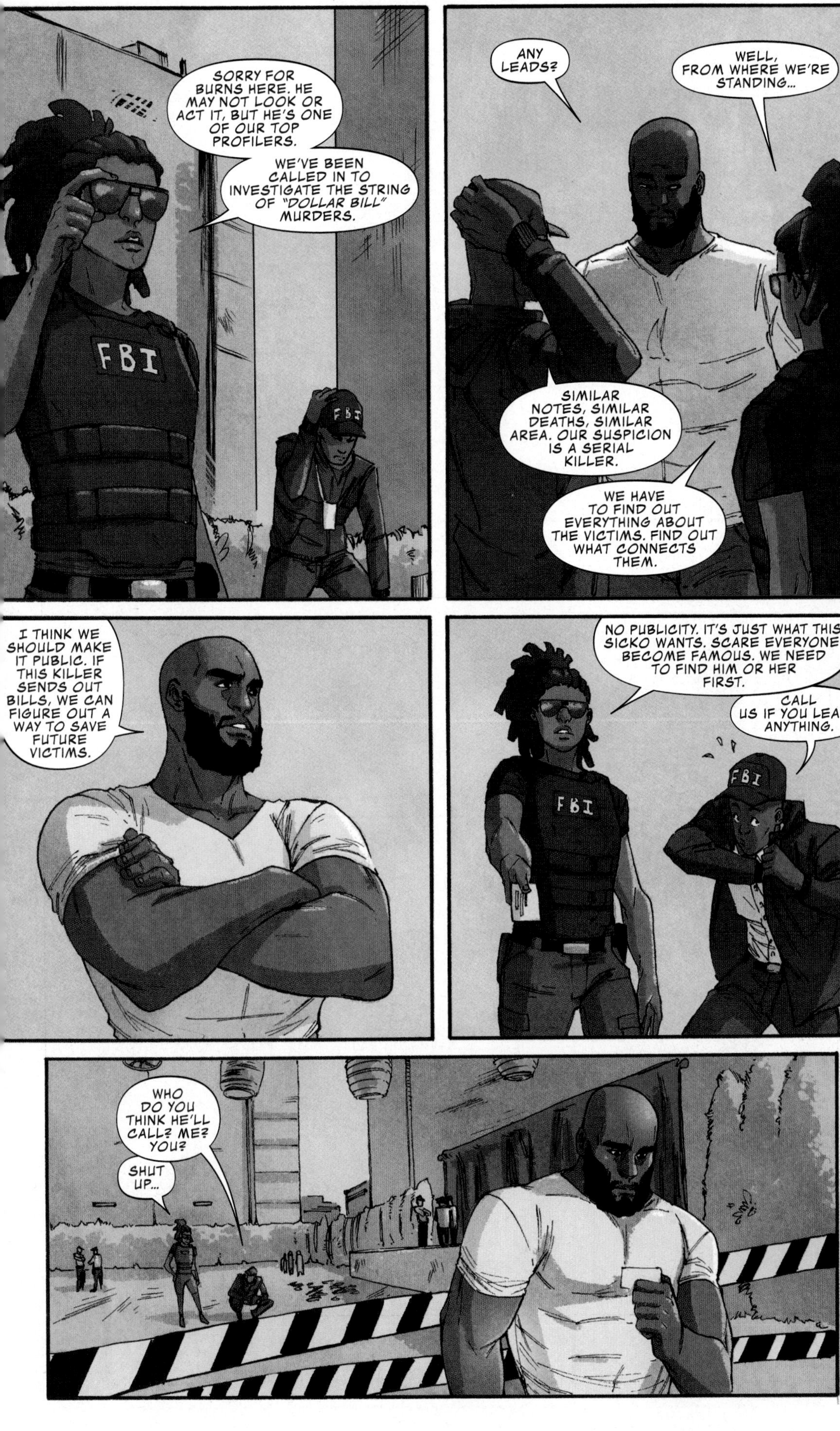
SORRY FOR BURNS HERE. HE MAY NOT LOOK OR ACT IT, BUT HE'S ONE OF OUR TOP PROFILERS.
WE'VE BEEN CALLED IN TO INVESTIGATE THE STRING OF "DOLLAR BILL" MURDERS.
FBI
FBI
ANY LEADS?
WELL, FROM WHERE WE'RE STANDING...
SIMILAR NOTES, SIMILAR DEATHS, SIMILAR AREA. OUR SUSPICION IS A SERIAL KILLER.
WE HAVE TO FIND OUT EVERYTHING ABOUT THE VICTIMS. FIND OUT WHAT CONNECTS THEM.
I THINK WE SHOULD MAKE IT PUBLIC. IF THIS KILLER SENDS OUT BILLS, WE CAN FIGURE OUT A WAY TO SAVE FUTURE VICTIMS.
NO PUBLICITY. IT'S JUST WHAT THIS SICKO WANTS. SCARE EVERYONE. BECOME FAMOUS. WE NEED TO FIND HIM OR HER FIRST.
CALL US IF YOU LEARN ANYTHING.
FBI
FBI
WHO DO YOU THINK HE'LL CALL? ME? YOU?
SHUT UP...

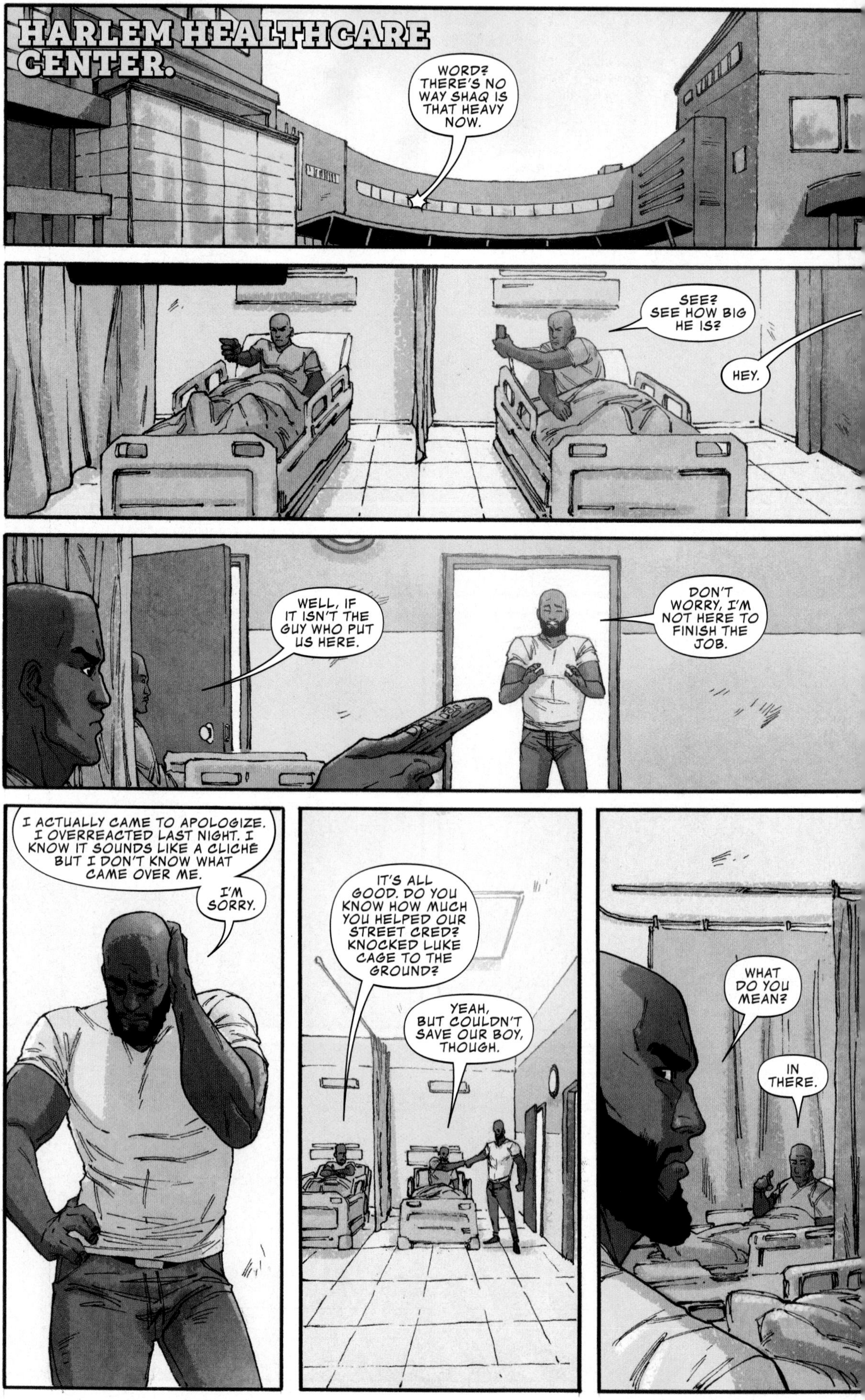
HARLEM HEALTHCARE CENTER.
WORD? THERE'S NO WAY SHAQ IS THAT HEAVY NOW.
SEE? SEE HOW BIG HE IS?
HEY.
WELL, IF IT ISN'T THE GUY WHO PUT US HERE.
DON'T WORRY, I'M NOT HERE TO FINISH THE JOB.
I ACTUALLY CAME TO APOLOGIZE. I OVERREACTED LAST NIGHT. I KNOW IT SOUNDS LIKE A CLICHÉ BUT I DON'T KNOW WHAT CAME OVER ME.
I'M SORRY.
IT'S ALL GOOD. DO YOU KNOW HOW MUCH YOU HELPED OUR STREET CRED? KNOCKED LUKE CAGE TO THE GROUND?
YEAH, BUT COULDN'T SAVE OUR BOY, THOUGH.
WHAT DO YOU MEAN?
IN THERE.

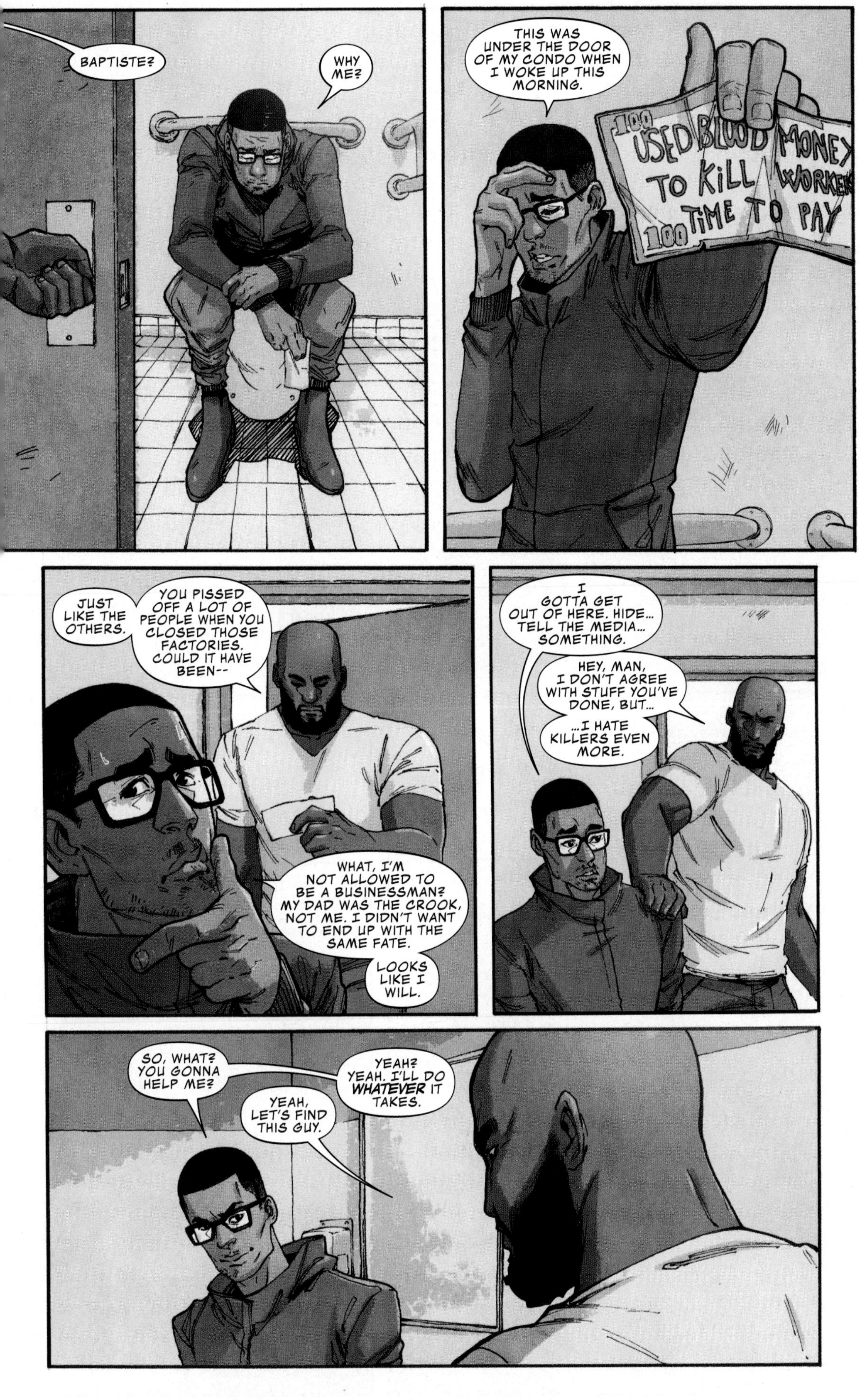
BAPTISTE?
WHY ME?
THIS WAS UNDER THE DOOR OF MY CONDO WHEN I WOKE UP THIS MORNING.
USED BLOOD MONEY TO KILL WORKERS TIME TO PAY
JUST LIKE THE OTHERS.
YOU PISSED OFF A LOT OF PEOPLE WHEN YOU CLOSED THOSE FACTORIES. COULD IT HAVE BEEN--
WHAT, I'M NOT ALLOWED TO BE A BUSINESSMAN? MY DAD WAS THE CROOK, NOT ME. I DIDN'T WANT TO END UP WITH THE SAME FATE.
LOOKS LIKE I WILL.
I GOTTA GET OUT OF HERE. HIDE... TELL THE MEDIA... SOMETHING.
HEY, MAN, I DON'T AGREE WITH STUFF YOU'VE DONE, BUT...
...I HATE KILLERS EVEN MORE.
SO, WHAT? YOU GONNA HELP ME?
YEAH? YEAH. I'LL DO *WHATEVER* IT TAKES.
YEAH, LET'S FIND THIS GUY.

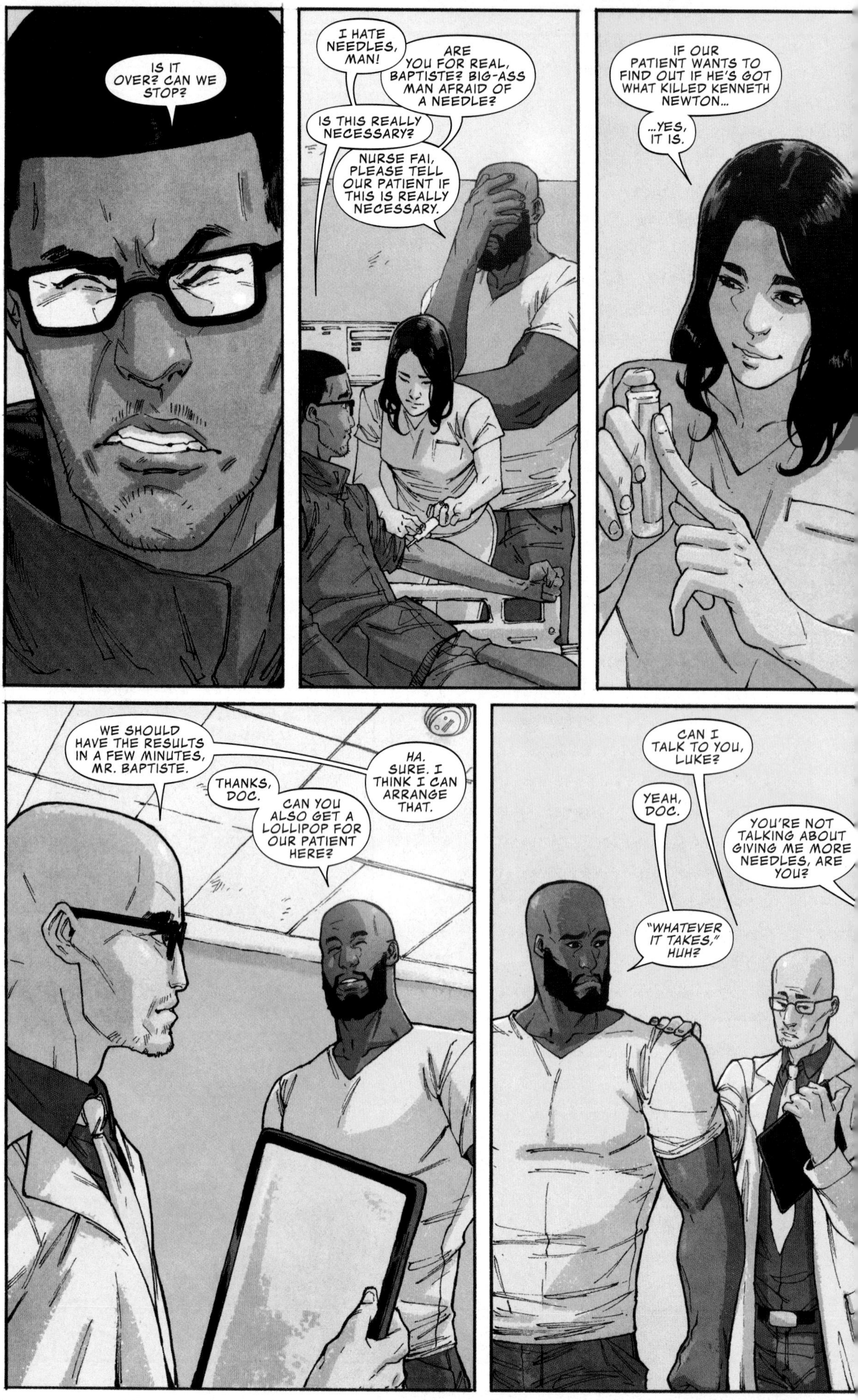
IS IT OVER? CAN WE STOP?
I HATE NEEDLES, MAN!
ARE YOU FOR REAL, BAPTISTE? BIG-ASS MAN AFRAID OF A NEEDLE?
IS THIS REALLY NECESSARY?
NURSE FAI, PLEASE TELL OUR PATIENT IF THIS IS REALLY NECESSARY.
IF OUR PATIENT WANTS TO FIND OUT IF HE'S GOT WHAT KILLED KENNETH NEWTON...
...YES, IT IS.
WE SHOULD HAVE THE RESULTS IN A FEW MINUTES, MR. BAPTISTE.
THANKS, DOC.
CAN YOU ALSO GET A LOLLIPOP FOR OUR PATIENT HERE?
HA. SURE. I THINK I CAN ARRANGE THAT.
CAN I TALK TO YOU, LUKE?
YEAH, DOC.
YOU'RE NOT TALKING ABOUT GIVING ME MORE NEEDLES, ARE YOU?
"WHATEVER IT TAKES," HUH?

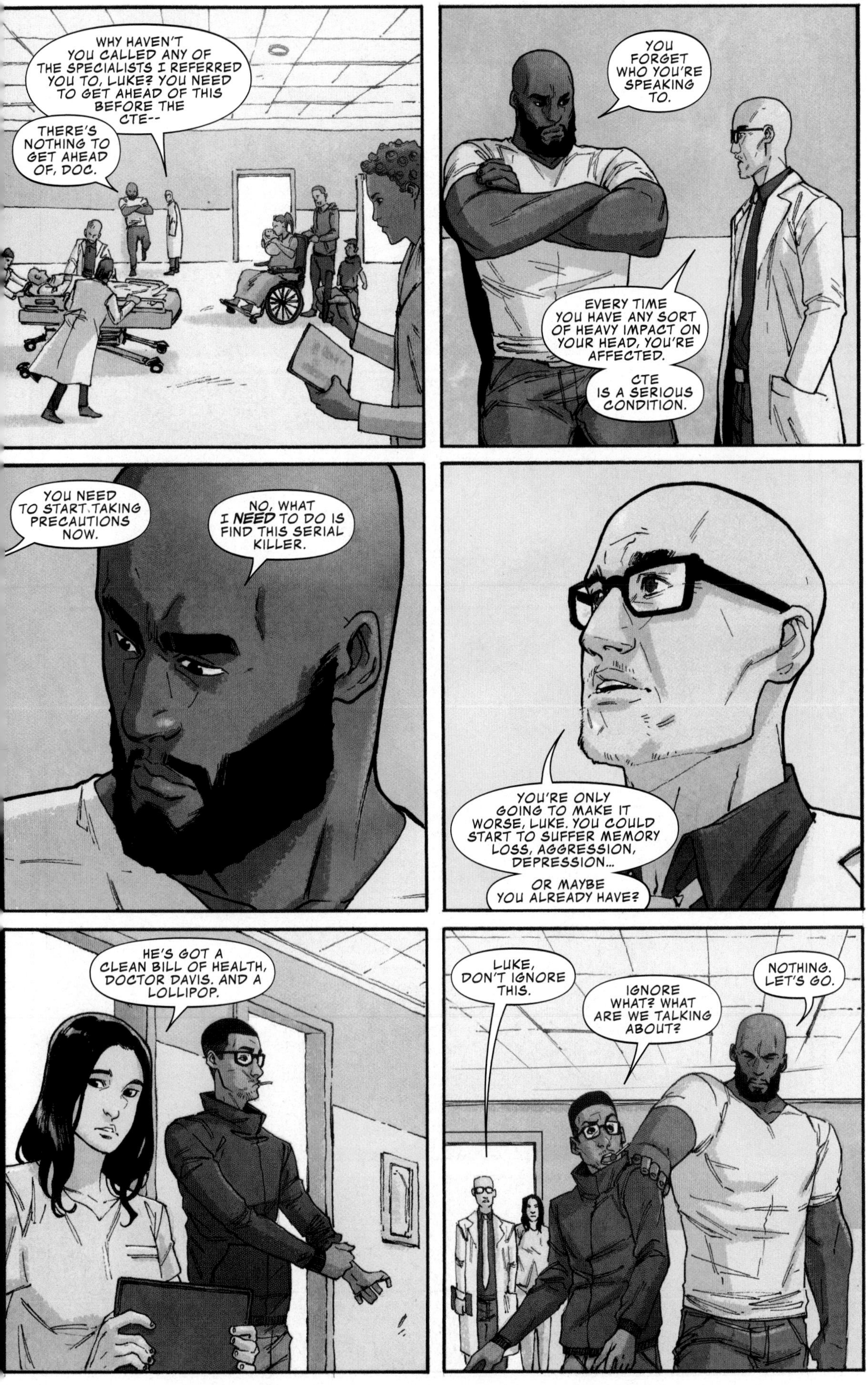
WHY HAVEN'T YOU CALLED ANY OF THE SPECIALISTS I REFERRED YOU TO, LUKE? YOU NEED TO GET AHEAD OF THIS BEFORE THE CTE--
THERE'S NOTHING TO GET AHEAD OF, DOC.
YOU FORGET WHO YOU'RE SPEAKING TO.
EVERY TIME YOU HAVE ANY SORT OF HEAVY IMPACT ON YOUR HEAD, YOU'RE AFFECTED.
CTE IS A SERIOUS CONDITION.
YOU NEED TO START TAKING PRECAUTIONS NOW.
NO, WHAT I NEED TO DO IS FIND THIS SERIAL KILLER.
YOU'RE ONLY GOING TO MAKE IT WORSE, LUKE. YOU COULD START TO SUFFER MEMORY LOSS, AGGRESSION, DEPRESSION...
OR MAYBE YOU ALREADY HAVE?
HE'S GOT A CLEAN BILL OF HEALTH, DOCTOR DAVIS. AND A LOLLIPOP.
LUKE, DON'T IGNORE THIS.
IGNORE WHAT? WHAT ARE WE TALKING ABOUT?
NOTHING. LET'S GO.

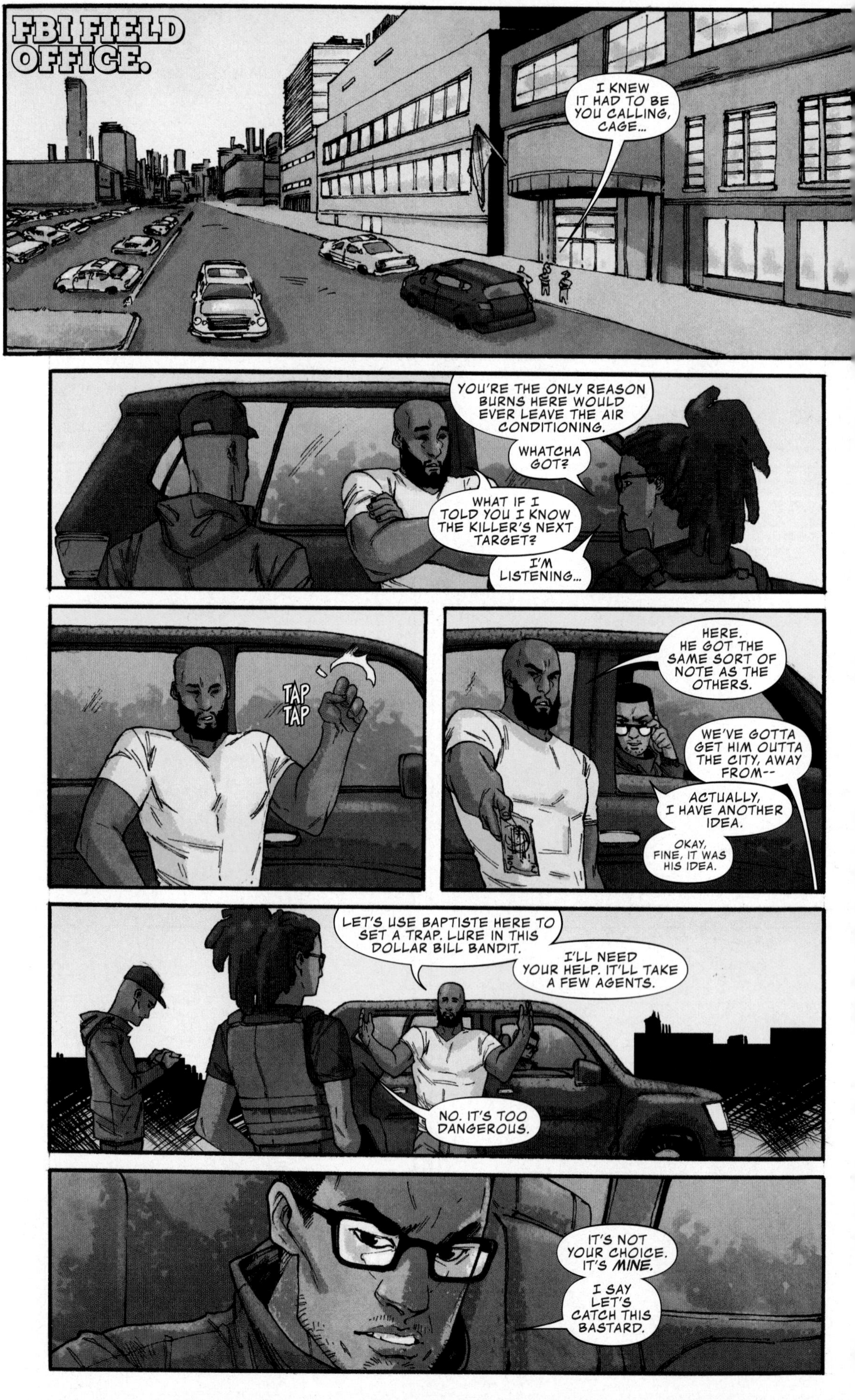
FBI FIELD OFFICE.
I KNEW IT HAD TO BE YOU CALLING, CAGE...
YOU'RE THE ONLY REASON BURNS HERE WOULD EVER LEAVE THE AIR CONDITIONING.
WHATCHA GOT?
WHAT IF I TOLD YOU I KNOW THE KILLER'S NEXT TARGET?
I'M LISTENING...
TAP TAP
HERE. HE GOT THE SAME SORT OF NOTE AS THE OTHERS.
WE'VE GOTTA GET HIM OUTTA THE CITY, AWAY FROM--
ACTUALLY, I HAVE ANOTHER IDEA.
OKAY, FINE, IT WAS HIS IDEA.
LET'S USE BAPTISTE HERE TO SET A TRAP. LURE IN THIS DOLLAR BILL BANDIT.
I'LL NEED YOUR HELP. IT'LL TAKE A FEW AGENTS.
NO. IT'S TOO DANGEROUS.
IT'S NOT YOUR CHOICE. IT'S *MINE.*
I SAY LET'S CATCH THIS BASTARD.

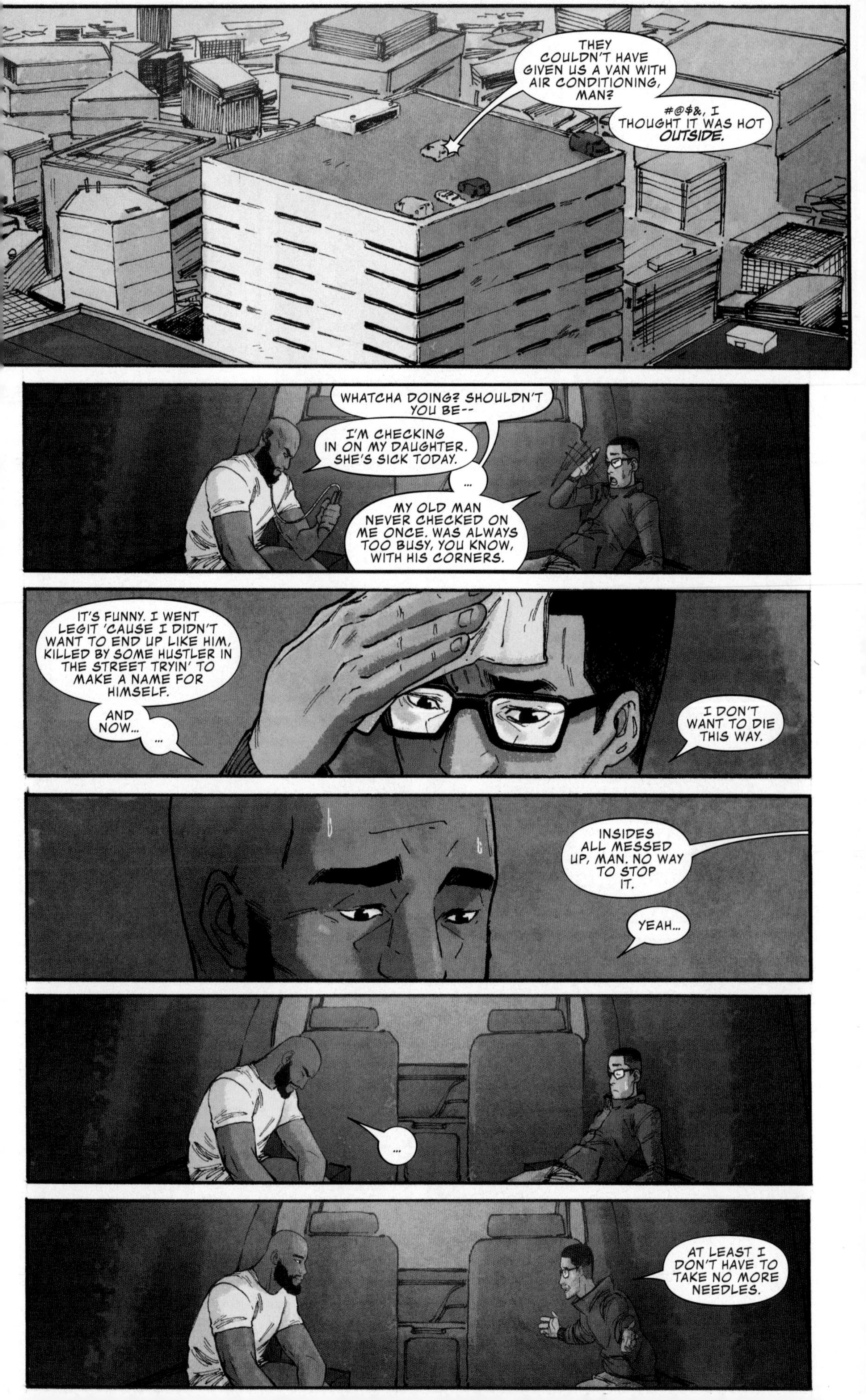
THEY COULDN'T HAVE GIVEN US A VAN WITH AIR CONDITIONING, MAN?
#@$&, I THOUGHT IT WAS HOT OUTSIDE.
WHATCHA DOING? SHOULDN'T YOU BE--
I'M CHECKING IN ON MY DAUGHTER. SHE'S SICK TODAY.
...
MY OLD MAN NEVER CHECKED ON ME ONCE. WAS ALWAYS TOO BUSY, YOU KNOW, WITH HIS CORNERS.
IT'S FUNNY. I WENT LEGIT 'CAUSE I DIDN'T WANT TO END UP LIKE HIM, KILLED BY SOME HUSTLER IN THE STREET TRYIN' TO MAKE A NAME FOR HIMSELF.
AND NOW...
...
I DON'T WANT TO DIE THIS WAY.
INSIDES ALL MESSED UP, MAN. NO WAY TO STOP IT.
YEAH...
...
AT LEAST I DON'T HAVE TO TAKE NO MORE NEEDLES.

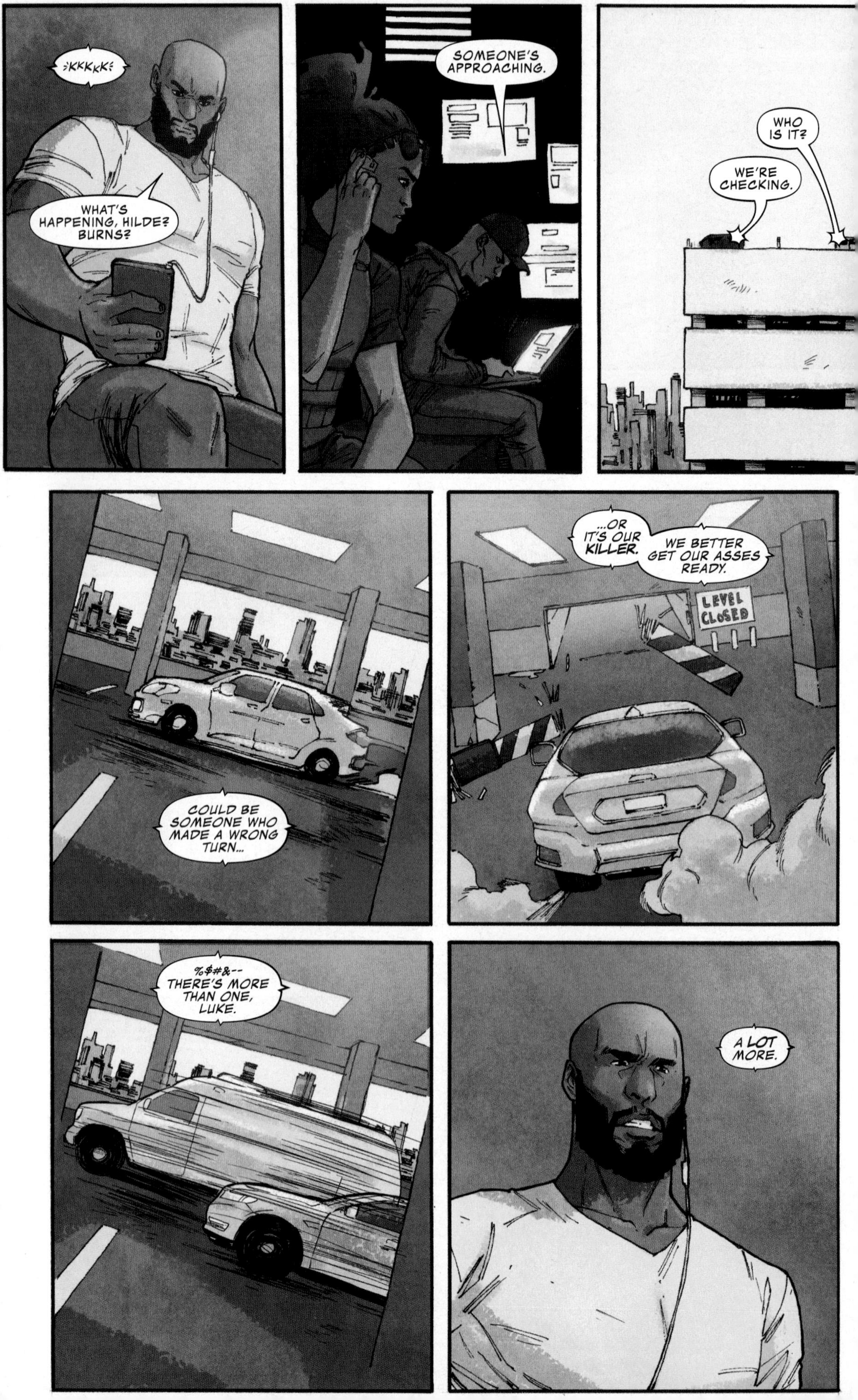

KKKKK
WHAT'S HAPPENING, HILDE? BURNS?
SOMEONE'S APPROACHING.
WHO IS IT?
WE'RE CHECKING.
COULD BE SOMEONE WHO MADE A WRONG TURN...
...OR IT'S OUR KILLER.
WE BETTER GET OUR ASSES READY.
LEVEL CLOSED
%$#&-- THERE'S MORE THAN ONE, LUKE.
A LOT MORE.

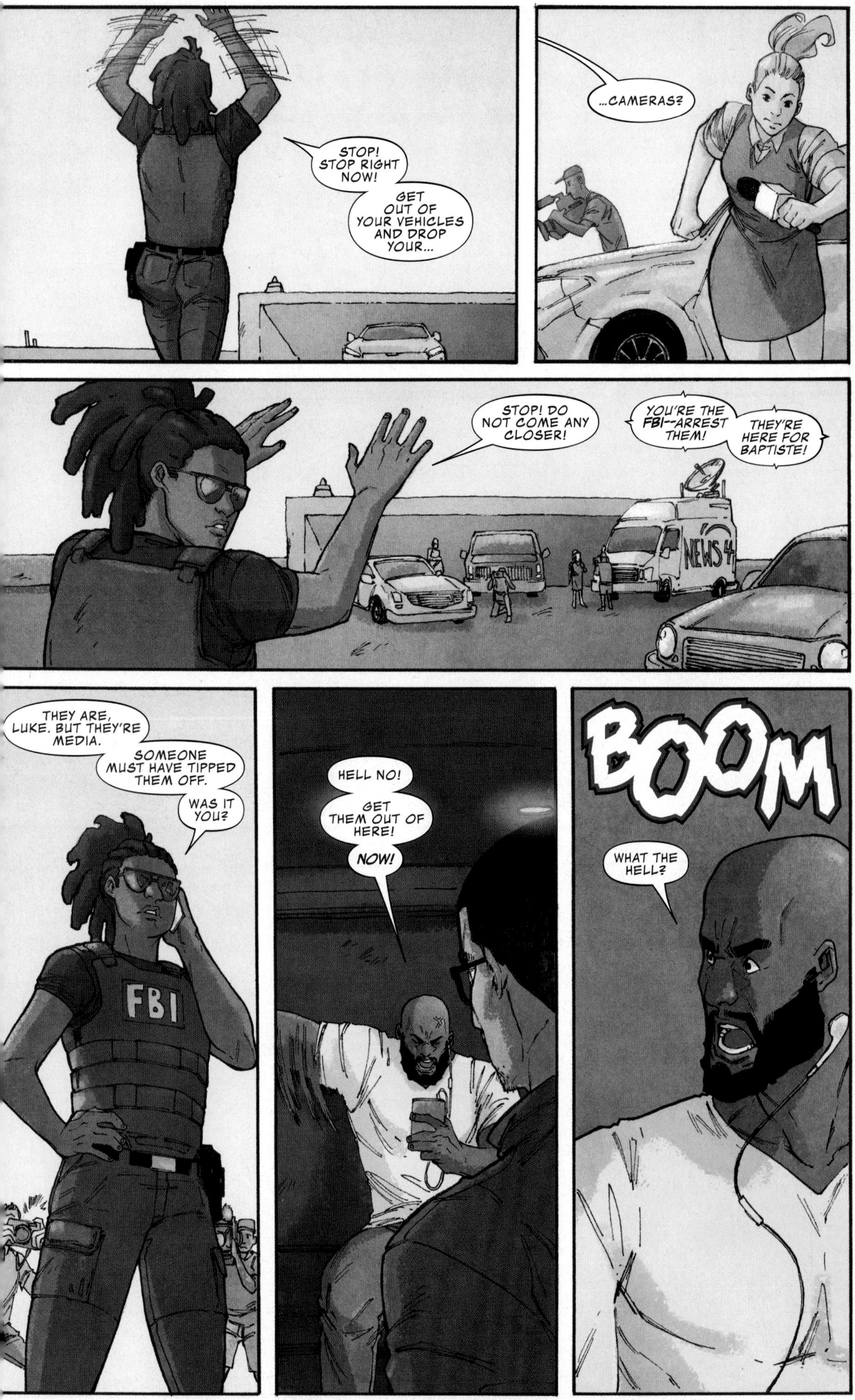
STOP! STOP RIGHT NOW!
GET OUT OF YOUR VEHICLES AND DROP YOUR...
...CAMERAS?
STOP! DO NOT COME ANY CLOSER!
YOU'RE THE FBI--ARREST THEM!
THEY'RE HERE FOR BAPTISTE!
NEWS 4
THEY ARE, LUKE. BUT THEY'RE MEDIA.
SOMEONE MUST HAVE TIPPED THEM OFF.
WAS IT YOU?
FBI
HELL NO!
GET THEM OUT OF HERE!
NOW!
BOOM
WHAT THE HELL?

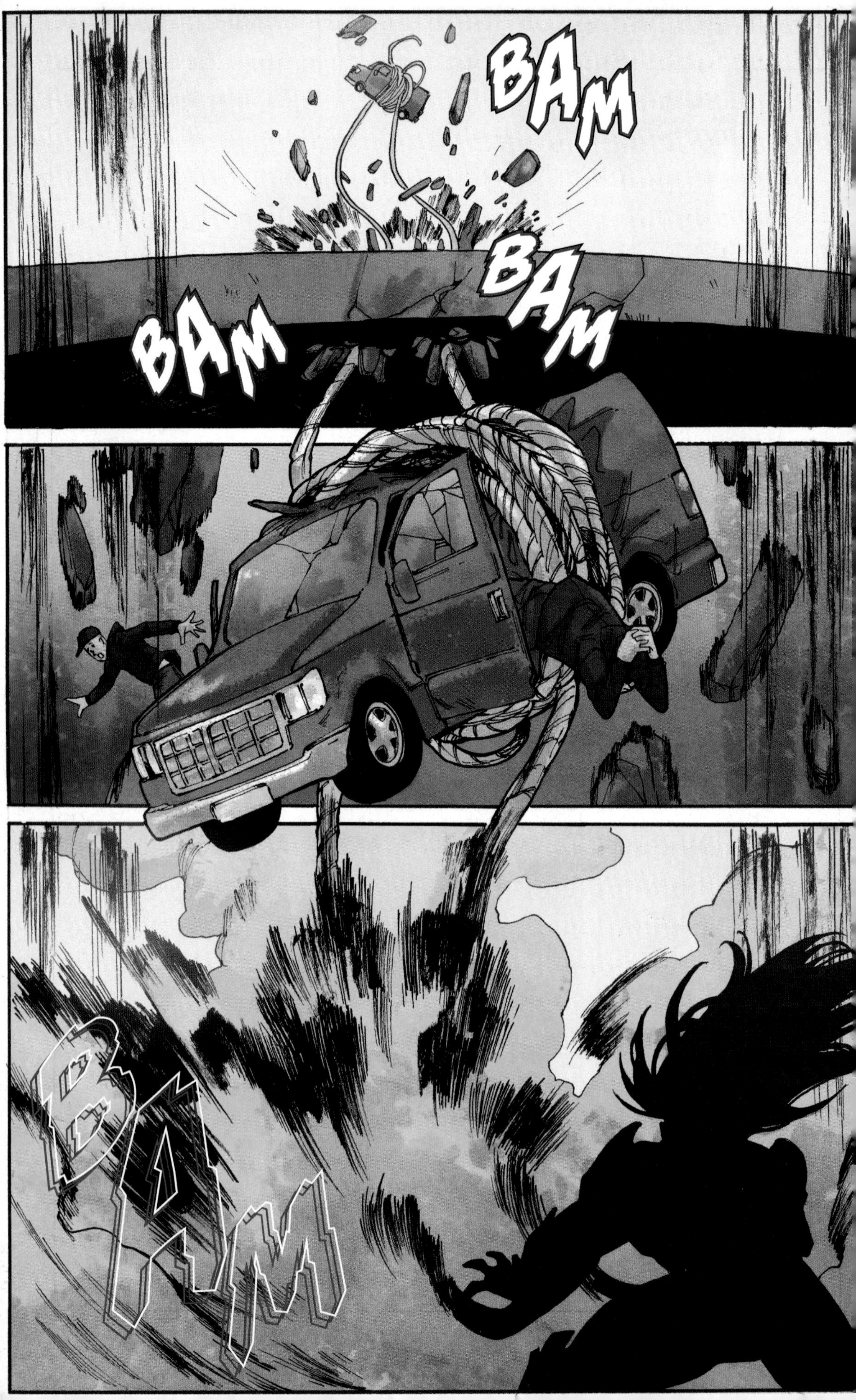
BAM
BAM
BAM
BAM

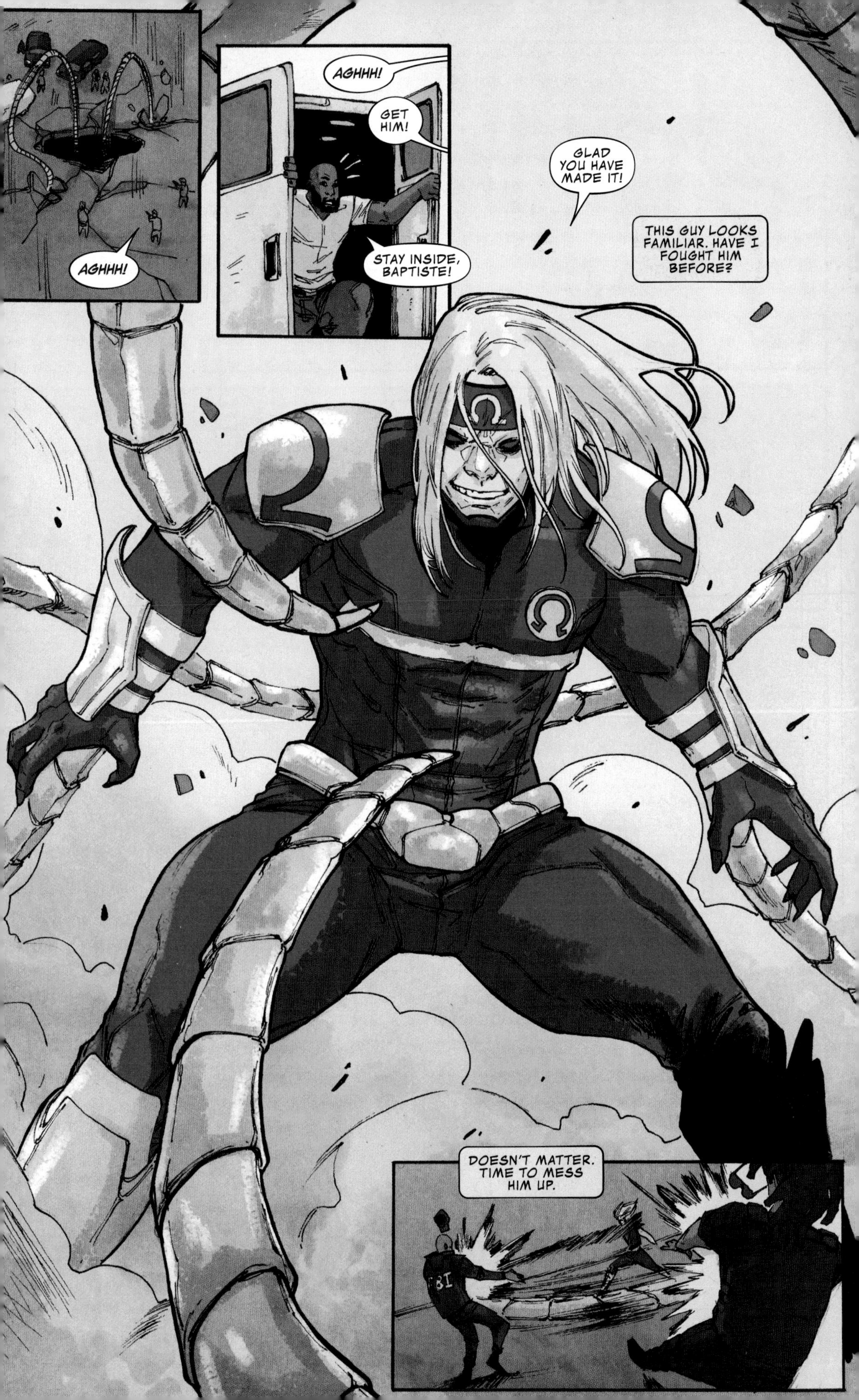
AGHHH!
AGHHH!
GET HIM!
STAY INSIDE, BAPTISTE!
GLAD YOU HAVE MADE IT!
THIS GUY LOOKS FAMILIAR. HAVE I FOUGHT HIM BEFORE?
DOESN'T MATTER. TIME TO MESS HIM UP.
FBI

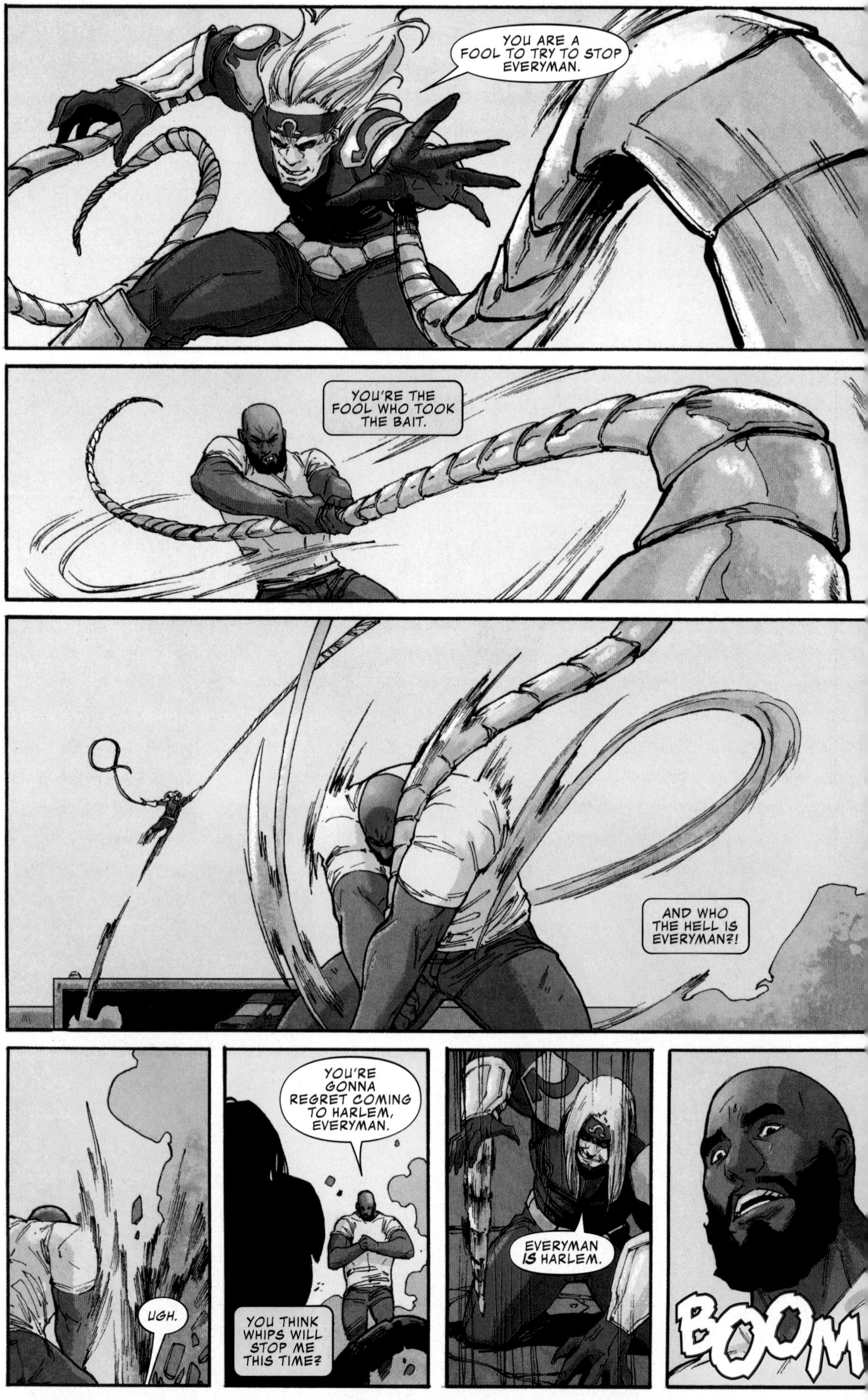
YOU ARE A FOOL TO TRY TO STOP EVERYMAN.
YOU'RE THE FOOL WHO TOOK THE BAIT.
AND WHO THE HELL IS EVERYMAN?!
UGH.
YOU'RE GONNA REGRET COMING TO HARLEM, EVERYMAN.
YOU THINK WHIPS WILL STOP ME THIS TIME?
EVERYMAN IS HARLEM.
BOOM

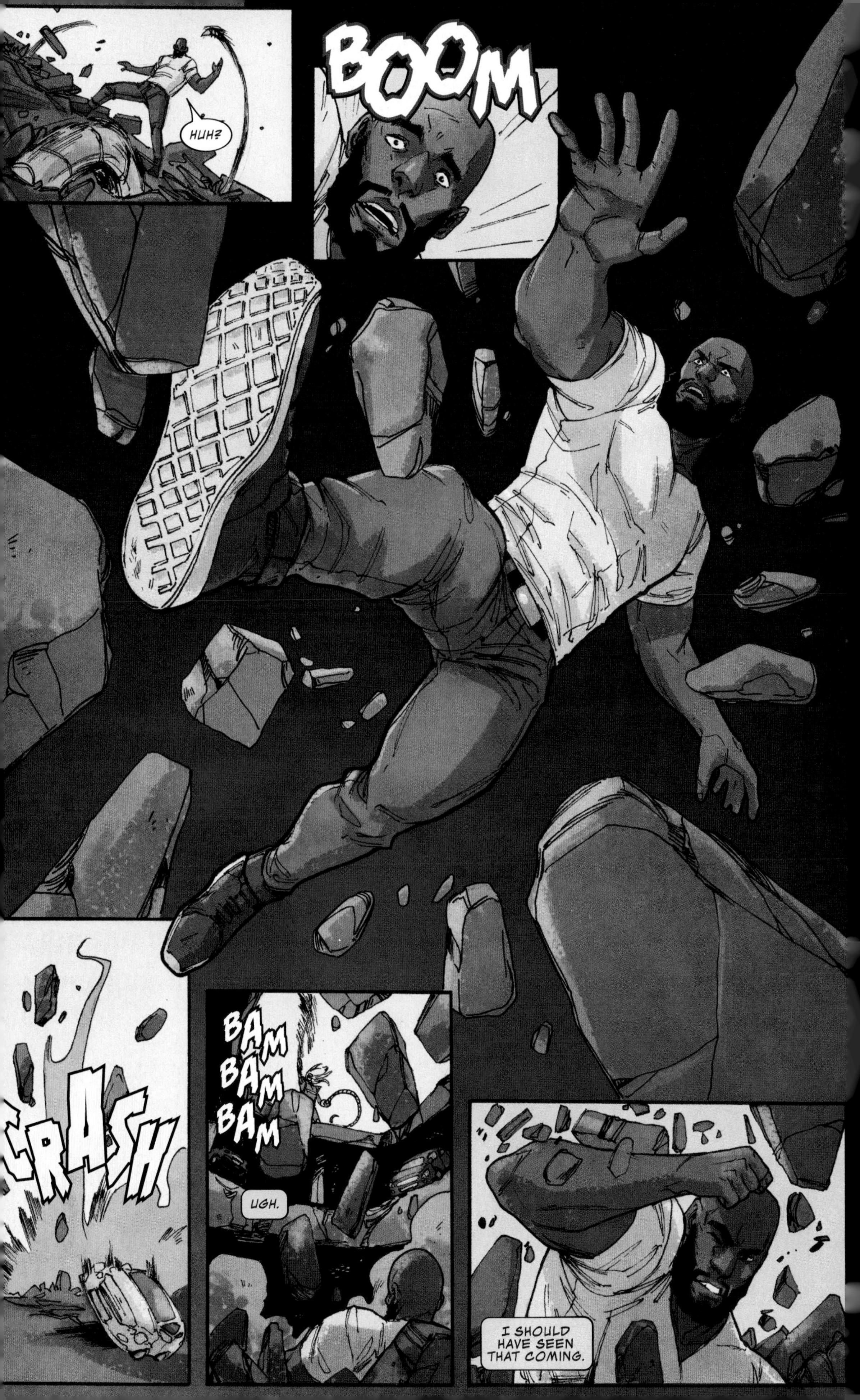
HUH?
BOOM
CRASH
BAM BAM BAM
UGH.
I SHOULD HAVE SEEN THAT COMING.

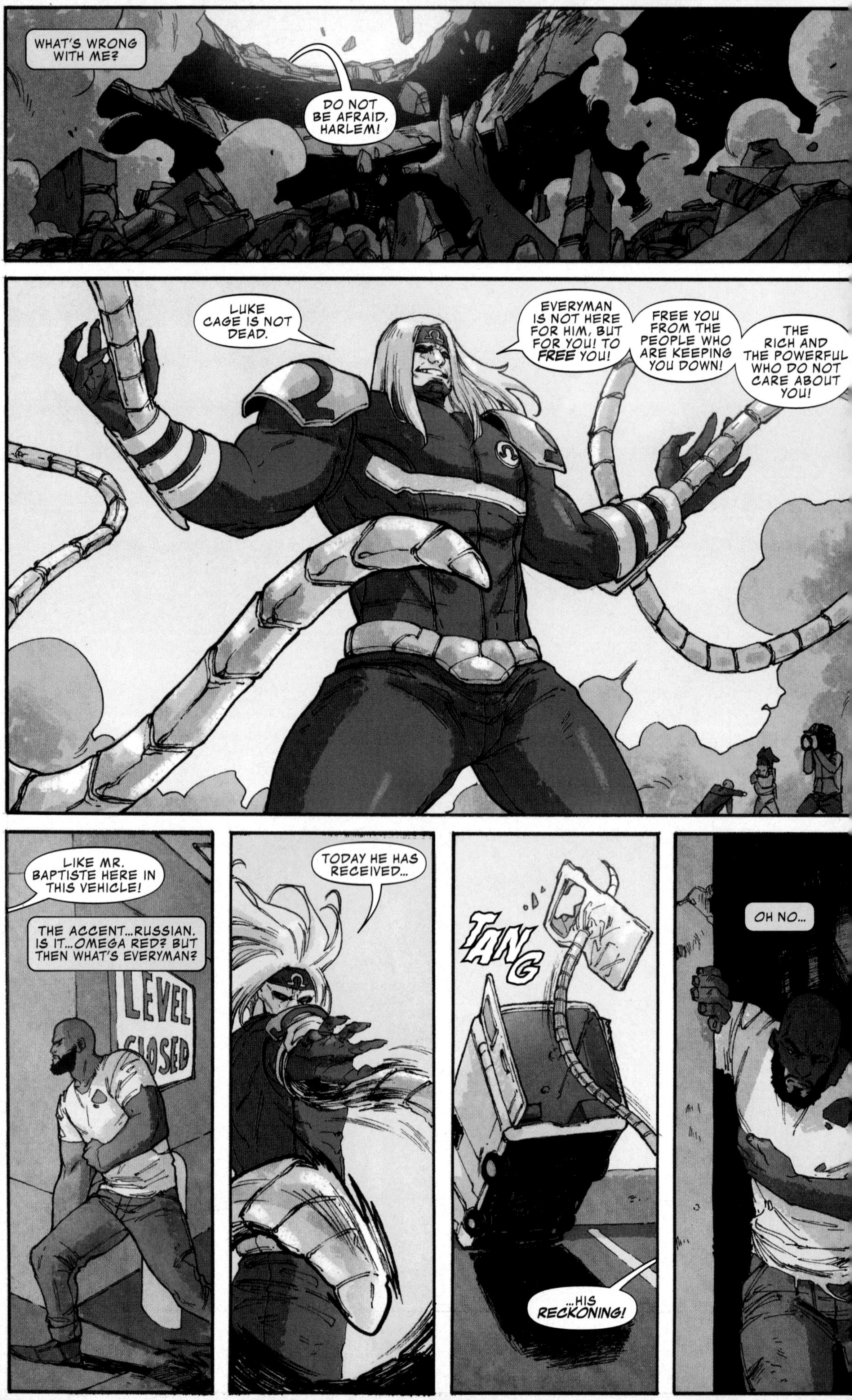
WHAT'S WRONG WITH ME?
DO NOT BE AFRAID, HARLEM!
LUKE CAGE IS NOT DEAD.
EVERYMAN IS NOT HERE FOR HIM, BUT FOR YOU! TO FREE YOU!
FREE YOU FROM THE PEOPLE WHO ARE KEEPING YOU DOWN!
THE RICH AND THE POWERFUL WHO DO NOT CARE ABOUT YOU!
LIKE MR. BAPTISTE HERE IN THIS VEHICLE!
THE ACCENT...RUSSIAN. IS IT...OMEGA RED? BUT THEN WHAT'S EVERYMAN?
LEVEL CLOSED
TODAY HE HAS RECEIVED...
TANG
...HIS RECKONING!
OH NO...

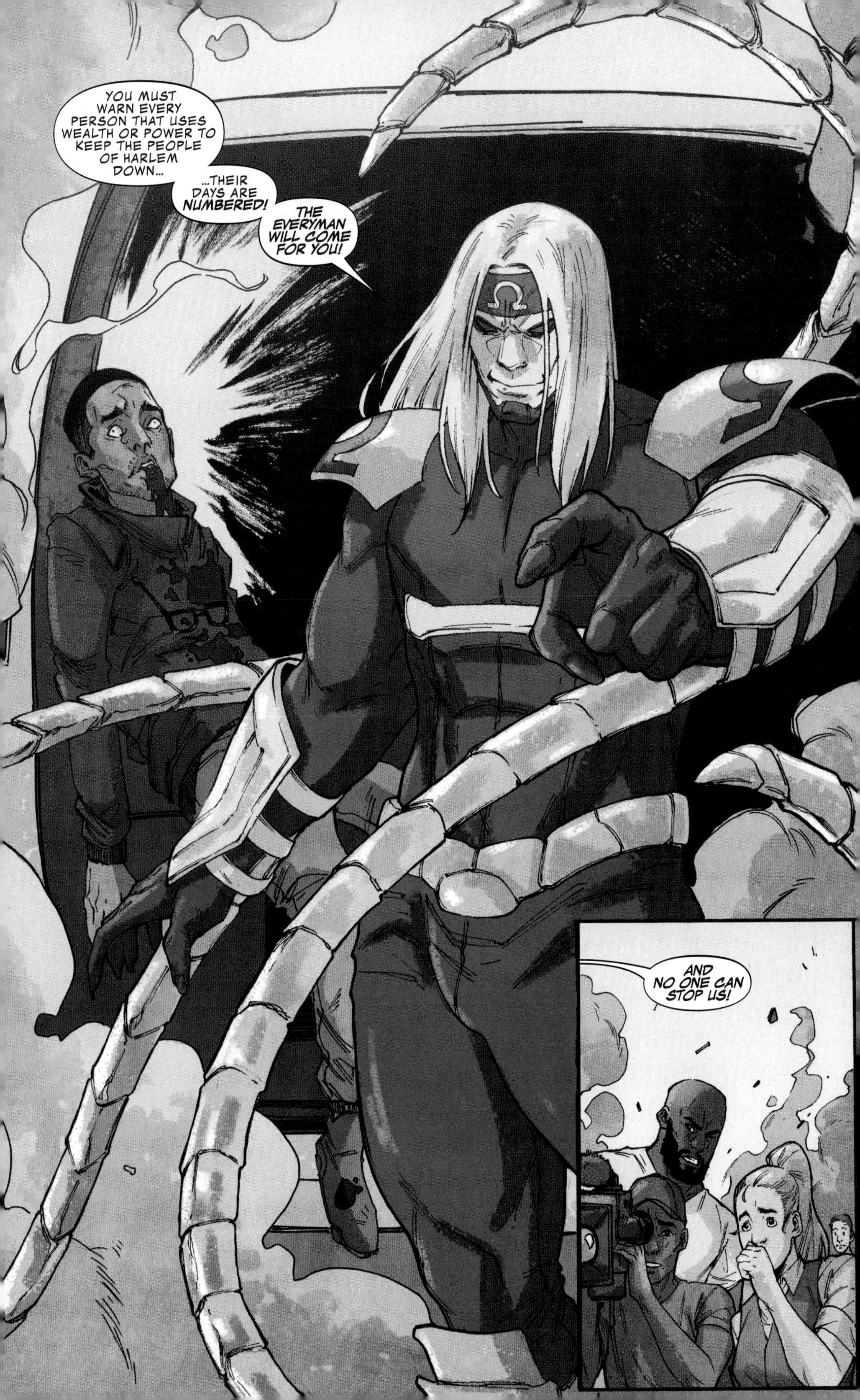
YOU MUST WARN EVERY PERSON THAT USES WEALTH OR POWER TO KEEP THE PEOPLE OF HARLEM DOWN...
...THEIR DAYS ARE NUMBERED!
THE EVERYMAN WILL COME FOR YOU!
AND NO ONE CAN STOP US!

EVERYMAN:
CHAPTER 3

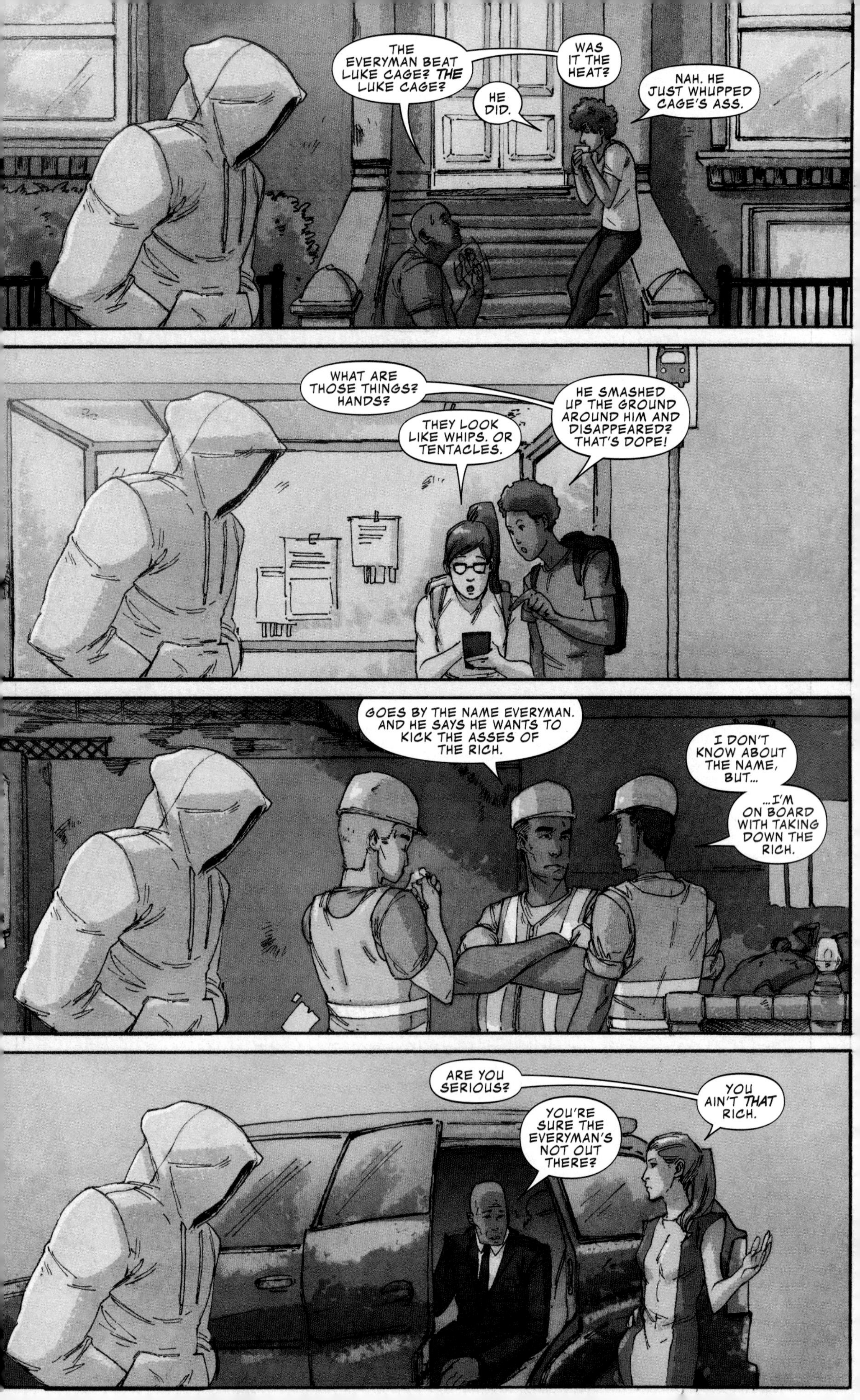

THE EVERYMAN BEAT LUKE CAGE? THE LUKE CAGE?
WAS IT THE HEAT?
HE DID.
NAH. HE JUST WHUPPED CAGE'S ASS.
WHAT ARE THOSE THINGS? HANDS?
HE SMASHED UP THE GROUND AROUND HIM AND DISAPPEARED? THAT'S DOPE!
THEY LOOK LIKE WHIPS. OR TENTACLES.
GOES BY THE NAME EVERYMAN. AND HE SAYS HE WANTS TO KICK THE ASSES OF THE RICH.
I DON'T KNOW ABOUT THE NAME, BUT...
...I'M ON BOARD WITH TAKING DOWN THE RICH.
ARE YOU SERIOUS?
YOU AIN'T THAT RICH.
YOU'RE SURE THE EVERYMAN'S NOT OUT THERE?

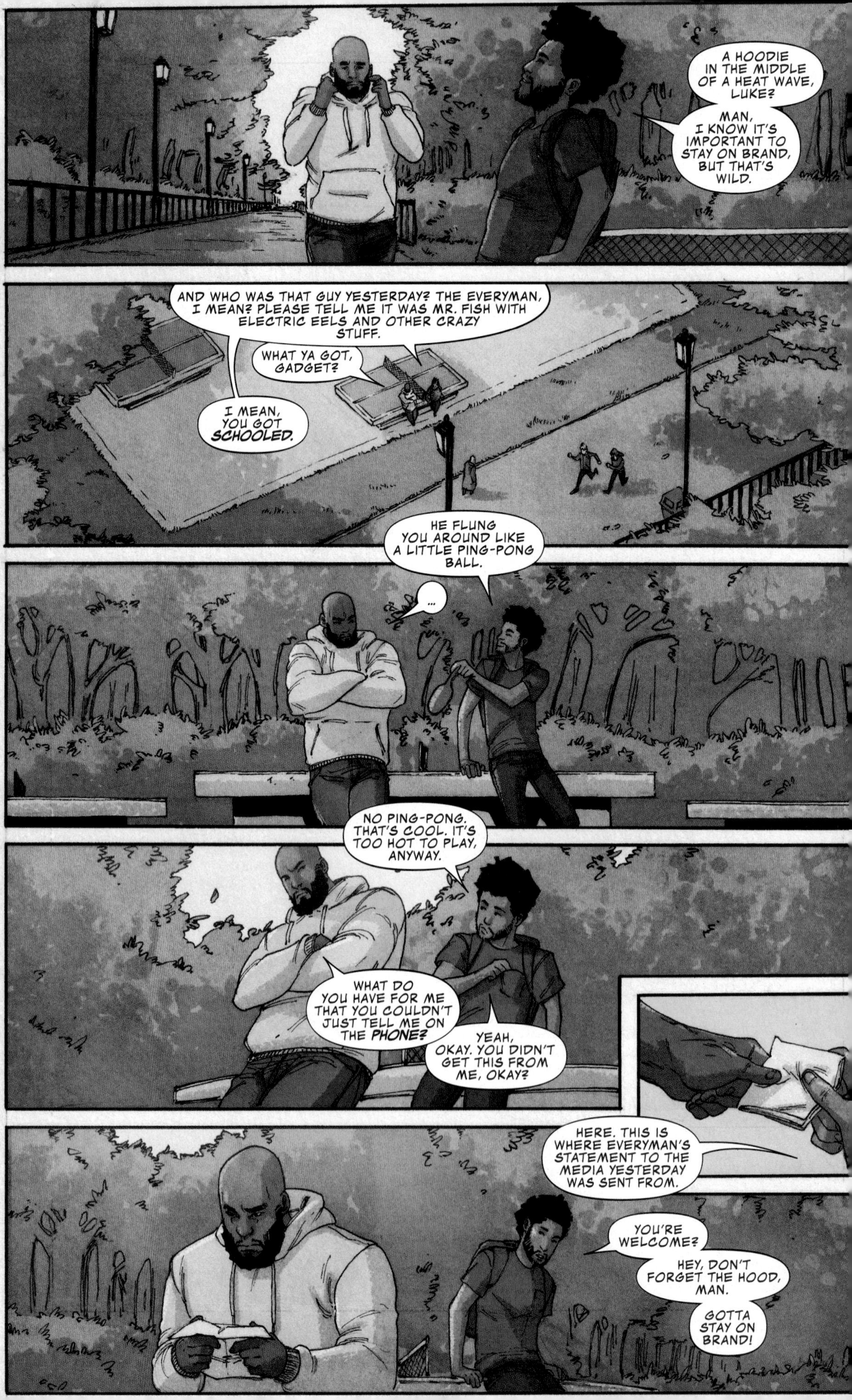
A HOODIE IN THE MIDDLE OF A HEAT WAVE, LUKE?
MAN, I KNOW IT'S IMPORTANT TO STAY ON BRAND, BUT THAT'S WILD.
AND WHO WAS THAT GUY YESTERDAY? THE EVERYMAN, I MEAN? PLEASE TELL ME IT WAS MR. FISH WITH ELECTRIC EELS AND OTHER CRAZY STUFF.
WHAT YA GOT, GADGET?
I MEAN, YOU GOT SCHOOLED.
HE FLUNG YOU AROUND LIKE A LITTLE PING-PONG BALL.
...
NO PING-PONG. THAT'S COOL. IT'S TOO HOT TO PLAY, ANYWAY.
WHAT DO YOU HAVE FOR ME THAT YOU COULDN'T JUST TELL ME ON THE PHONE?
YEAH, OKAY. YOU DIDN'T GET THIS FROM ME, OKAY?
HERE. THIS IS WHERE EVERYMAN'S STATEMENT TO THE MEDIA YESTERDAY WAS SENT FROM.
YOU'RE WELCOME?
HEY, DON'T FORGET THE HOOD, MAN.
GOTTA STAY ON BRAND!

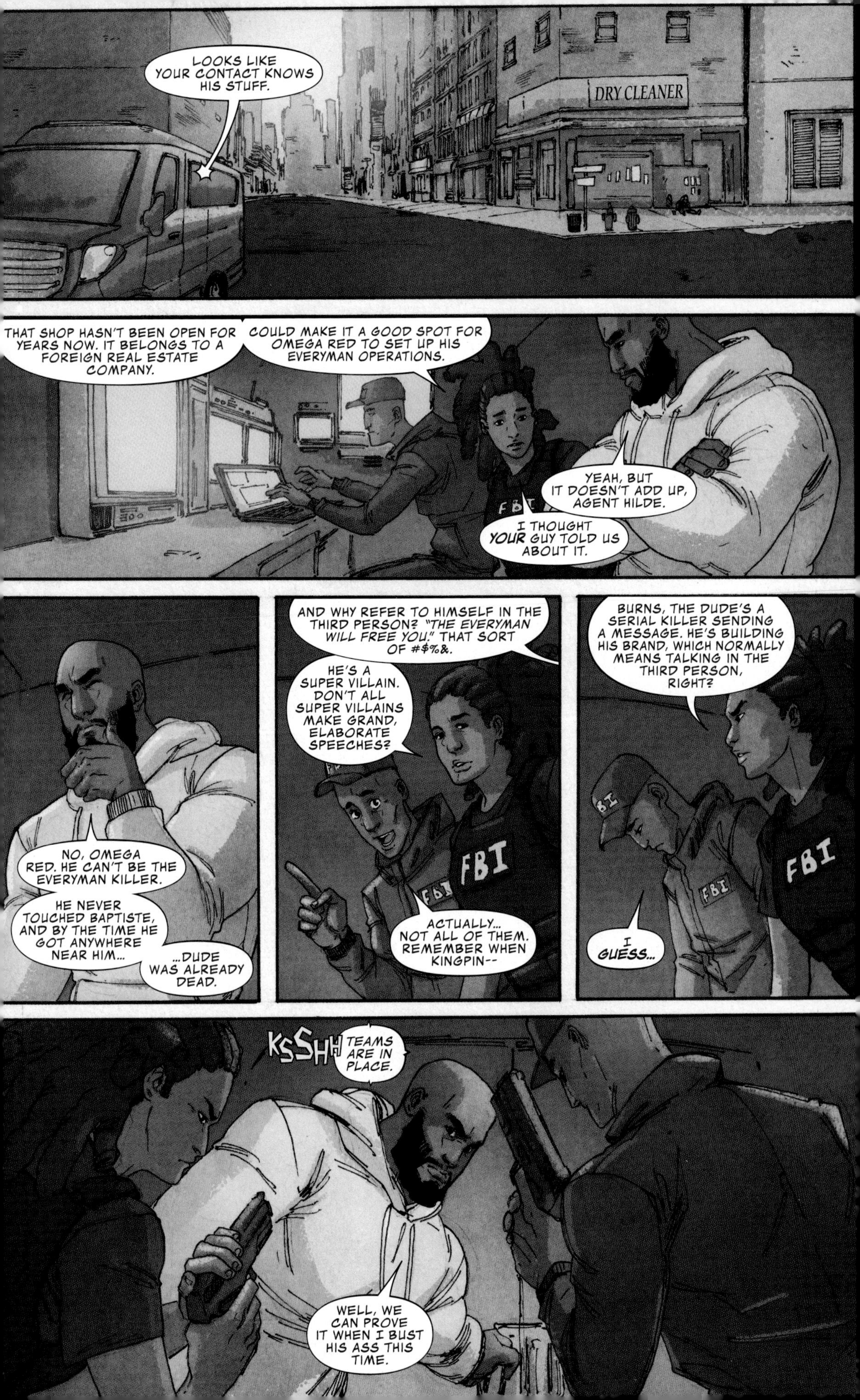
LOOKS LIKE YOUR CONTACT KNOWS HIS STUFF.
DRY CLEANER
THAT SHOP HASN'T BEEN OPEN FOR YEARS NOW. IT BELONGS TO A FOREIGN REAL ESTATE COMPANY.
COULD MAKE IT A GOOD SPOT FOR OMEGA RED TO SET UP HIS EVERYMAN OPERATIONS.
YEAH, BUT IT DOESN'T ADD UP, AGENT HILDE.
I THOUGHT YOUR GUY TOLD US ABOUT IT.
NO, OMEGA RED. HE CAN'T BE THE EVERYMAN KILLER.
HE NEVER TOUCHED BAPTISTE, AND BY THE TIME HE GOT ANYWHERE NEAR HIM...
...DUDE WAS ALREADY DEAD.
AND WHY REFER TO HIMSELF IN THE THIRD PERSON? "THE EVERYMAN WILL FREE YOU." THAT SORT OF #$%&.
HE'S A SUPER VILLAIN. DON'T ALL SUPER VILLAINS MAKE GRAND, ELABORATE SPEECHES?
ACTUALLY... NOT ALL OF THEM. REMEMBER WHEN KINGPIN--
BURNS, THE DUDE'S A SERIAL KILLER SENDING A MESSAGE. HE'S BUILDING HIS BRAND, WHICH NORMALLY MEANS TALKING IN THE THIRD PERSON, RIGHT?
I GUESS...
KSSHH
TEAMS ARE IN PLACE.
WELL, WE CAN PROVE IT WHEN I BUST HIS ASS THIS TIME.

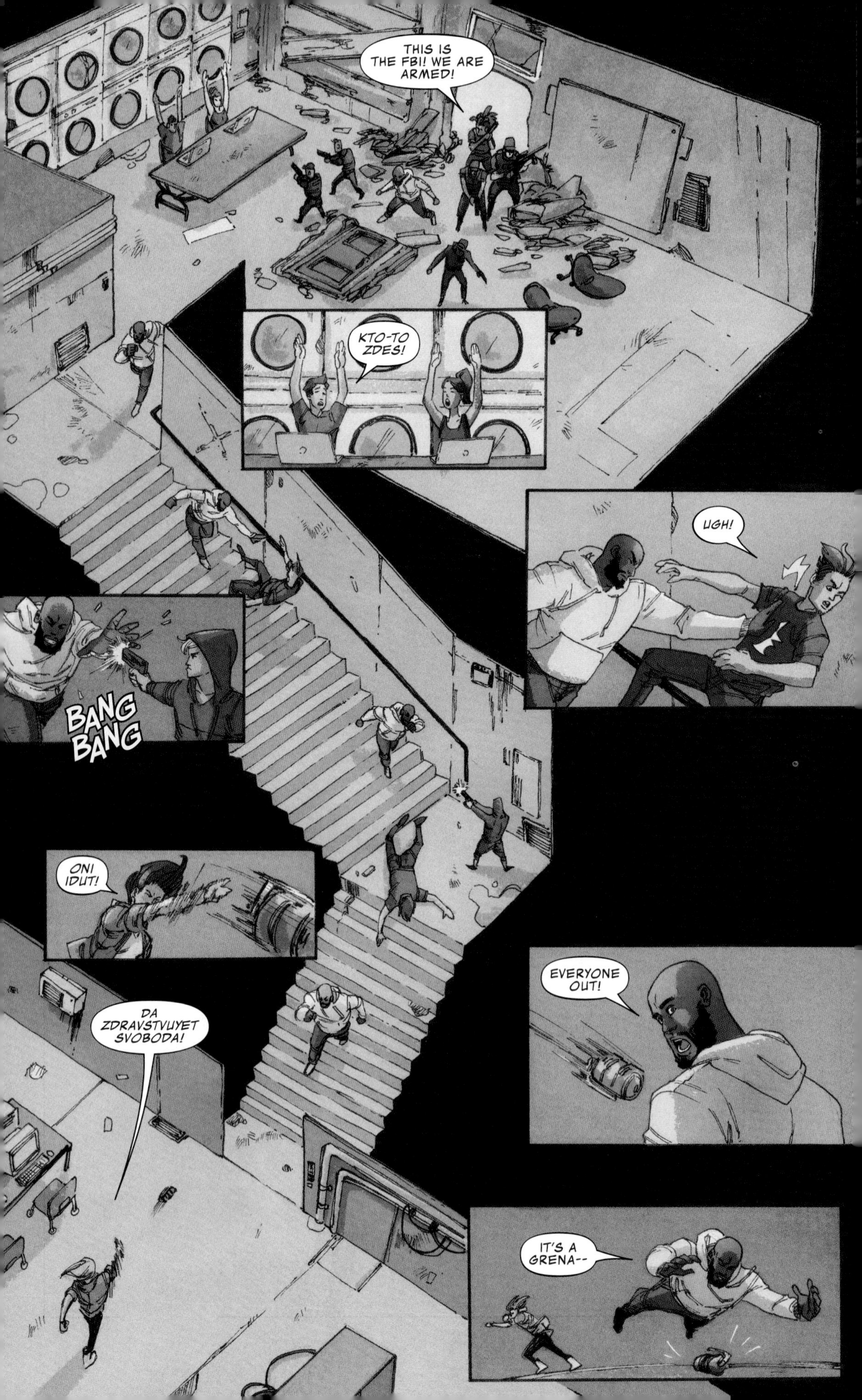
THIS IS THE FBI! WE ARE ARMED!
KTO-TO ZDES!
UGH!
BANG BANG
ONI IDUT!
EVERYONE OUT!
DA ZDRAVSTVUYET SVOBODA!
IT'S A GRENA--

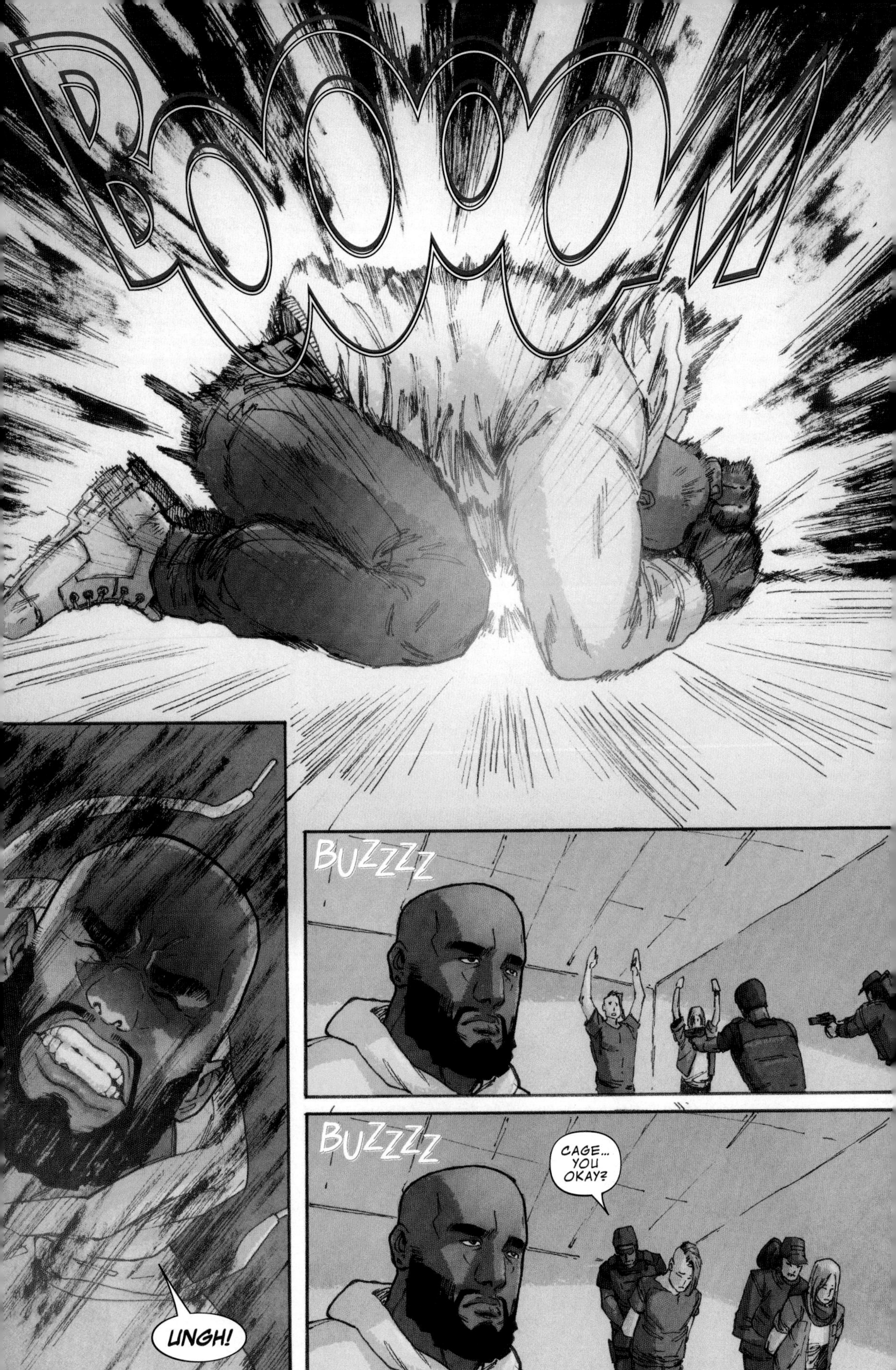
BOOOOOM
UNGH!
BUZZZZ
BUZZZZ
CAGE... YOU OKAY?

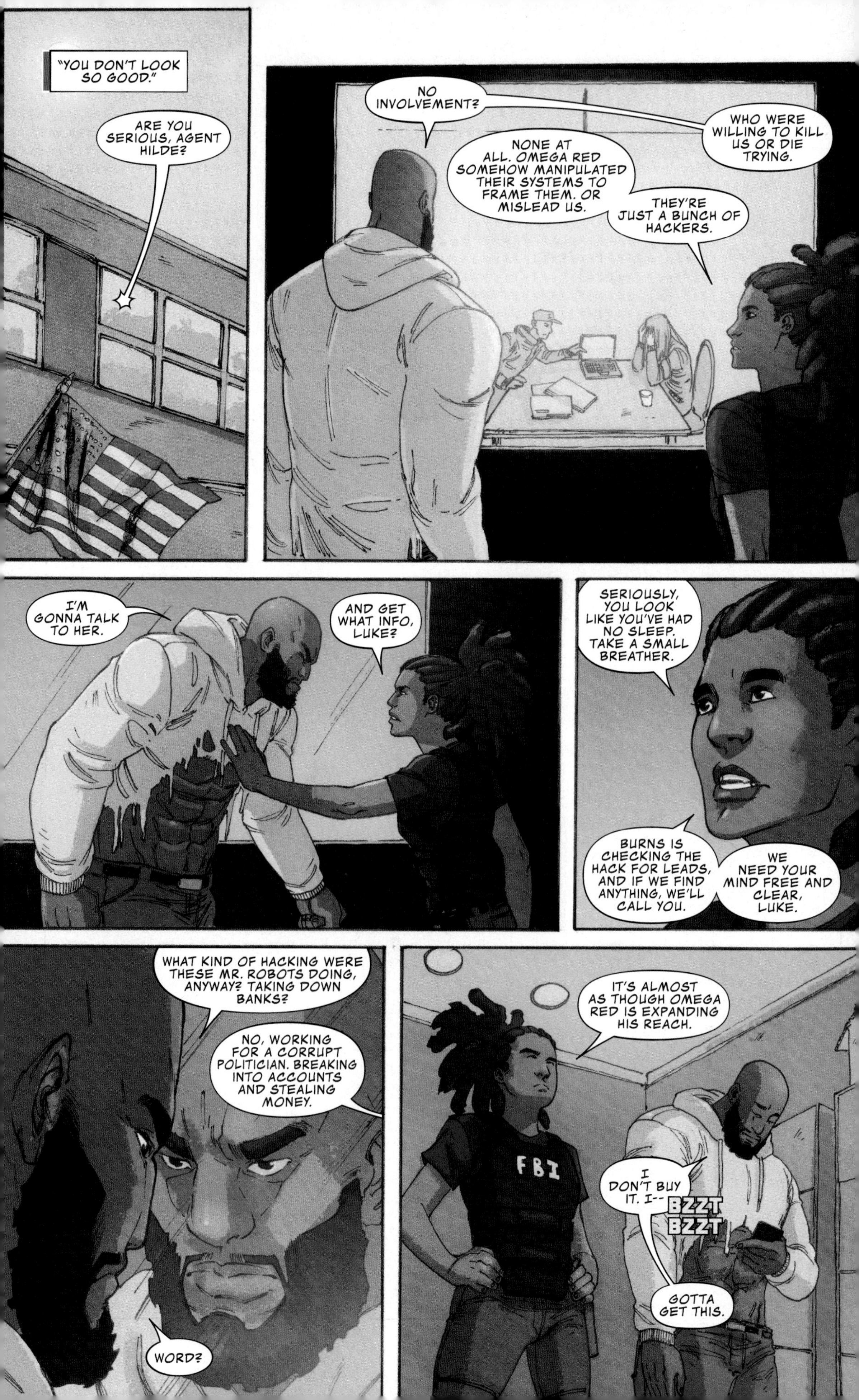
"YOU DON'T LOOK SO GOOD."
ARE YOU SERIOUS, AGENT HILDE?
NO INVOLVEMENT?
NONE AT ALL. OMEGA RED SOMEHOW MANIPULATED THEIR SYSTEMS TO FRAME THEM. OR MISLEAD US.
WHO WERE WILLING TO KILL US OR DIE TRYING.
THEY'RE JUST A BUNCH OF HACKERS.
I'M GONNA TALK TO HER.
AND GET WHAT INFO, LUKE?
SERIOUSLY, YOU LOOK LIKE YOU'VE HAD NO SLEEP. TAKE A SMALL BREATHER.
BURNS IS CHECKING THE HACK FOR LEADS, AND IF WE FIND ANYTHING, WE'LL CALL YOU.
WE NEED YOUR MIND FREE AND CLEAR, LUKE.
WHAT KIND OF HACKING WERE THESE MR. ROBOTS DOING, ANYWAY? TAKING DOWN BANKS?
NO, WORKING FOR A CORRUPT POLITICIAN. BREAKING INTO ACCOUNTS AND STEALING MONEY.
WORD?
IT'S ALMOST AS THOUGH OMEGA RED IS EXPANDING HIS REACH.
FBI
I DON'T BUY IT. I--
BZZT
BZZT
GOTTA GET THIS.

HEY, BABY MAMA.

HEY THERE, BABY DADDY.

IT'S GOOD TO HEAR FROM YOU, JESS. FIGURE OUT HOW TO USE THOSE EUROPEAN OUTLETS YET?

YEAH, WHAT'S UP WITH THAT GARBAGE? WHY DO THEY HAVE TO DO EVERYTHING SO BACKWARDS?

THINGS ARE GOOD. HAWKEYE AND I ARE ABOUT TO BLOW THIS CASE WIDE OPEN.

I SAW THE FOOTAGE OF THE ATTACK BY BORIS THE RUSSIAN. YOU OKAY? THAT HIT WAS PRETTY HARD.

YEAH. YEAH. I'M FINE.

YOU DON'T SOUND FINE.

I'M ALL GOOD. I'M ON OMEGA RED'S TRAIL RIGHT NOW.

HERE IT COMES...

...

SHE KNOWS I'M HIDING SOMETHING.

BUZZ

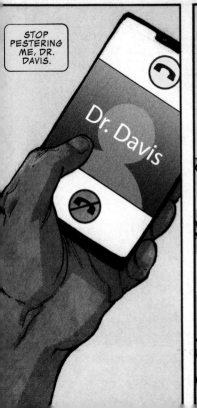

STOP PESTERING ME, DR. DAVIS.

Dr. Davis

I, UH... I'VE GOT A CALL ON THE OTHER LINE. GOTTA TAKE IT.

I...GOTTA TAKE THIS. IT'S A LEAD. I LOVE YOU.

REALLY? YOU'RE BAILING ON ME?

THERE'S NOTHING TO TELL JESSICA. OR DAVIS.

THERE'S NOTHING WRONG WITH ME.

RIGHT?

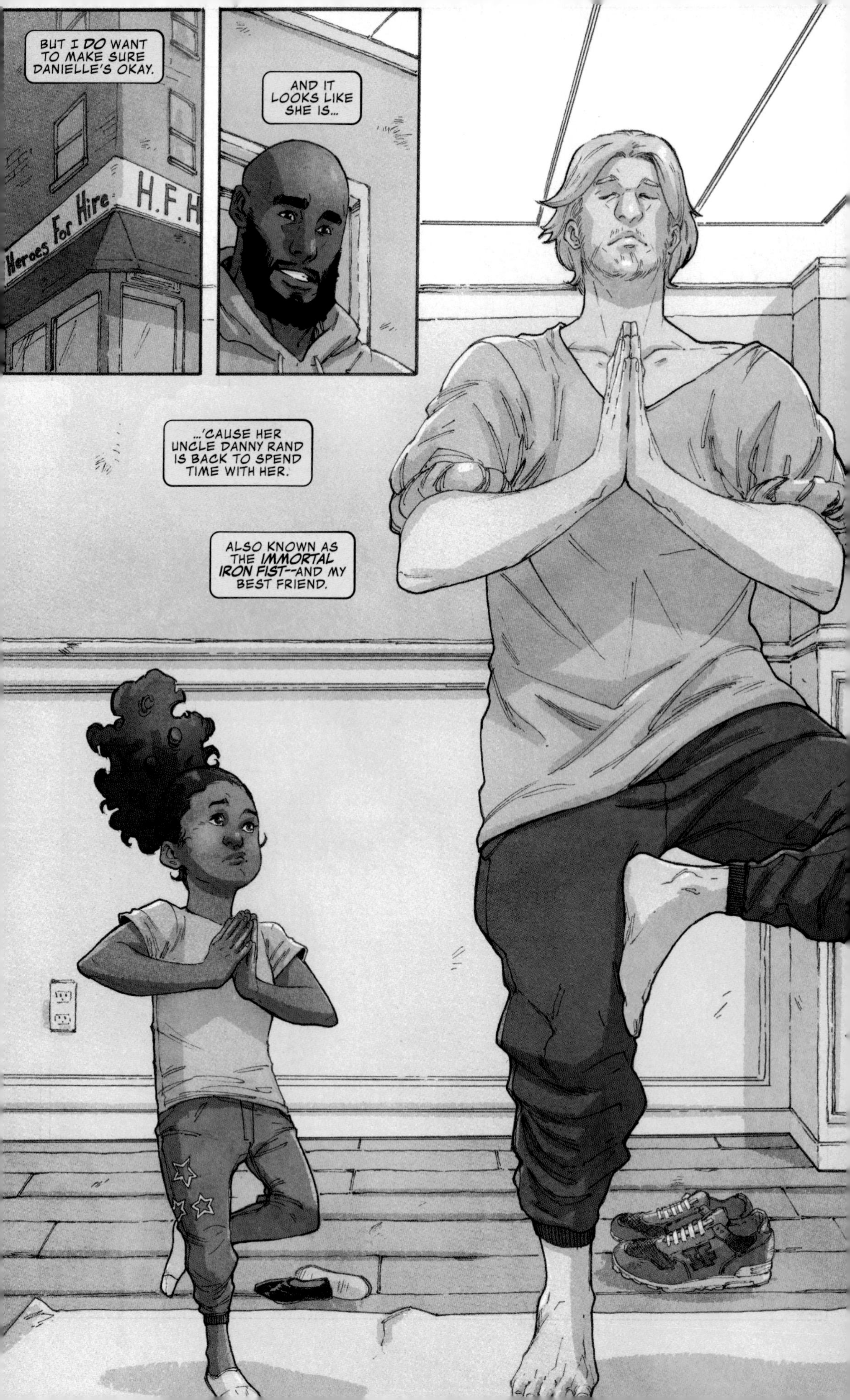

BUT I DO WANT TO MAKE SURE DANIELLE'S OKAY.
Heroes For Hire
H.F.H
AND IT LOOKS LIKE SHE IS...
...'CAUSE HER UNCLE DANNY RAND IS BACK TO SPEND TIME WITH HER.
ALSO KNOWN AS THE IMMORTAL IRON FIST--AND MY BEST FRIEND.

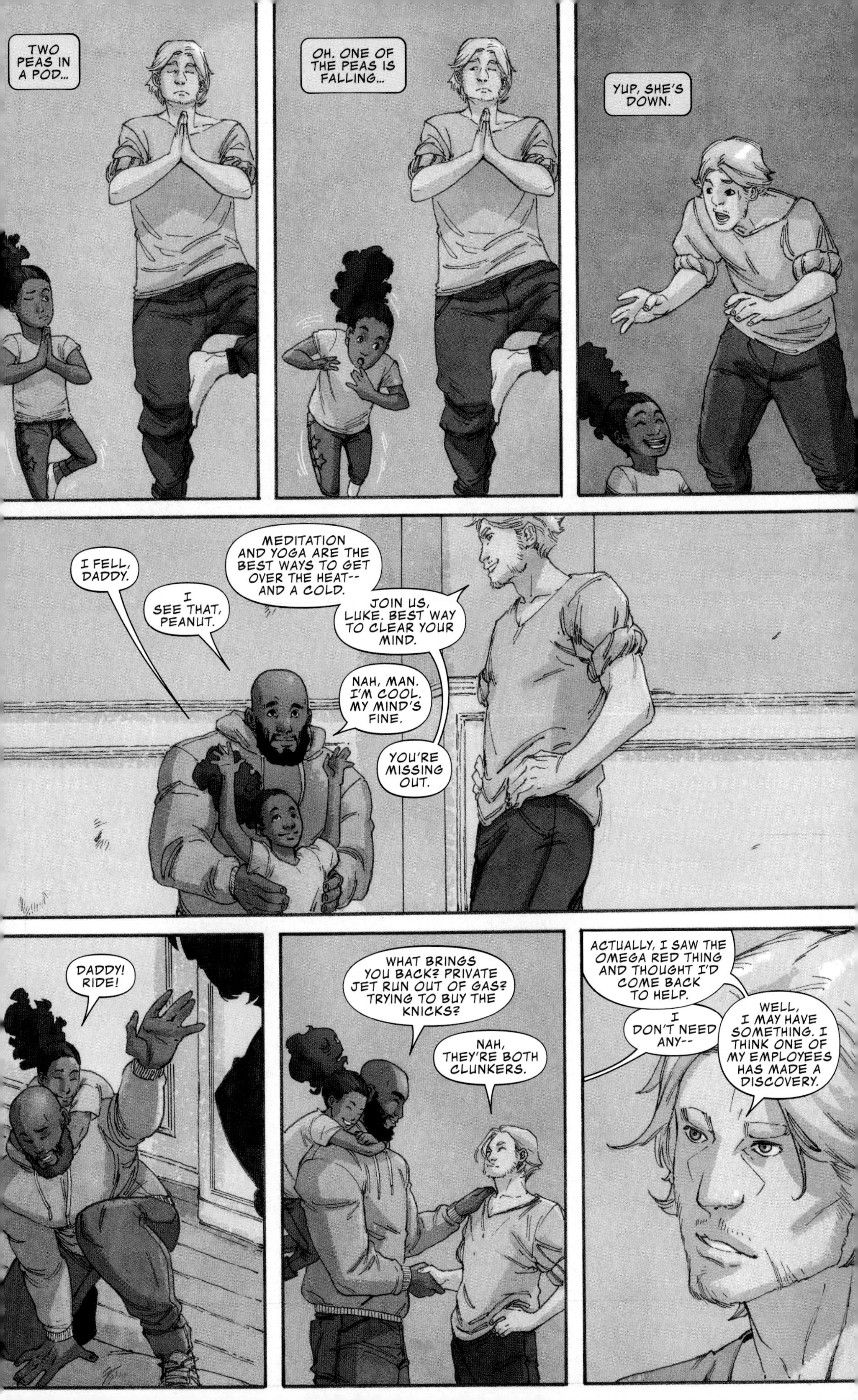
TWO PEAS IN A POD...
OH. ONE OF THE PEAS IS FALLING...
YUP, SHE'S DOWN.
I FELL, DADDY.
I SEE THAT, PEANUT.
MEDITATION AND YOGA ARE THE BEST WAYS TO GET OVER THE HEAT-- AND A COLD.
JOIN US, LUKE. BEST WAY TO CLEAR YOUR MIND.
NAH, MAN. I'M COOL. MY MIND'S FINE.
YOU'RE MISSING OUT.
DADDY! RIDE!
WHAT BRINGS YOU BACK? PRIVATE JET RUN OUT OF GAS? TRYING TO BUY THE KNICKS?
NAH, THEY'RE BOTH CLUNKERS.
ACTUALLY, I SAW THE OMEGA RED THING AND THOUGHT I'D COME BACK TO HELP.
I DON'T NEED ANY--
WELL, I MAY HAVE SOMETHING. I THINK ONE OF MY EMPLOYEES HAS MADE A DISCOVERY.

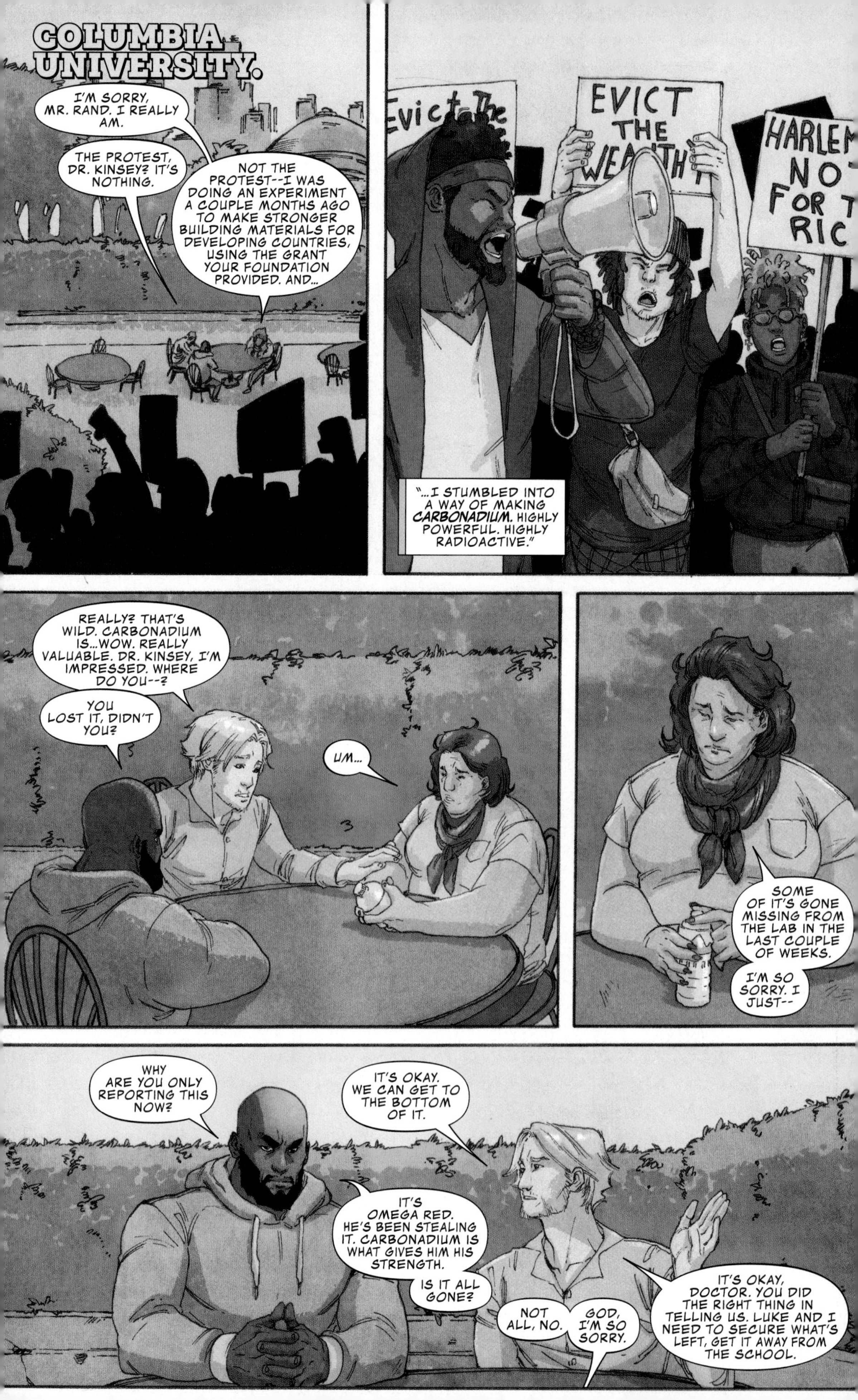
COLUMBIA UNIVERSITY.
I'M SORRY, MR. RAND. I REALLY AM.
THE PROTEST, DR. KINSEY? IT'S NOTHING.
NOT THE PROTEST--I WAS DOING AN EXPERIMENT A COUPLE MONTHS AGO TO MAKE STRONGER BUILDING MATERIALS FOR DEVELOPING COUNTRIES, USING THE GRANT YOUR FOUNDATION PROVIDED. AND...
Evict The
EVICT THE WEALTHY
HARLEM NOT FOR T RIC
"...I STUMBLED INTO A WAY OF MAKING CARBONADIUM. HIGHLY POWERFUL. HIGHLY RADIOACTIVE."
REALLY? THAT'S WILD. CARBONADIUM IS...WOW. REALLY VALUABLE. DR. KINSEY, I'M IMPRESSED. WHERE DO YOU--?
YOU LOST IT, DIDN'T YOU?
UM...
SOME OF IT'S GONE MISSING FROM THE LAB IN THE LAST COUPLE OF WEEKS.
I'M SO SORRY. I JUST--
WHY ARE YOU ONLY REPORTING THIS NOW?
IT'S OKAY. WE CAN GET TO THE BOTTOM OF IT.
IT'S OMEGA RED. HE'S BEEN STEALING IT. CARBONADIUM IS WHAT GIVES HIM HIS STRENGTH.
IS IT ALL GONE?
NOT ALL, NO.
GOD, I'M SO SORRY.
IT'S OKAY, DOCTOR. YOU DID THE RIGHT THING IN TELLING US. LUKE AND I NEED TO SECURE WHAT'S LEFT, GET IT AWAY FROM THE SCHOOL.

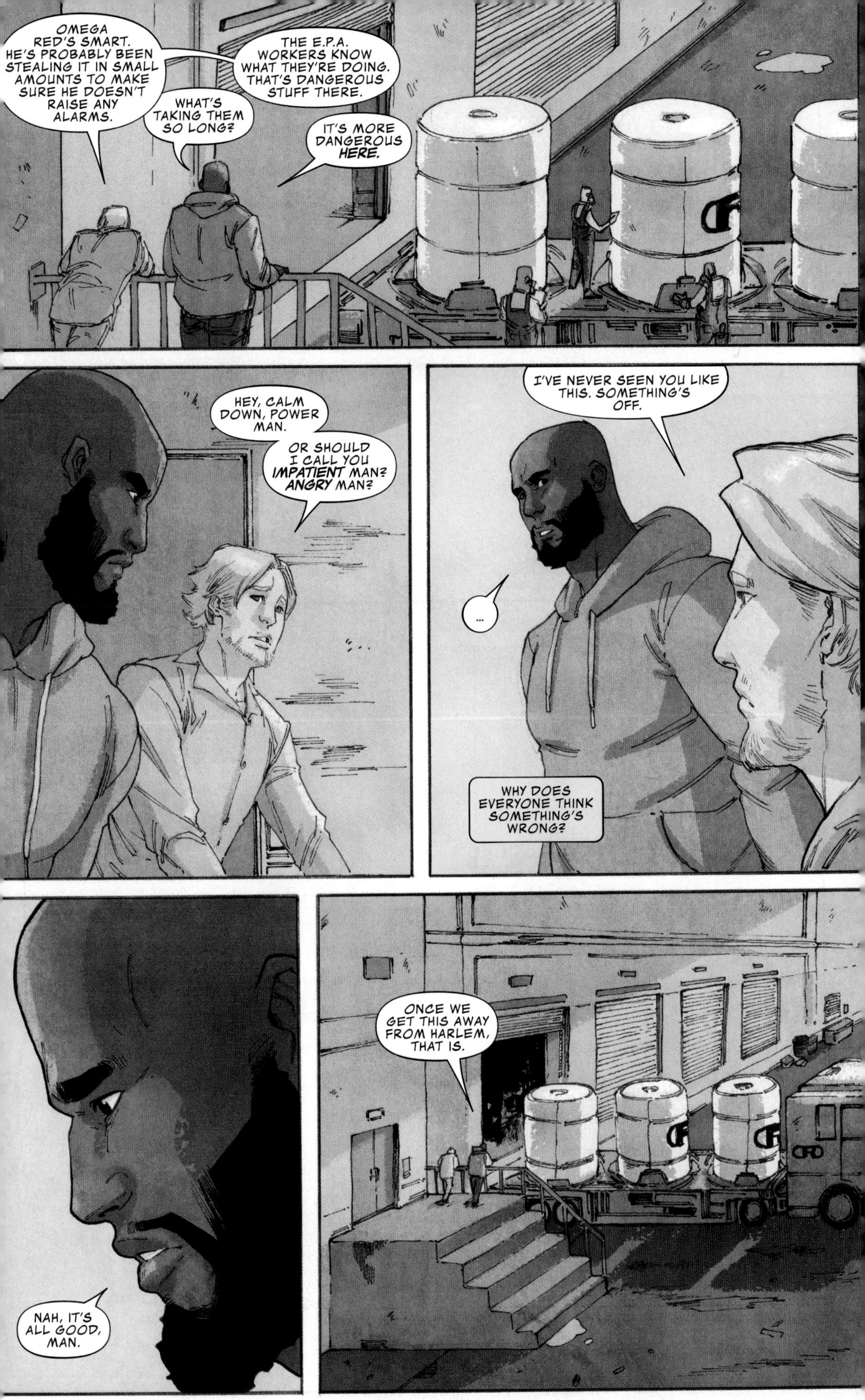
OMEGA RED'S SMART. HE'S PROBABLY BEEN STEALING IT IN SMALL AMOUNTS TO MAKE SURE HE DOESN'T RAISE ANY ALARMS.
THE E.P.A. WORKERS KNOW WHAT THEY'RE DOING. THAT'S DANGEROUS STUFF THERE.
WHAT'S TAKING THEM SO LONG?
IT'S MORE DANGEROUS HERE.
HEY, CALM DOWN, POWER MAN.
OR SHOULD I CALL YOU IMPATIENT MAN? ANGRY MAN?
I'VE NEVER SEEN YOU LIKE THIS. SOMETHING'S OFF.
...
WHY DOES EVERYONE THINK SOMETHING'S WRONG?
NAH, IT'S ALL GOOD, MAN.
ONCE WE GET THIS AWAY FROM HARLEM, THAT IS.

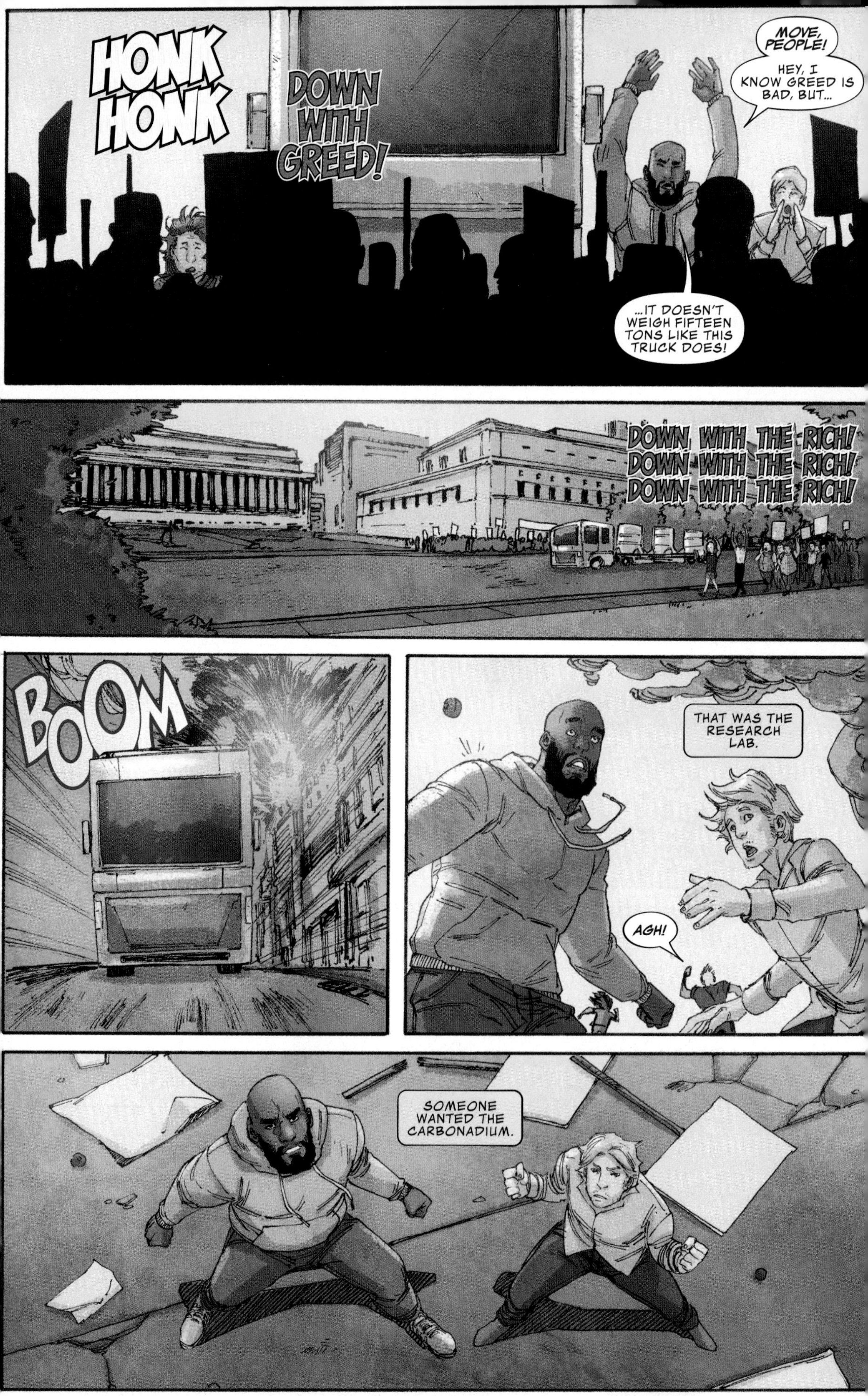
HONK HONK
DOWN WITH GREED!
MOVE, PEOPLE!
HEY, I KNOW GREED IS BAD, BUT...
...IT DOESN'T WEIGH FIFTEEN TONS LIKE THIS TRUCK DOES!
DOWN WITH THE RICH! DOWN WITH THE RICH! DOWN WITH THE RICH!
BOOM
THAT WAS THE RESEARCH LAB.
AGH!
SOMEONE WANTED THE CARBONADIUM.

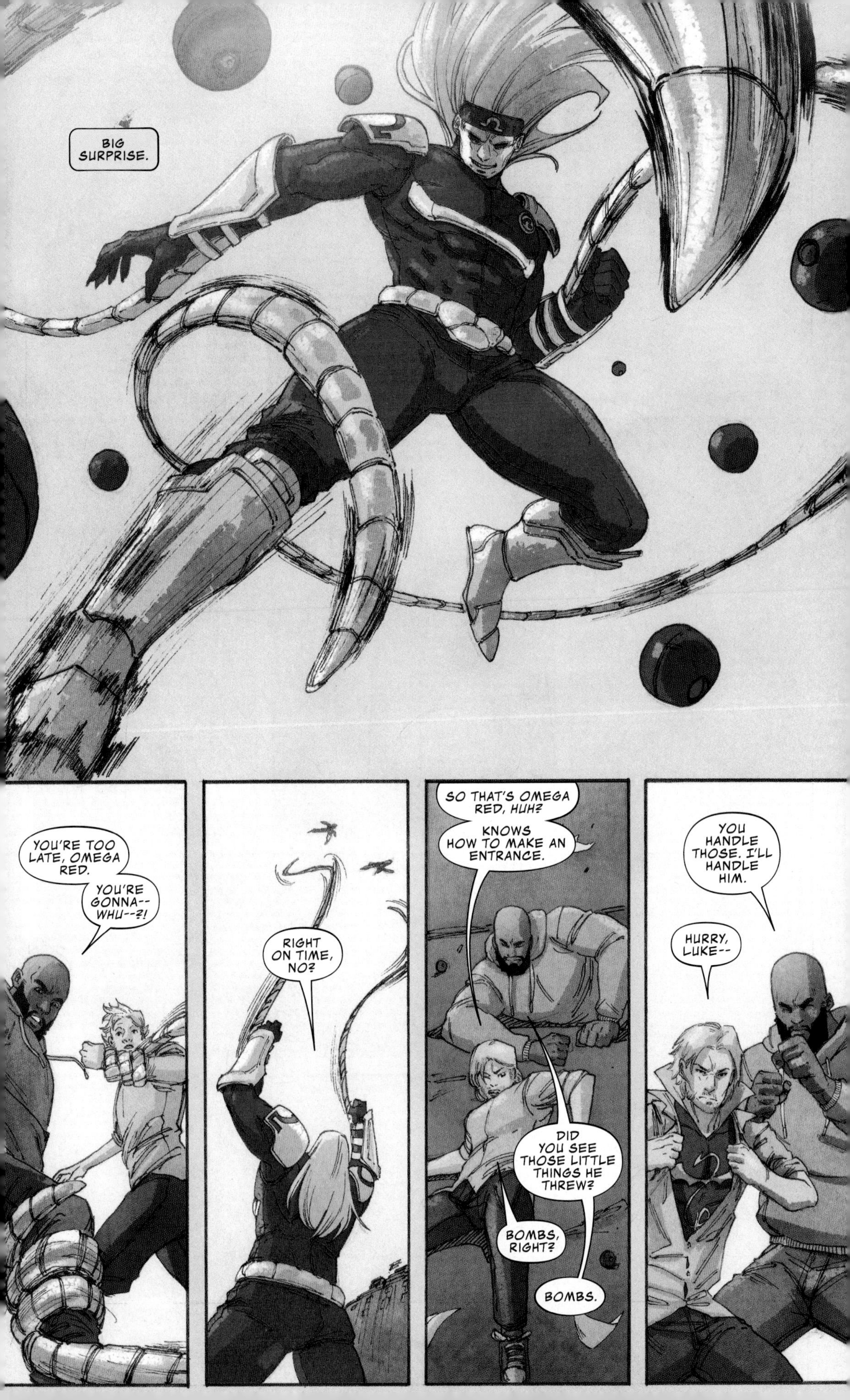
BIG SURPRISE.
YOU'RE TOO LATE, OMEGA RED.
YOU'RE GONNA-- WHU--?!
RIGHT ON TIME, NO?
SO THAT'S OMEGA RED, HUH?
KNOWS HOW TO MAKE AN ENTRANCE.
DID YOU SEE THOSE LITTLE THINGS HE THREW?
BOMBS, RIGHT?
BOMBS.
YOU HANDLE THOSE. I'LL HANDLE HIM.
HURRY, LUKE--

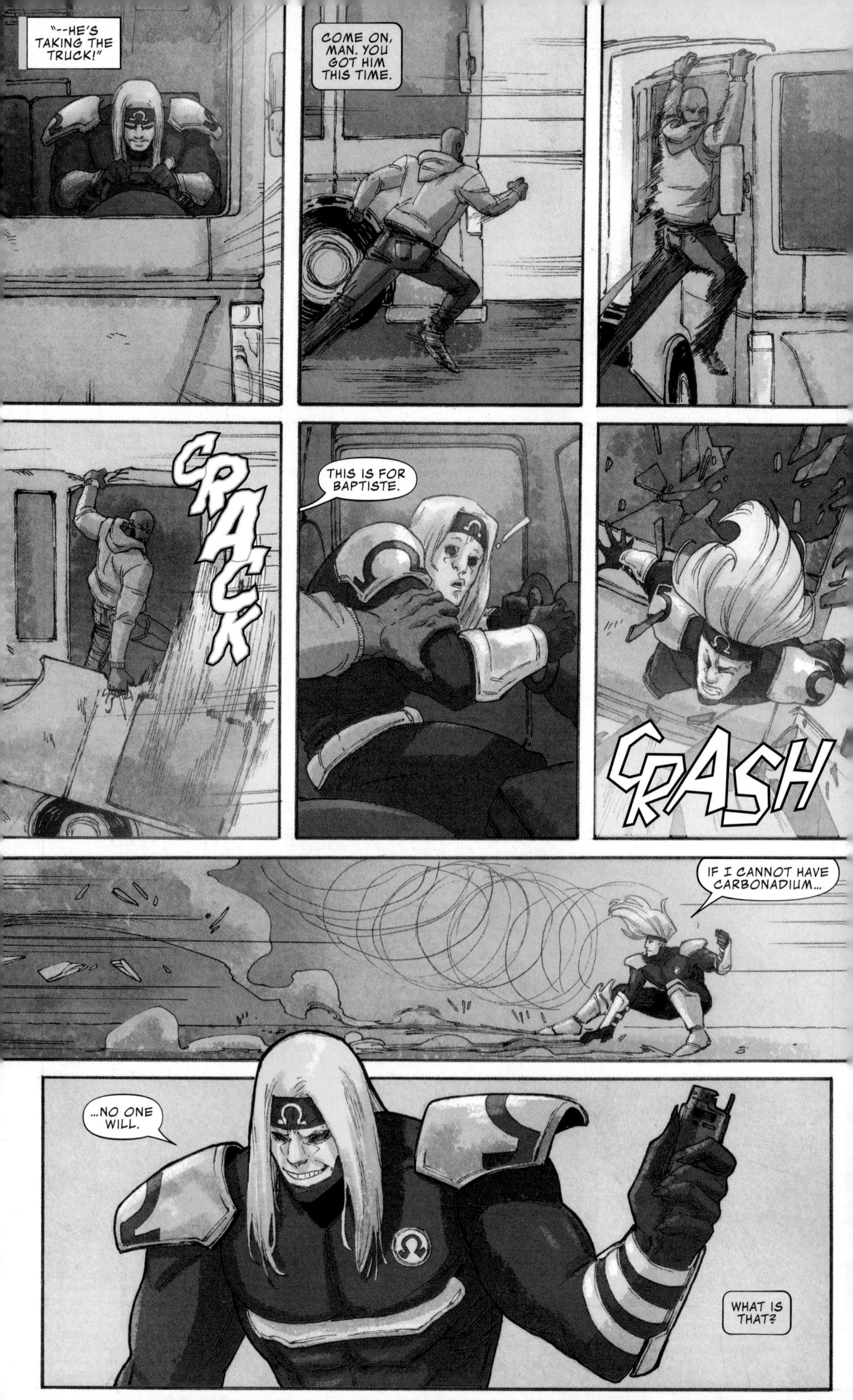
"--HE'S TAKING THE TRUCK!"
COME ON, MAN. YOU GOT HIM THIS TIME.
CRACK
THIS IS FOR BAPTISTE.
CRASH
IF I CANNOT HAVE CARBONADIUM...
...NO ONE WILL.
WHAT IS THAT?

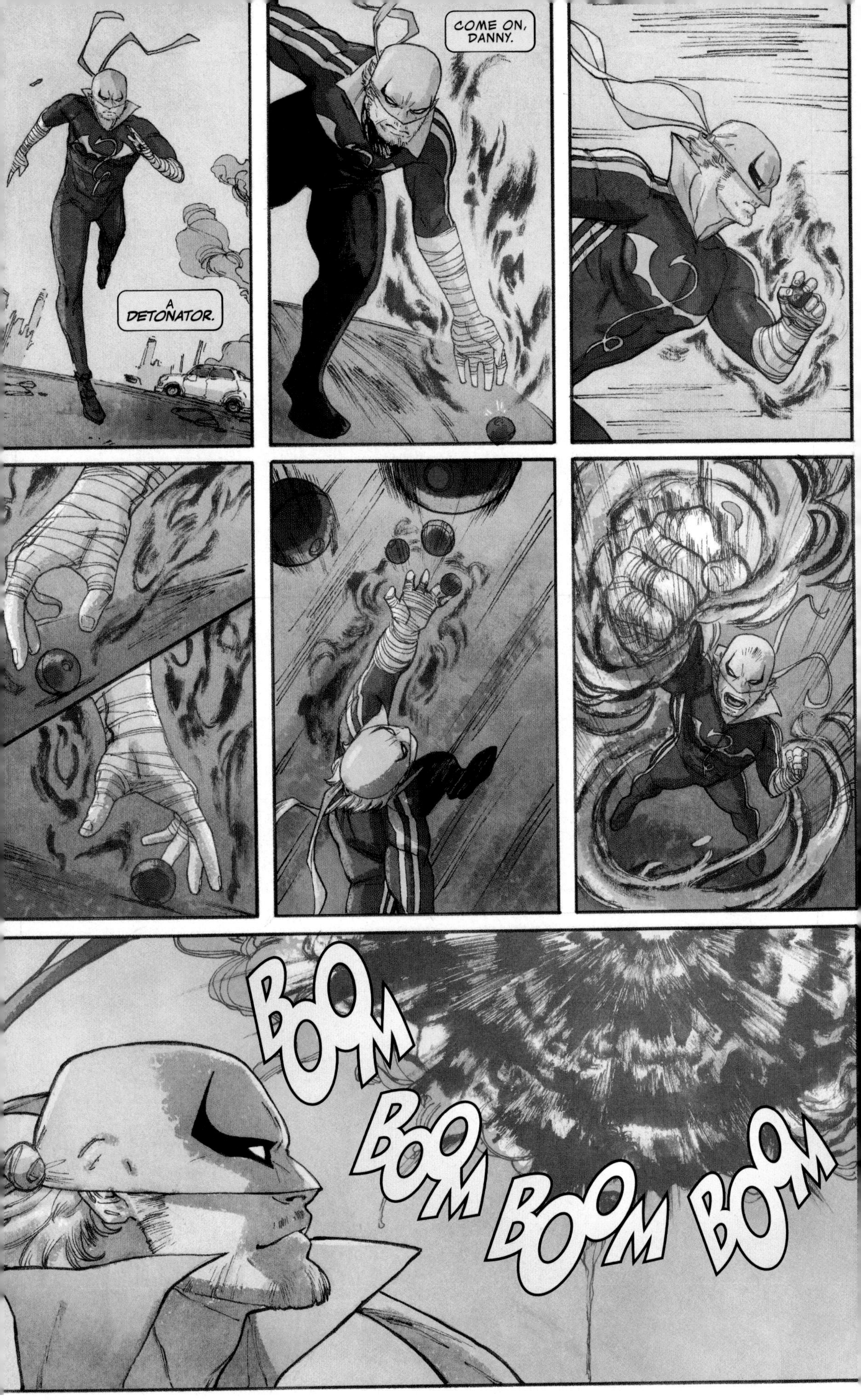
A DETONATOR.
COME ON, DANNY.
BOOM
BOOM
BOOM
BOOM

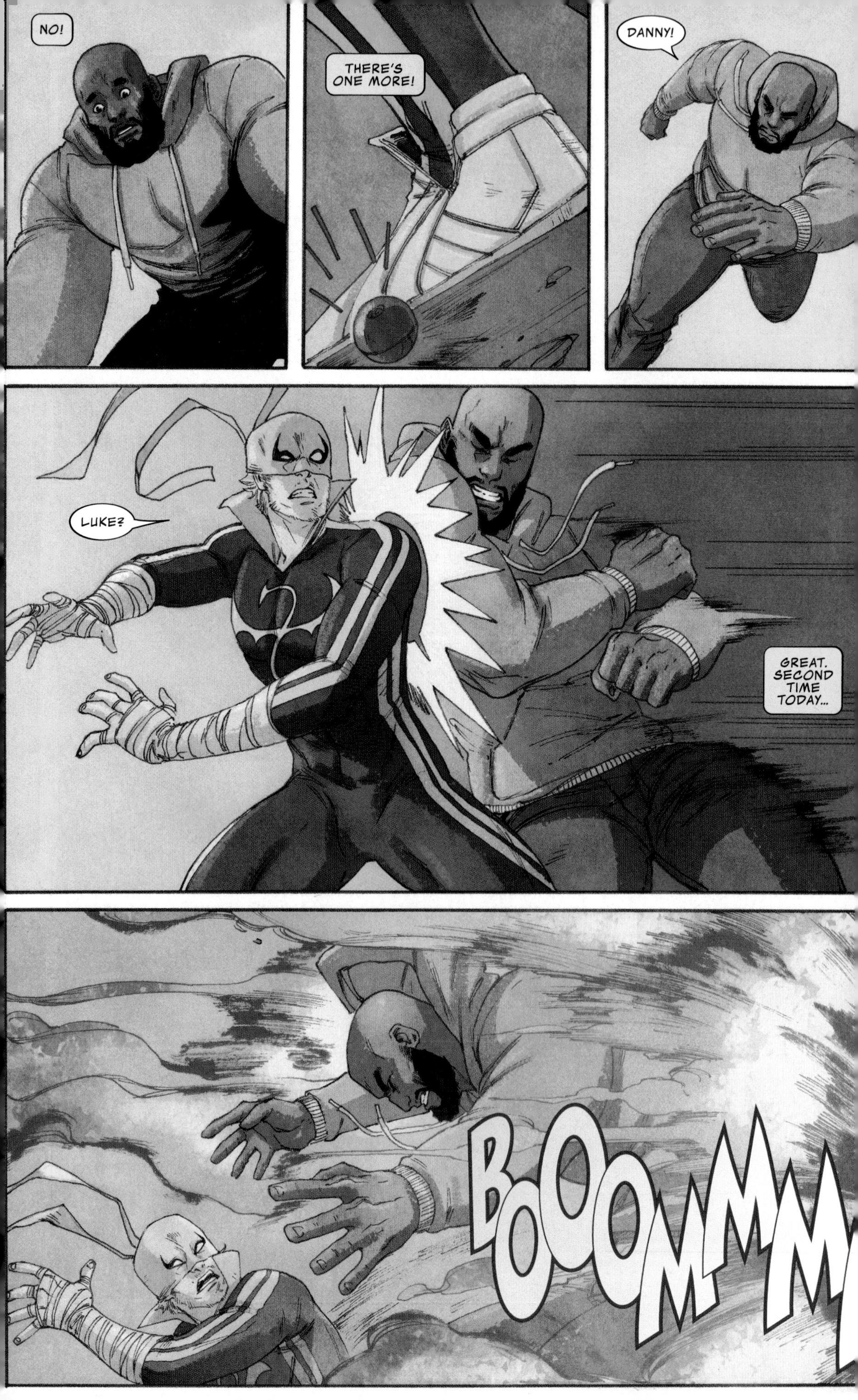
NO!
THERE'S ONE MORE!
DANNY!
LUKE?
GREAT. SECOND TIME TODAY...
BOOOMMMM

BUZZZZ

BUZZZZ

MY HEAD...

BUZZZZ

WHAT THE...

BUZZZZ

WHO'S THERE WITH HIM?

HE DOESN'T LOOK HAPPY.

YOU GOT LUCKY, COMRADES!

I WAS RIGHT. OMEGA RED REPORTS TO SOMEONE.

I ALMOST HAD HIM... I COULD HAVE GOTTEN...

COULD HAVE GOTTEN...

THE EVERYMAN.

THE EVERYMAN.

LUKE? I NEED HELP WITH THE TANKS.

THE EVERYMAN.

THE EVERYMAN.

THE EVERYMAN.

THE EVER

THE EVERYMAN.

THE EVERYMAN.

THE EVERYMA

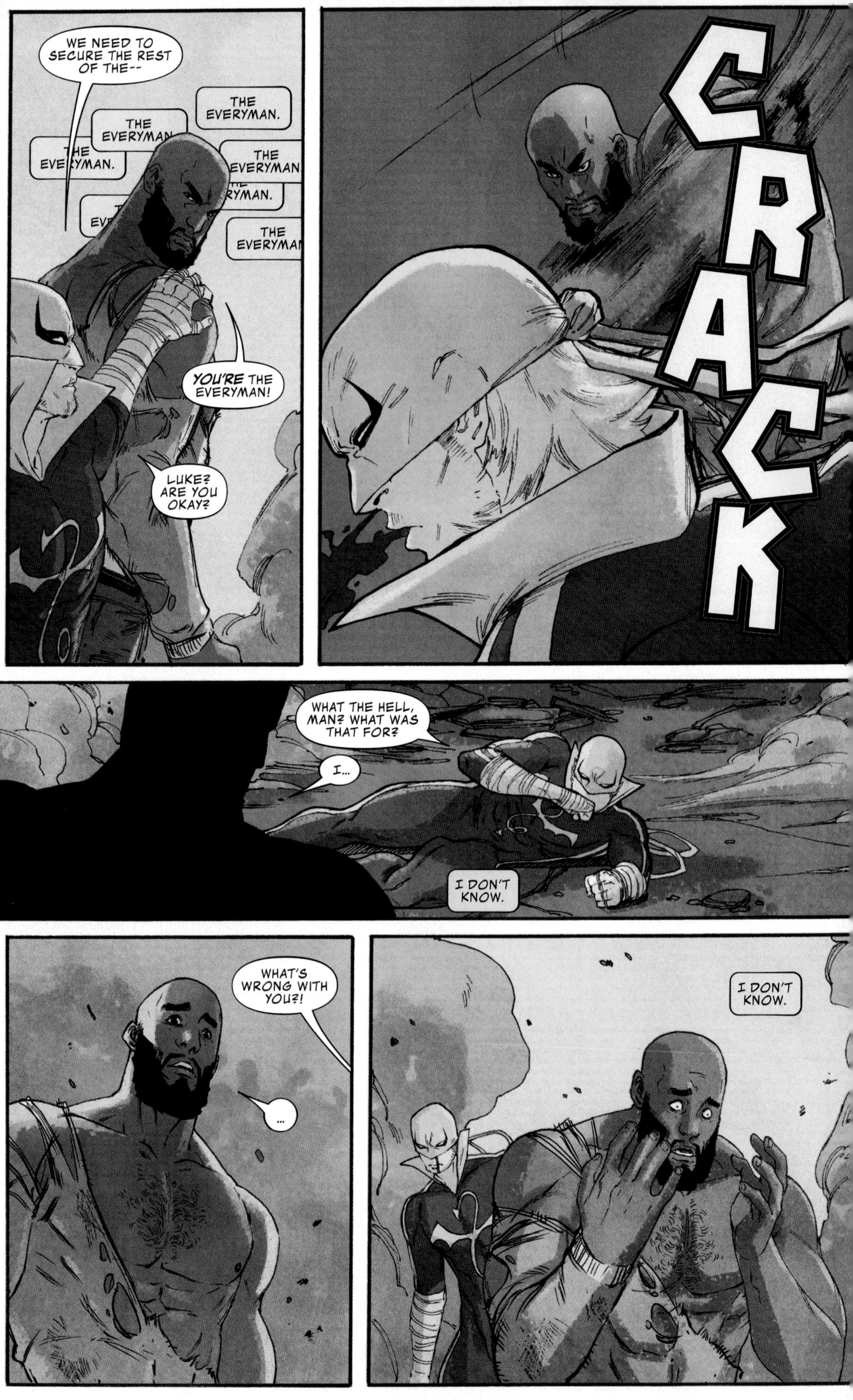
WE NEED TO SECURE THE REST OF THE--
THE EVERYMAN.
THE EVERYMAN.
THE EVERYMAN.
THE EVERYMAN.
THE EVERYMAN.
YOU'RE THE EVERYMAN!
LUKE? ARE YOU OKAY?
CRACK
WHAT THE HELL, MAN? WHAT WAS THAT FOR?
I...
I DON'T KNOW.
WHAT'S WRONG WITH YOU?!
...
I DON'T KNOW.

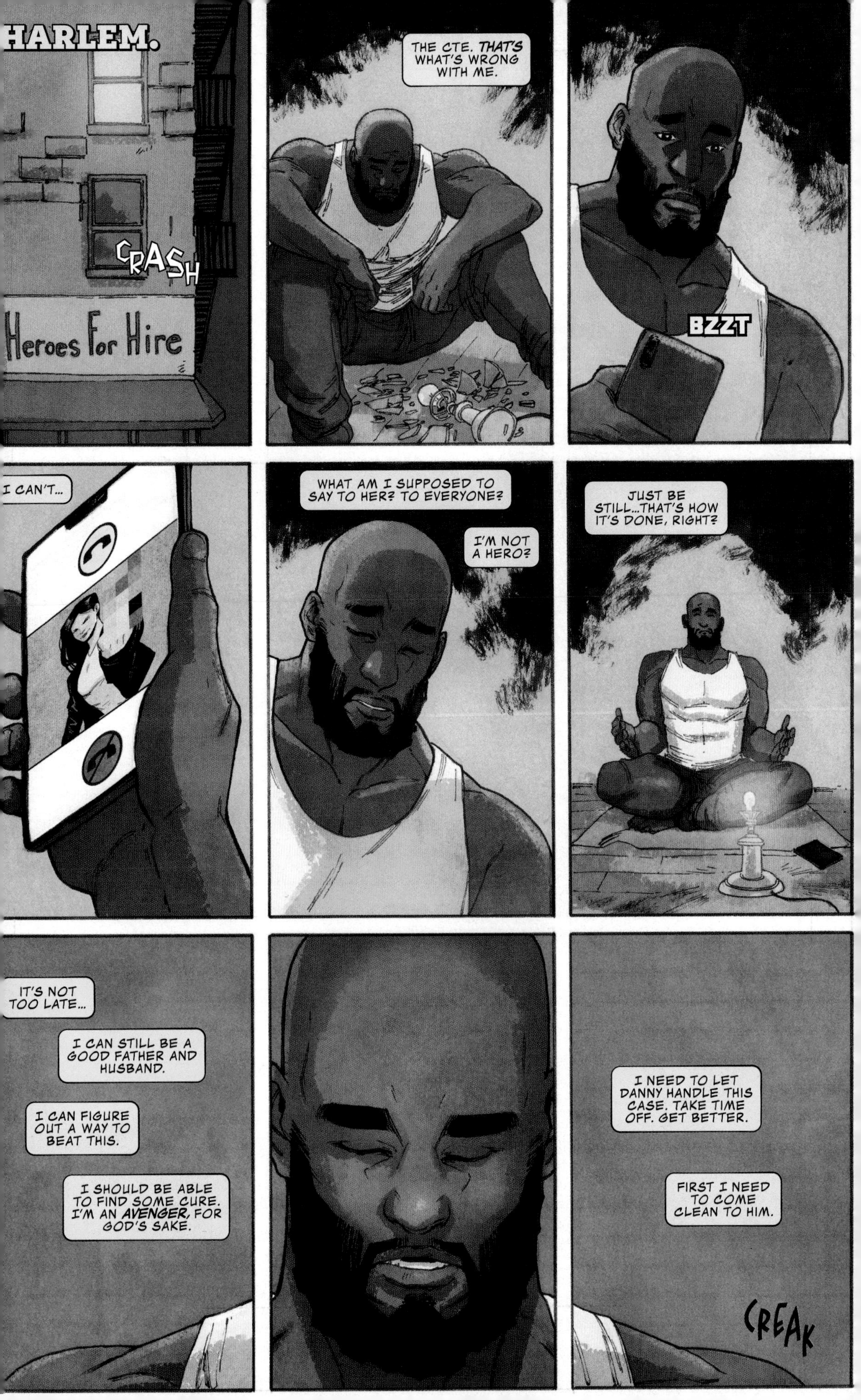
HARLEM.
CRASH
Heroes For Hire
THE CTE. THAT'S WHAT'S WRONG WITH ME.
BZZT
I CAN'T...
WHAT AM I SUPPOSED TO SAY TO HER? TO EVERYONE?
I'M NOT A HERO?
JUST BE STILL...THAT'S HOW IT'S DONE, RIGHT?
IT'S NOT TOO LATE...
I CAN STILL BE A GOOD FATHER AND HUSBAND.
I CAN FIGURE OUT A WAY TO BEAT THIS.
I SHOULD BE ABLE TO FIND SOME CURE. I'M AN AVENGER, FOR GOD'S SAKE.
I NEED TO LET DANNY HANDLE THIS CASE. TAKE TIME OFF. GET BETTER.
FIRST I NEED TO COME CLEAN TO HIM.
CREAK

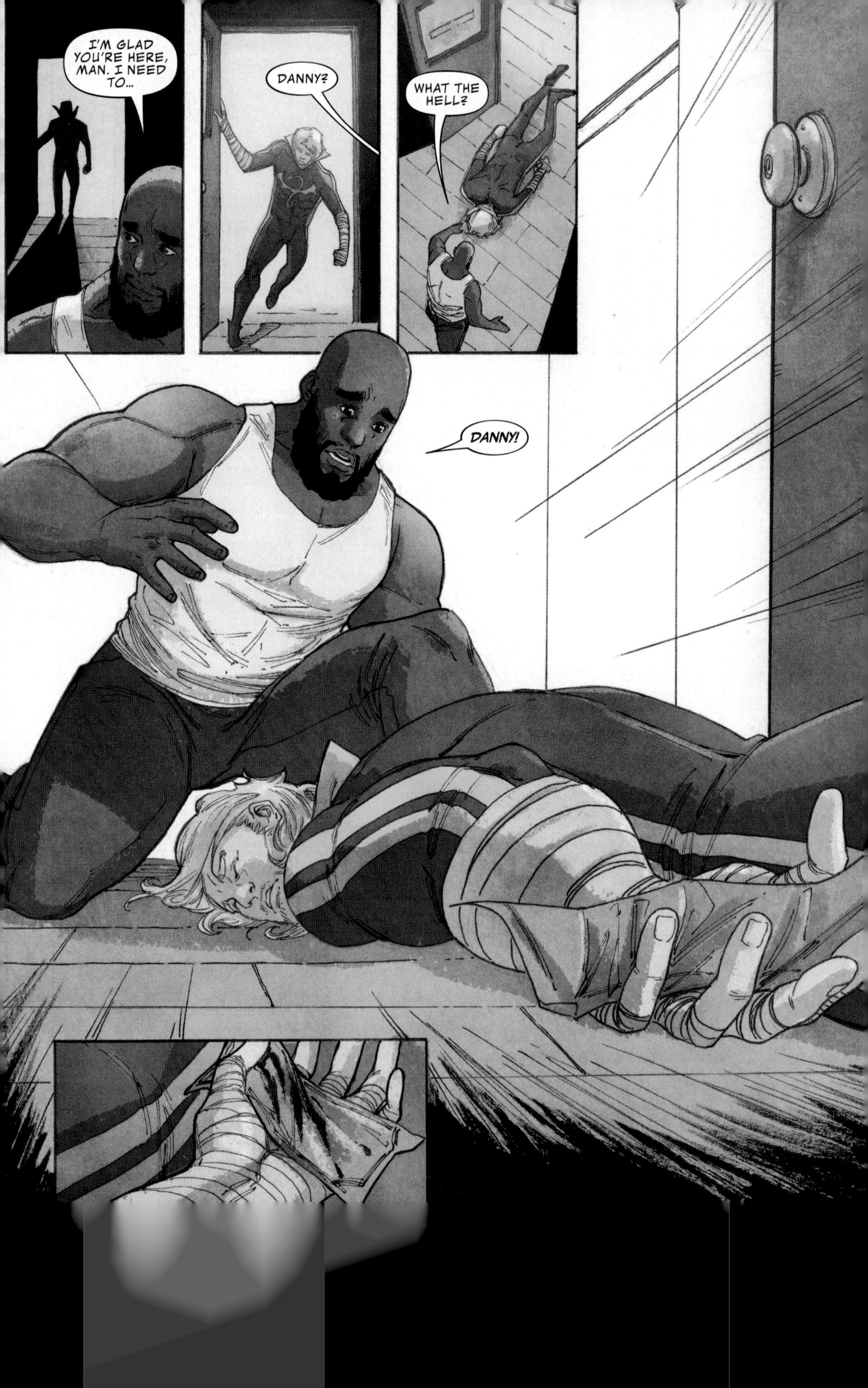
I'M GLAD YOU'RE HERE, MAN. I NEED TO...
DANNY?
WHAT THE HELL?
DANNY!

EVERYMAN:
CHAPTER 4

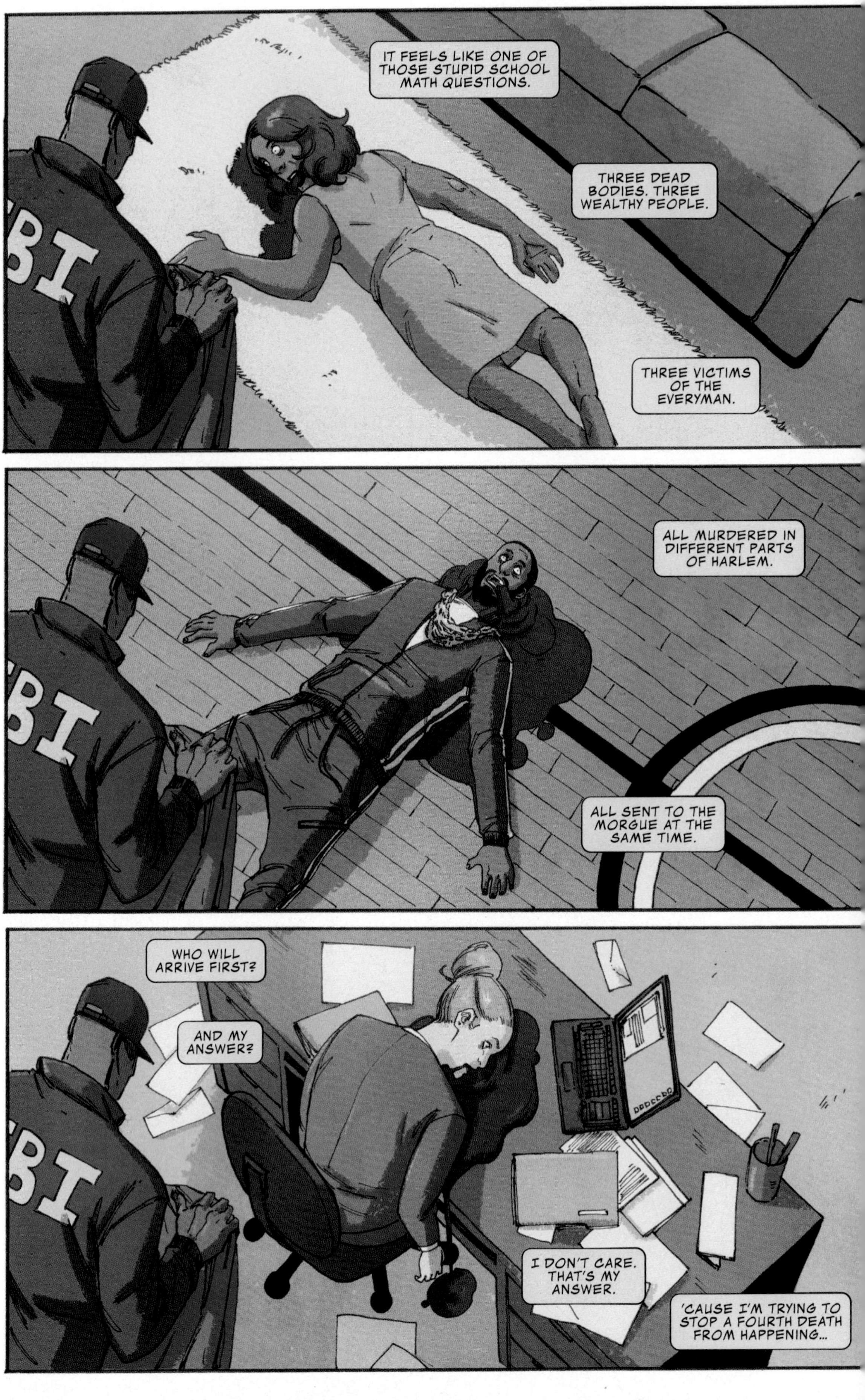
IT FEELS LIKE ONE OF THOSE STUPID SCHOOL MATH QUESTIONS.
THREE DEAD BODIES. THREE WEALTHY PEOPLE.
THREE VICTIMS OF THE EVERYMAN.
FBI
ALL MURDERED IN DIFFERENT PARTS OF HARLEM.
ALL SENT TO THE MORGUE AT THE SAME TIME.
FBI
WHO WILL ARRIVE FIRST?
AND MY ANSWER?
FBI
I DON'T CARE. THAT'S MY ANSWER.
'CAUSE I'M TRYING TO STOP A FOURTH DEATH FROM HAPPENING...

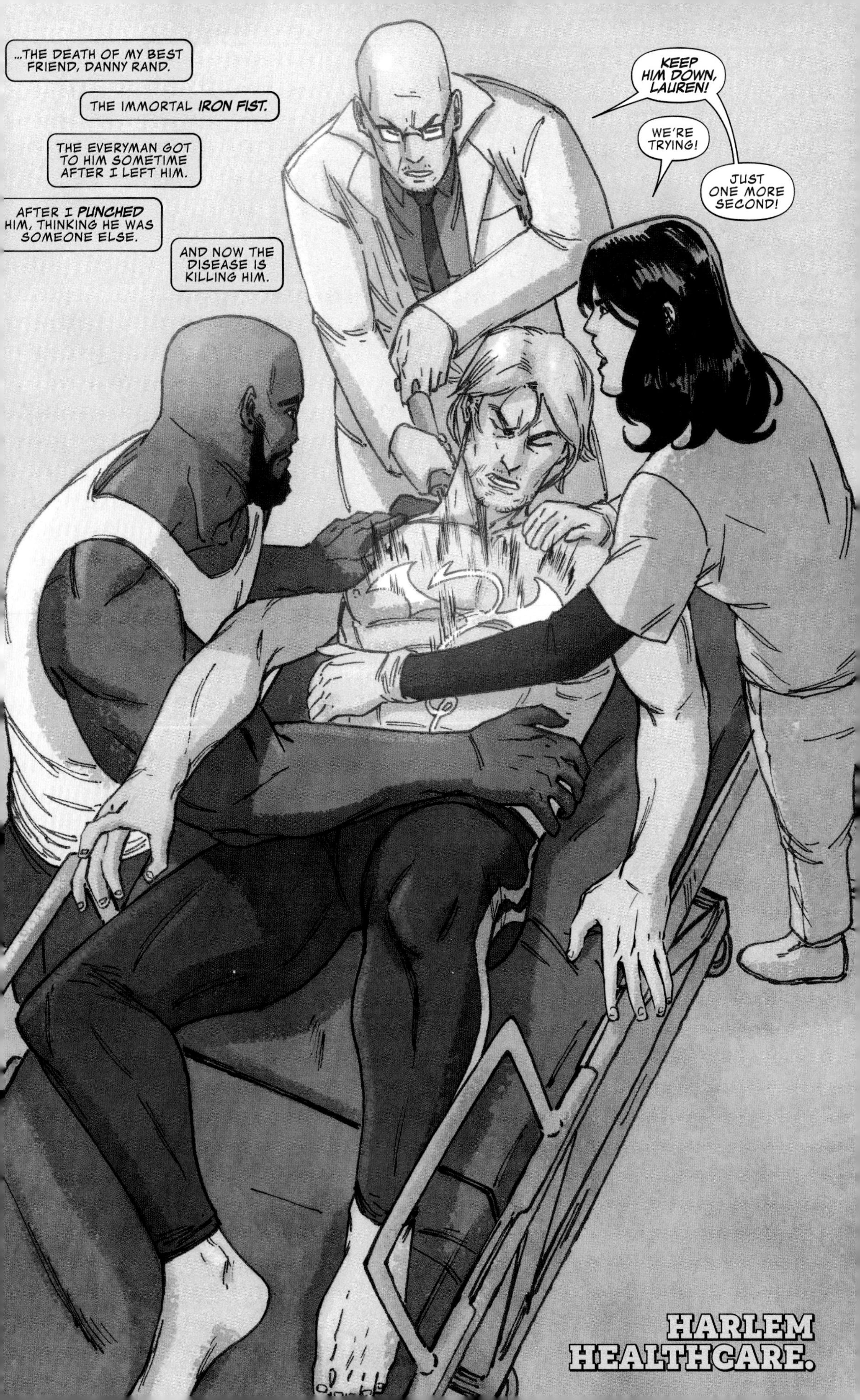
...THE DEATH OF MY BEST FRIEND, DANNY RAND.
THE IMMORTAL IRON FIST.
THE EVERYMAN GOT TO HIM SOMETIME AFTER I LEFT HIM.
AFTER I PUNCHED HIM, THINKING HE WAS SOMEONE ELSE.
AND NOW THE DISEASE IS KILLING HIM.
KEEP HIM DOWN, LAUREN!
WE'RE TRYING!
JUST ONE MORE SECOND!
HARLEM HEALTHCARE.

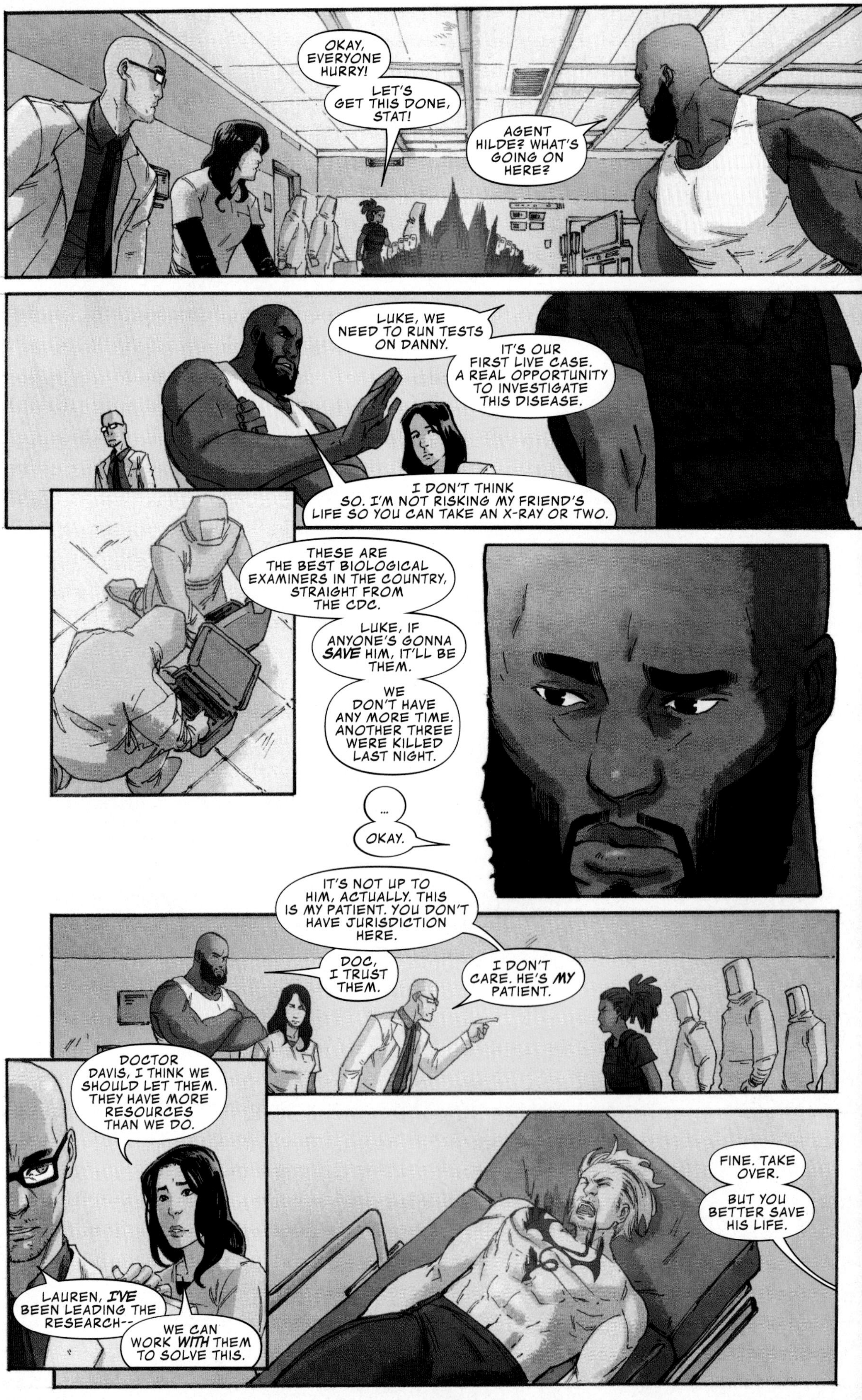
OKAY, EVERYONE HURRY!
LET'S GET THIS DONE, STAT!
AGENT HILDE? WHAT'S GOING ON HERE?
LUKE, WE NEED TO RUN TESTS ON DANNY.
IT'S OUR FIRST LIVE CASE. A REAL OPPORTUNITY TO INVESTIGATE THIS DISEASE.
I DON'T THINK SO. I'M NOT RISKING MY FRIEND'S LIFE SO YOU CAN TAKE AN X-RAY OR TWO.
THESE ARE THE BEST BIOLOGICAL EXAMINERS IN THE COUNTRY, STRAIGHT FROM THE CDC.
LUKE, IF ANYONE'S GONNA SAVE HIM, IT'LL BE THEM.
WE DON'T HAVE ANY MORE TIME. ANOTHER THREE WERE KILLED LAST NIGHT.
...
OKAY.
IT'S NOT UP TO HIM, ACTUALLY. THIS IS MY PATIENT. YOU DON'T HAVE JURISDICTION HERE.
DOC, I TRUST THEM.
I DON'T CARE. HE'S MY PATIENT.
DOCTOR DAVIS, I THINK WE SHOULD LET THEM. THEY HAVE MORE RESOURCES THAN WE DO.
LAUREN, I'VE BEEN LEADING THE RESEARCH--
WE CAN WORK WITH THEM TO SOLVE THIS.
FINE. TAKE OVER.
BUT YOU BETTER SAVE HIS LIFE.

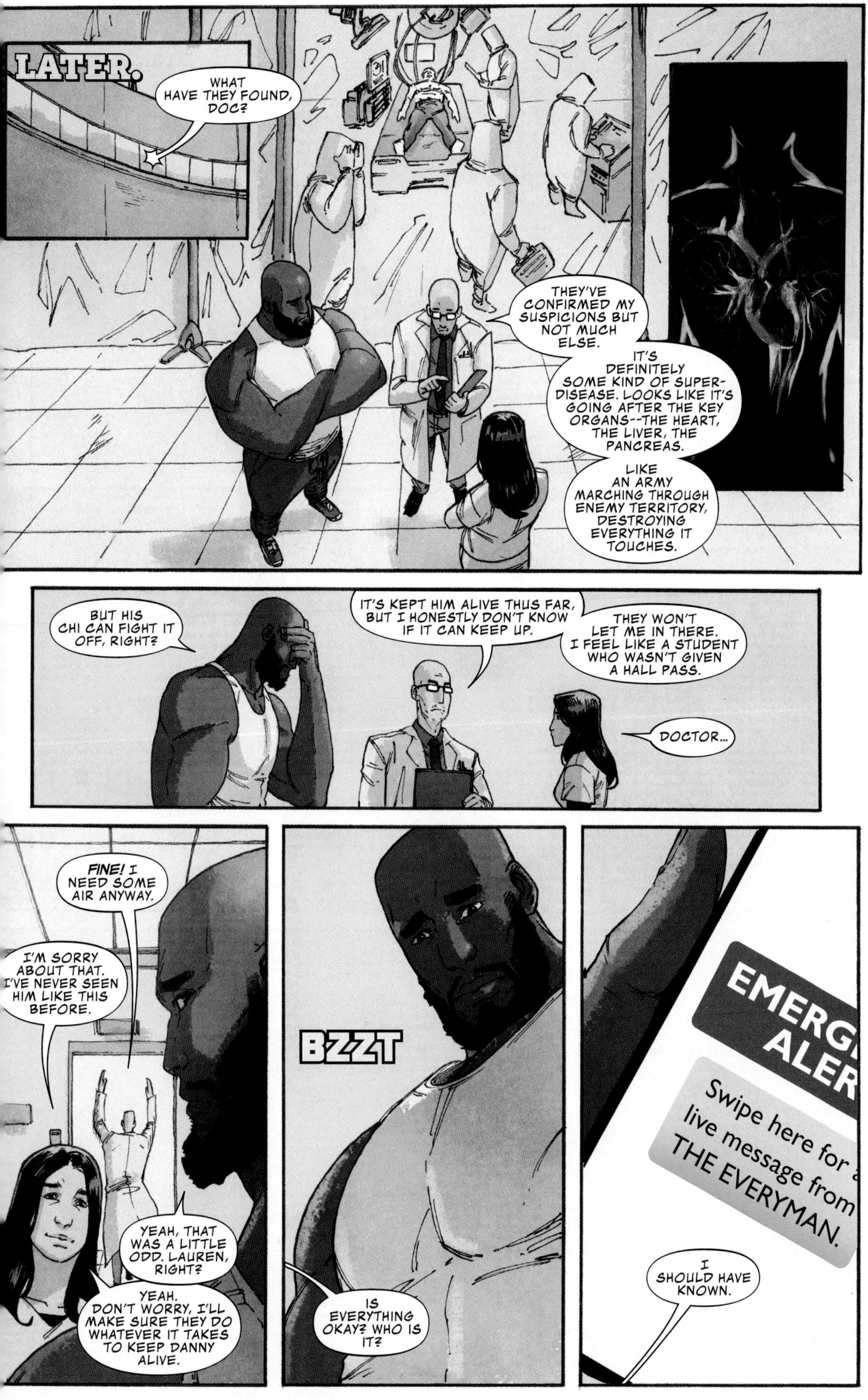
LATER.
WHAT HAVE THEY FOUND, DOC?
THEY'VE CONFIRMED MY SUSPICIONS BUT NOT MUCH ELSE.
IT'S DEFINITELY SOME KIND OF SUPER-DISEASE. LOOKS LIKE IT'S GOING AFTER THE KEY ORGANS--THE HEART, THE LIVER, THE PANCREAS.
LIKE AN ARMY MARCHING THROUGH ENEMY TERRITORY, DESTROYING EVERYTHING IT TOUCHES.
BUT HIS CHI CAN FIGHT IT OFF, RIGHT?
IT'S KEPT HIM ALIVE THUS FAR, BUT I HONESTLY DON'T KNOW IF IT CAN KEEP UP.
THEY WON'T LET ME IN THERE. I FEEL LIKE A STUDENT WHO WASN'T GIVEN A HALL PASS.
DOCTOR...
FINE! I NEED SOME AIR ANYWAY.
I'M SORRY ABOUT THAT. I'VE NEVER SEEN HIM LIKE THIS BEFORE.
YEAH, THAT WAS A LITTLE ODD. LAUREN, RIGHT?
YEAH. DON'T WORRY, I'LL MAKE SURE THEY DO WHATEVER IT TAKES TO KEEP DANNY ALIVE.
BZZT
IS EVERYTHING OKAY? WHO IS IT?
EMERG
ALER
Swipe here for
live message from
THE EVERYMAN.
I SHOULD HAVE KNOWN.

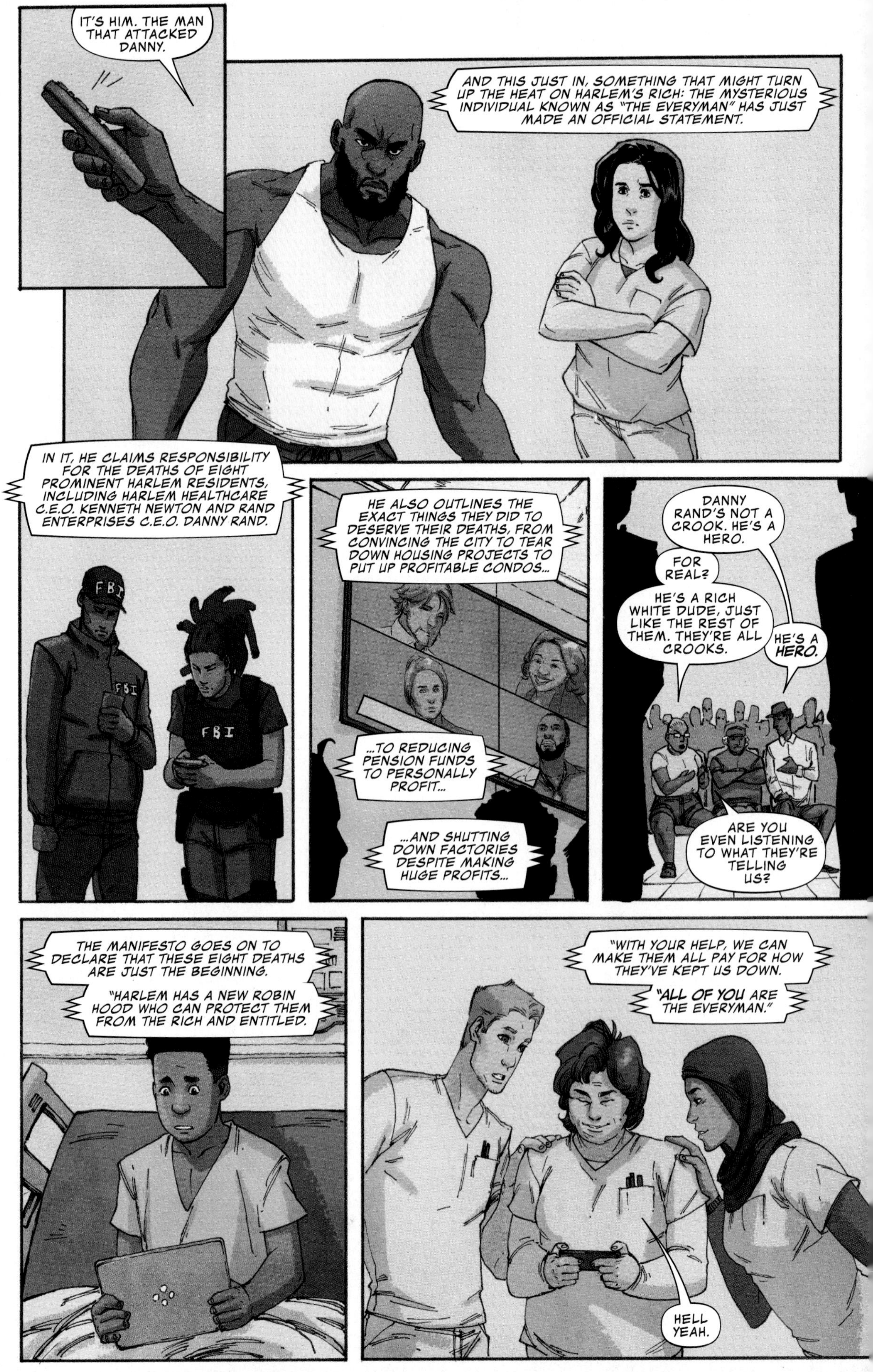
IT'S HIM. THE MAN THAT ATTACKED DANNY.
AND THIS JUST IN, SOMETHING THAT MIGHT TURN UP THE HEAT ON HARLEM'S RICH: THE MYSTERIOUS INDIVIDUAL KNOWN AS "THE EVERYMAN" HAS JUST MADE AN OFFICIAL STATEMENT.
IN IT, HE CLAIMS RESPONSIBILITY FOR THE DEATHS OF EIGHT PROMINENT HARLEM RESIDENTS, INCLUDING HARLEM HEALTHCARE C.E.O. KENNETH NEWTON AND RAND ENTERPRISES C.E.O. DANNY RAND.
FBI
FBI
FBI
HE ALSO OUTLINES THE EXACT THINGS THEY DID TO DESERVE THEIR DEATHS, FROM CONVINCING THE CITY TO TEAR DOWN HOUSING PROJECTS TO PUT UP PROFITABLE CONDOS...
...TO REDUCING PENSION FUNDS TO PERSONALLY PROFIT...
...AND SHUTTING DOWN FACTORIES DESPITE MAKING HUGE PROFITS...
DANNY RAND'S NOT A CROOK. HE'S A HERO.
FOR REAL?
HE'S A RICH WHITE DUDE, JUST LIKE THE REST OF THEM. THEY'RE ALL CROOKS.
HE'S A HERO.
ARE YOU EVEN LISTENING TO WHAT THEY'RE TELLING US?
THE MANIFESTO GOES ON TO DECLARE THAT THESE EIGHT DEATHS ARE JUST THE BEGINNING.
"HARLEM HAS A NEW ROBIN HOOD WHO CAN PROTECT THEM FROM THE RICH AND ENTITLED.
"WITH YOUR HELP, WE CAN MAKE THEM ALL PAY FOR HOW THEY'VE KEPT US DOWN.
"ALL OF YOU ARE THE EVERYMAN."
HELL YEAH.

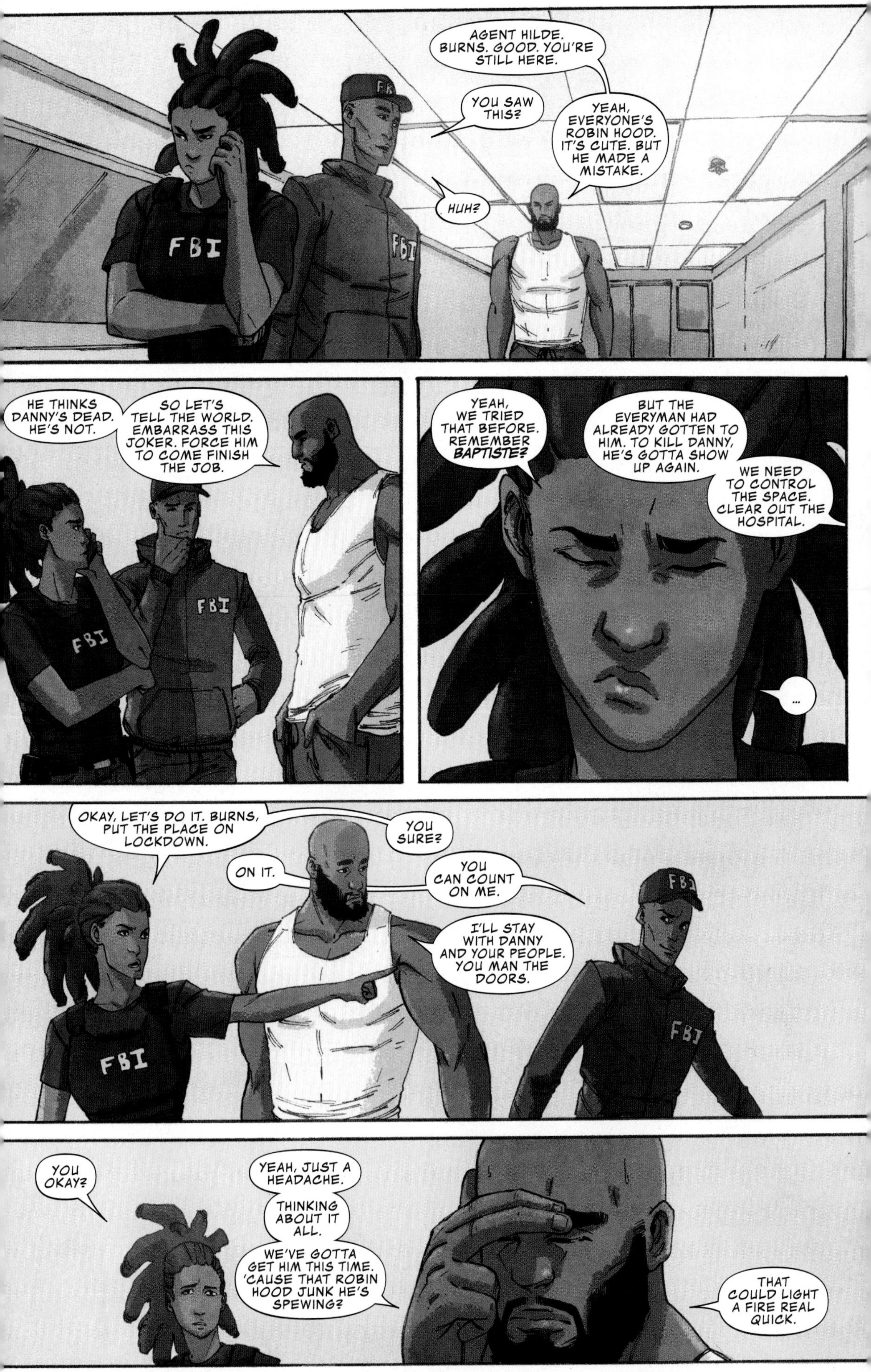

AGENT HILDE. BURNS. GOOD. YOU'RE STILL HERE.
YOU SAW THIS?
YEAH, EVERYONE'S ROBIN HOOD. IT'S CUTE. BUT HE MADE A MISTAKE.
HUH?
HE THINKS DANNY'S DEAD. HE'S NOT.
SO LET'S TELL THE WORLD. EMBARRASS THIS JOKER. FORCE HIM TO COME FINISH THE JOB.
YEAH, WE TRIED THAT BEFORE. REMEMBER *BAPTISTE?*
BUT THE EVERYMAN HAD ALREADY GOTTEN TO HIM. TO KILL DANNY, HE'S GOTTA SHOW UP AGAIN.
WE NEED TO CONTROL THE SPACE. CLEAR OUT THE HOSPITAL.
...
OKAY, LET'S DO IT. BURNS, PUT THE PLACE ON LOCKDOWN.
YOU SURE?
ON IT.
YOU CAN COUNT ON ME.
I'LL STAY WITH DANNY AND YOUR PEOPLE. YOU MAN THE DOORS.
YOU OKAY?
YEAH, JUST A HEADACHE.
THINKING ABOUT IT ALL.
WE'VE GOTTA GET HIM THIS TIME. 'CAUSE THAT ROBIN HOOD JUNK HE'S SPEWING?
THAT COULD LIGHT A FIRE REAL QUICK.

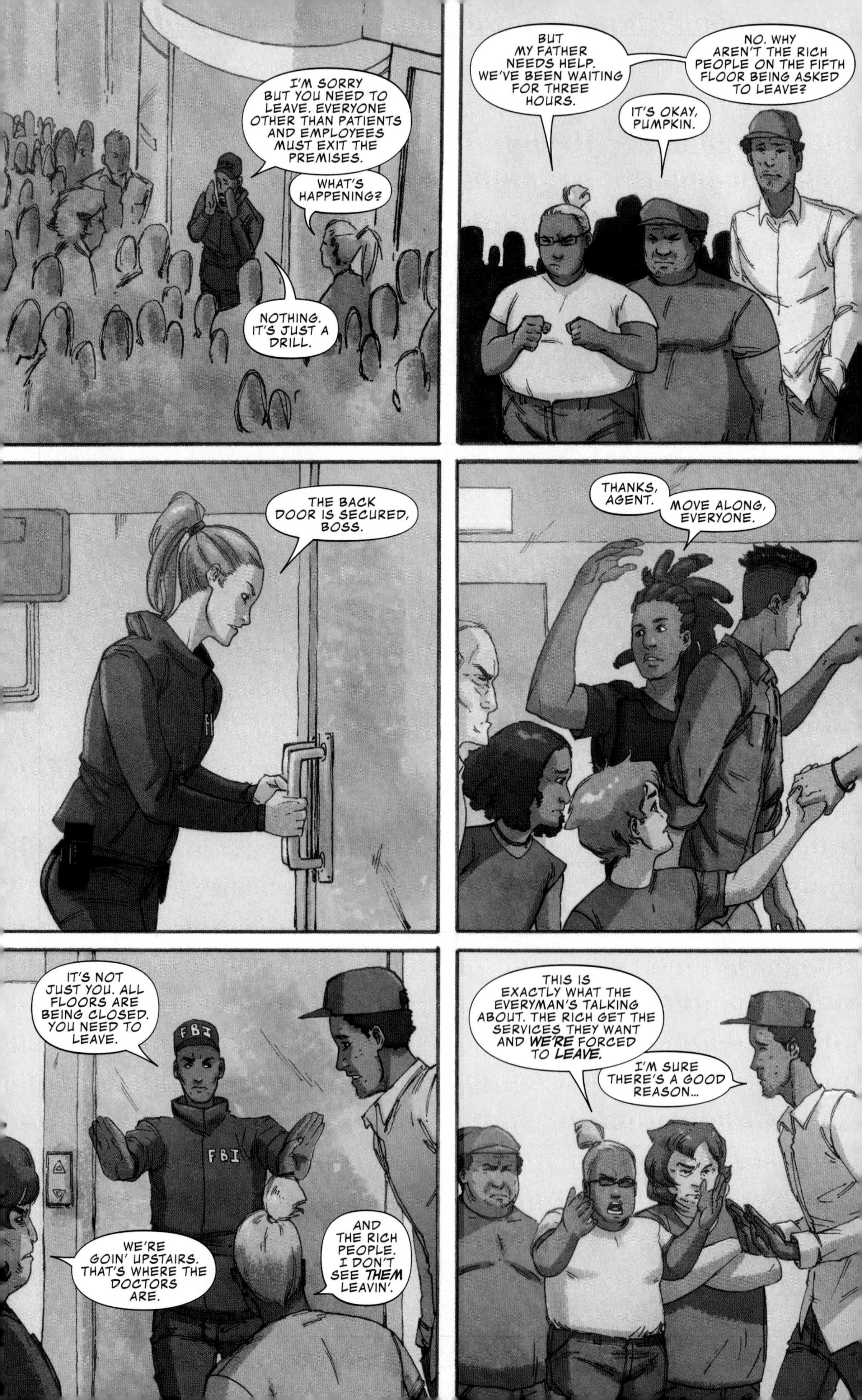
I'M SORRY BUT YOU NEED TO LEAVE. EVERYONE OTHER THAN PATIENTS AND EMPLOYEES MUST EXIT THE PREMISES.
WHAT'S HAPPENING?
NOTHING. IT'S JUST A DRILL.
BUT MY FATHER NEEDS HELP. WE'VE BEEN WAITING FOR THREE HOURS.
NO. WHY AREN'T THE RICH PEOPLE ON THE FIFTH FLOOR BEING ASKED TO LEAVE?
IT'S OKAY, PUMPKIN.
THE BACK DOOR IS SECURED, BOSS.
THANKS, AGENT.
MOVE ALONG, EVERYONE.
IT'S NOT JUST YOU. ALL FLOORS ARE BEING CLOSED. YOU NEED TO LEAVE.
FBI
FBI
WE'RE GOIN' UPSTAIRS. THAT'S WHERE THE DOCTORS ARE.
AND THE RICH PEOPLE. I DON'T SEE THEM LEAVIN'.
THIS IS EXACTLY WHAT THE EVERYMAN'S TALKING ABOUT. THE RICH GET THE SERVICES THEY WANT AND WE'RE FORCED TO LEAVE.
I'M SURE THERE'S A GOOD REASON...

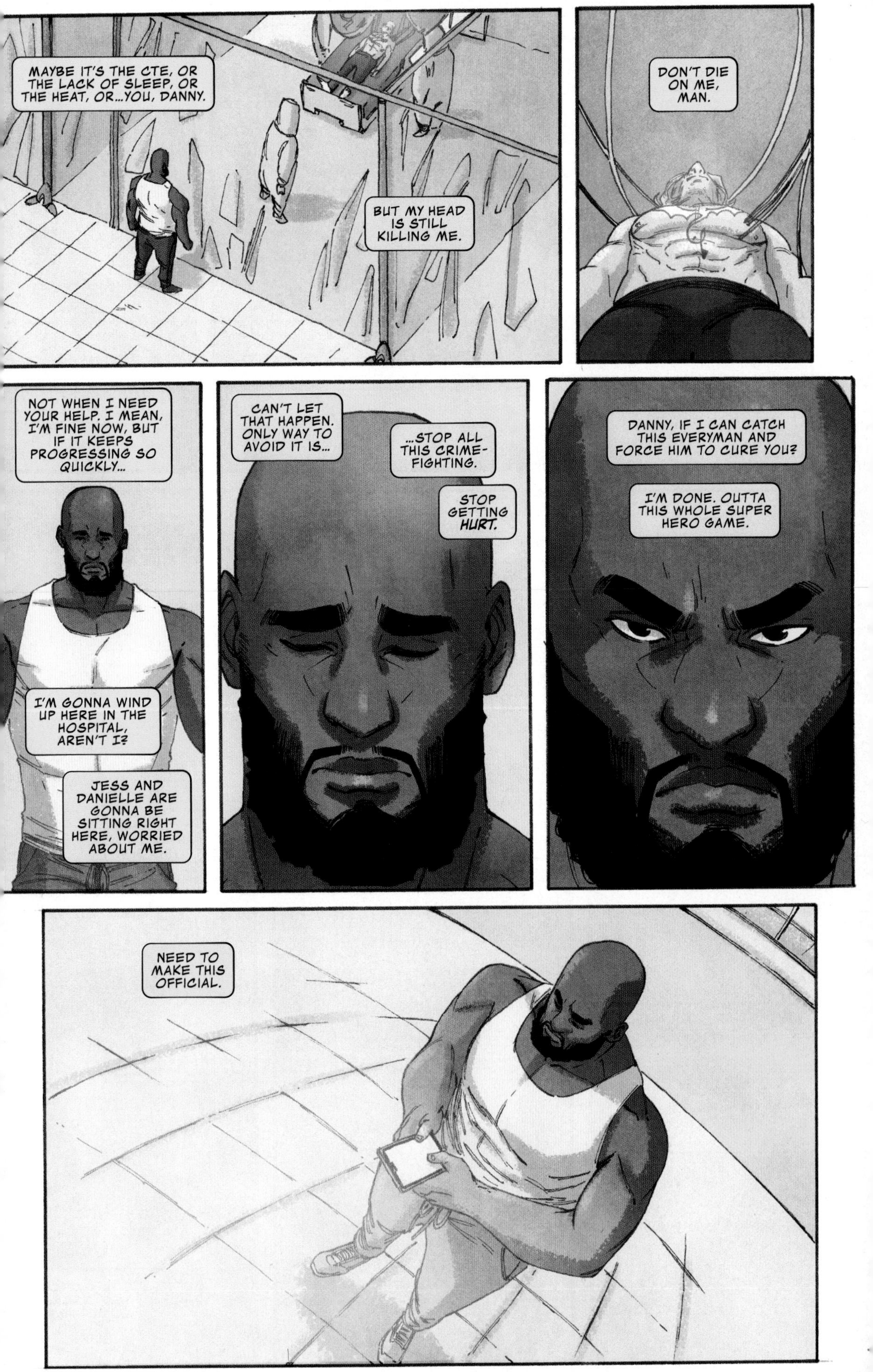
MAYBE IT'S THE CTE, OR THE LACK OF SLEEP, OR THE HEAT, OR...YOU, DANNY.
BUT MY HEAD IS STILL KILLING ME.
DON'T DIE ON ME, MAN.
NOT WHEN I NEED YOUR HELP. I MEAN, I'M FINE NOW, BUT IF IT KEEPS PROGRESSING SO QUICKLY...
I'M GONNA WIND UP HERE IN THE HOSPITAL, AREN'T I?
JESS AND DANIELLE ARE GONNA BE SITTING RIGHT HERE, WORRIED ABOUT ME.
CAN'T LET THAT HAPPEN. ONLY WAY TO AVOID IT IS...
...STOP ALL THIS CRIME-FIGHTING.
STOP GETTING *HURT.*
DANNY, IF I CAN CATCH THIS EVERYMAN AND FORCE HIM TO CURE YOU?
I'M DONE. OUTTA THIS WHOLE SUPER HERO GAME.
NEED TO MAKE THIS OFFICIAL.

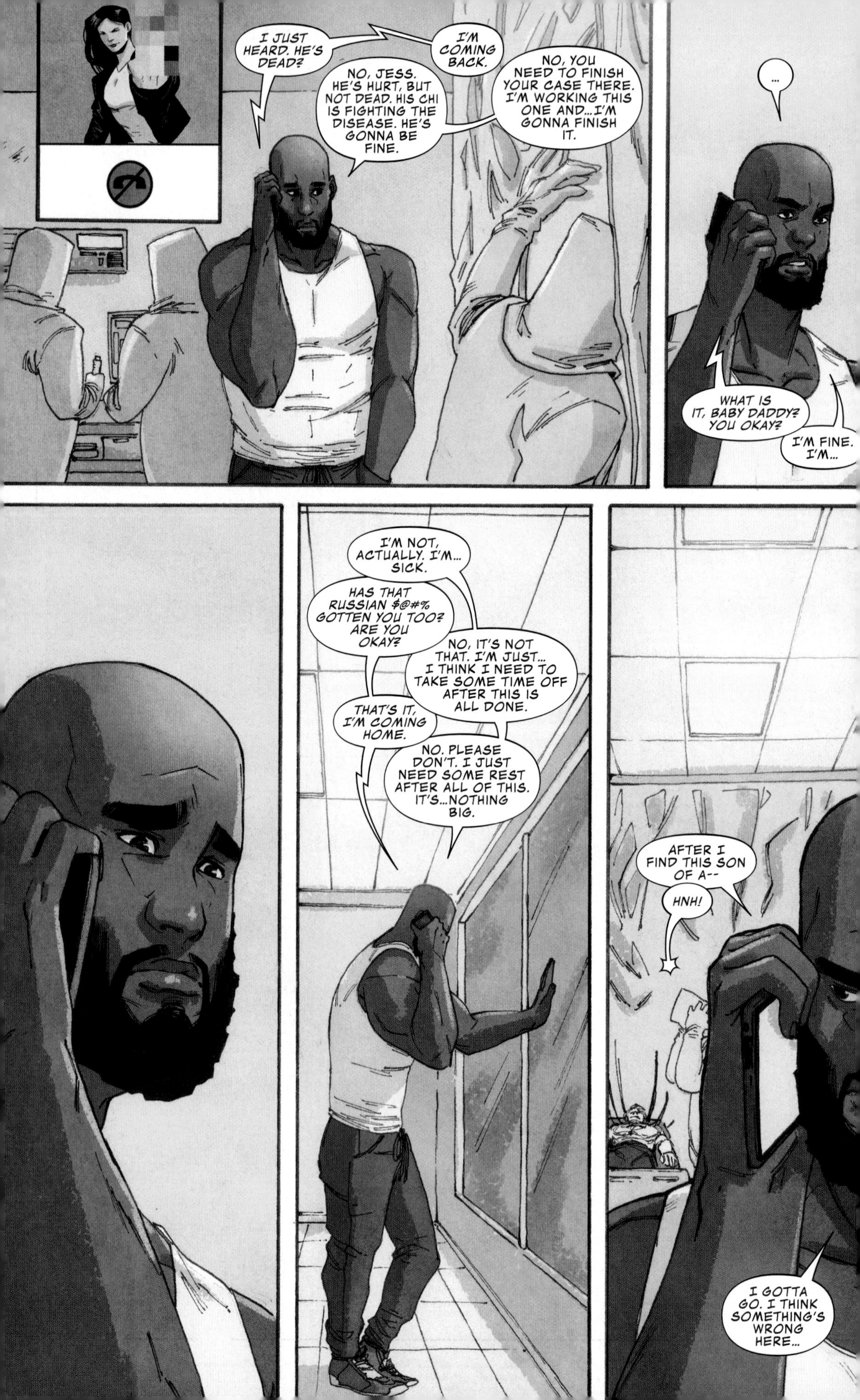
I JUST HEARD. HE'S DEAD?
I'M COMING BACK.
NO, JESS. HE'S HURT, BUT NOT DEAD. HIS CHI IS FIGHTING THE DISEASE. HE'S GONNA BE FINE.
NO, YOU NEED TO FINISH YOUR CASE THERE. I'M WORKING THIS ONE AND...I'M GONNA FINISH IT.
...
WHAT IS IT, BABY DADDY? YOU OKAY?
I'M FINE. I'M...
I'M NOT, ACTUALLY. I'M... SICK.
HAS THAT RUSSIAN $@#% GOTTEN YOU TOO? ARE YOU OKAY?
NO, IT'S NOT THAT. I'M JUST... I THINK I NEED TO TAKE SOME TIME OFF AFTER THIS IS ALL DONE.
THAT'S IT, I'M COMING HOME.
NO. PLEASE DON'T. I JUST NEED SOME REST AFTER ALL OF THIS. IT'S...NOTHING BIG.
AFTER I FIND THIS SON OF A--
HNH!
I GOTTA GO. I THINK SOMETHING'S WRONG HERE...

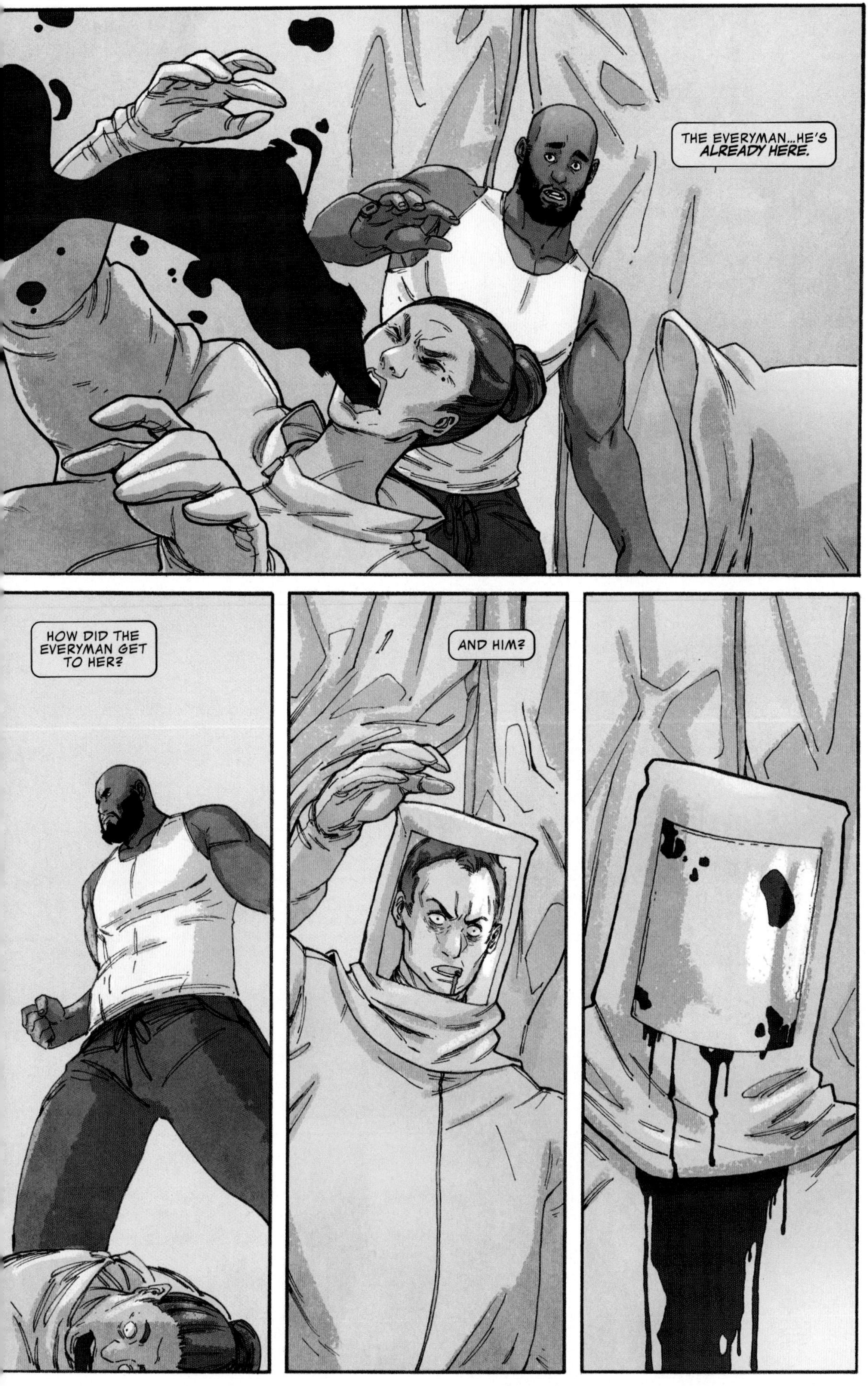
THE EVERYMAN...HE'S ALREADY HERE.
HOW DID THE EVERYMAN GET TO HER?
AND HIM?

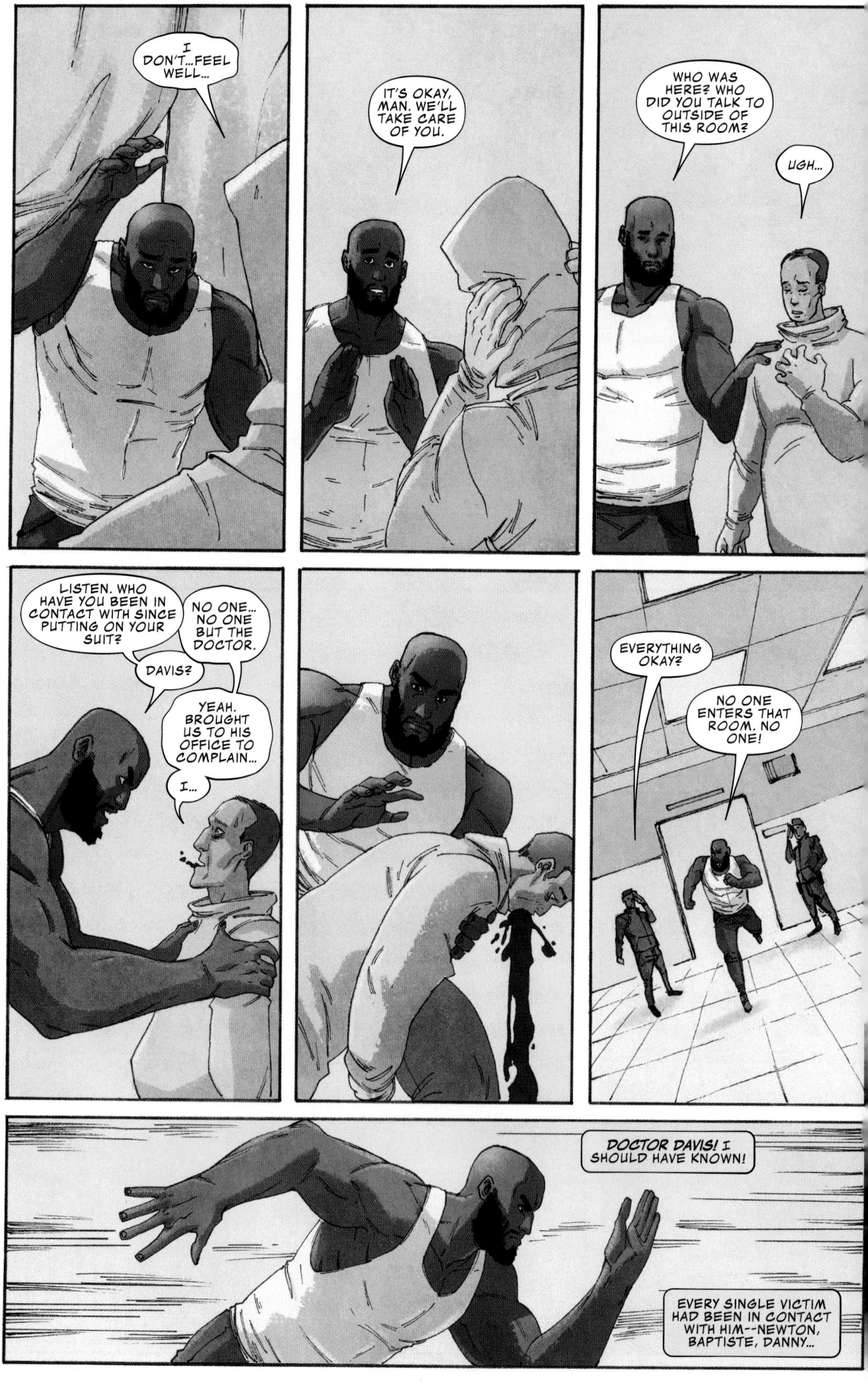
I DON'T...FEEL WELL...
IT'S OKAY, MAN. WE'LL TAKE CARE OF YOU.
WHO WAS HERE? WHO DID YOU TALK TO OUTSIDE OF THIS ROOM?
UGH...
LISTEN. WHO HAVE YOU BEEN IN CONTACT WITH SINCE PUTTING ON YOUR SUIT?
NO ONE... NO ONE BUT THE DOCTOR.
DAVIS?
YEAH. BROUGHT US TO HIS OFFICE TO COMPLAIN...
I...
EVERYTHING OKAY?
NO ONE ENTERS THAT ROOM. NO ONE!
DOCTOR DAVIS! I SHOULD HAVE KNOWN!
EVERY SINGLE VICTIM HAD BEEN IN CONTACT WITH HIM--NEWTON, BAPTISTE, DANNY...

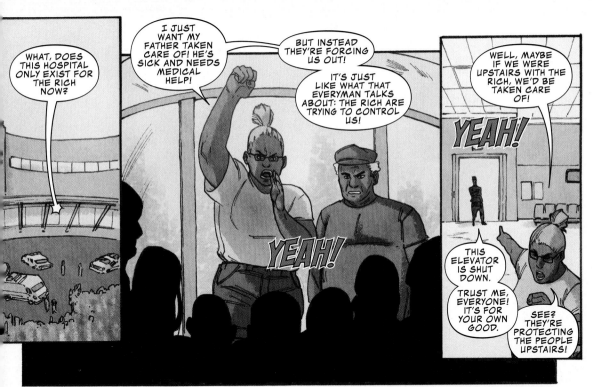

WHAT, DOES THIS HOSPITAL ONLY EXIST FOR THE RICH NOW?

I JUST WANT MY FATHER TAKEN CARE OF! HE'S SICK AND NEEDS MEDICAL HELP!

BUT INSTEAD THEY'RE FORCING US OUT!

IT'S JUST LIKE WHAT THAT EVERYMAN TALKS ABOUT: THE RICH ARE TRYING TO CONTROL US!

YEAH!

WELL, MAYBE IF WE WERE UPSTAIRS WITH THE RICH, WE'D BE TAKEN CARE OF!

YEAH!

THIS ELEVATOR IS SHUT DOWN.

TRUST ME, EVERYONE! IT'S FOR YOUR OWN GOOD.

SEE? THEY'RE PROTECTING THE PEOPLE UPSTAIRS!

EVERYONE! PLEASE, IT'S NOT SAFE UP THERE!

WOULD ROBIN HOOD LET THEM TELL US WHAT TO DO? WOULD THE EVERYMAN?

NO!

IT'S TIME FOR THEM TO GET WHAT THEY DESERVE!

AGH!

WHUMP WHUMP WHUMP

LET'S GET WHAT WE'RE OWED!

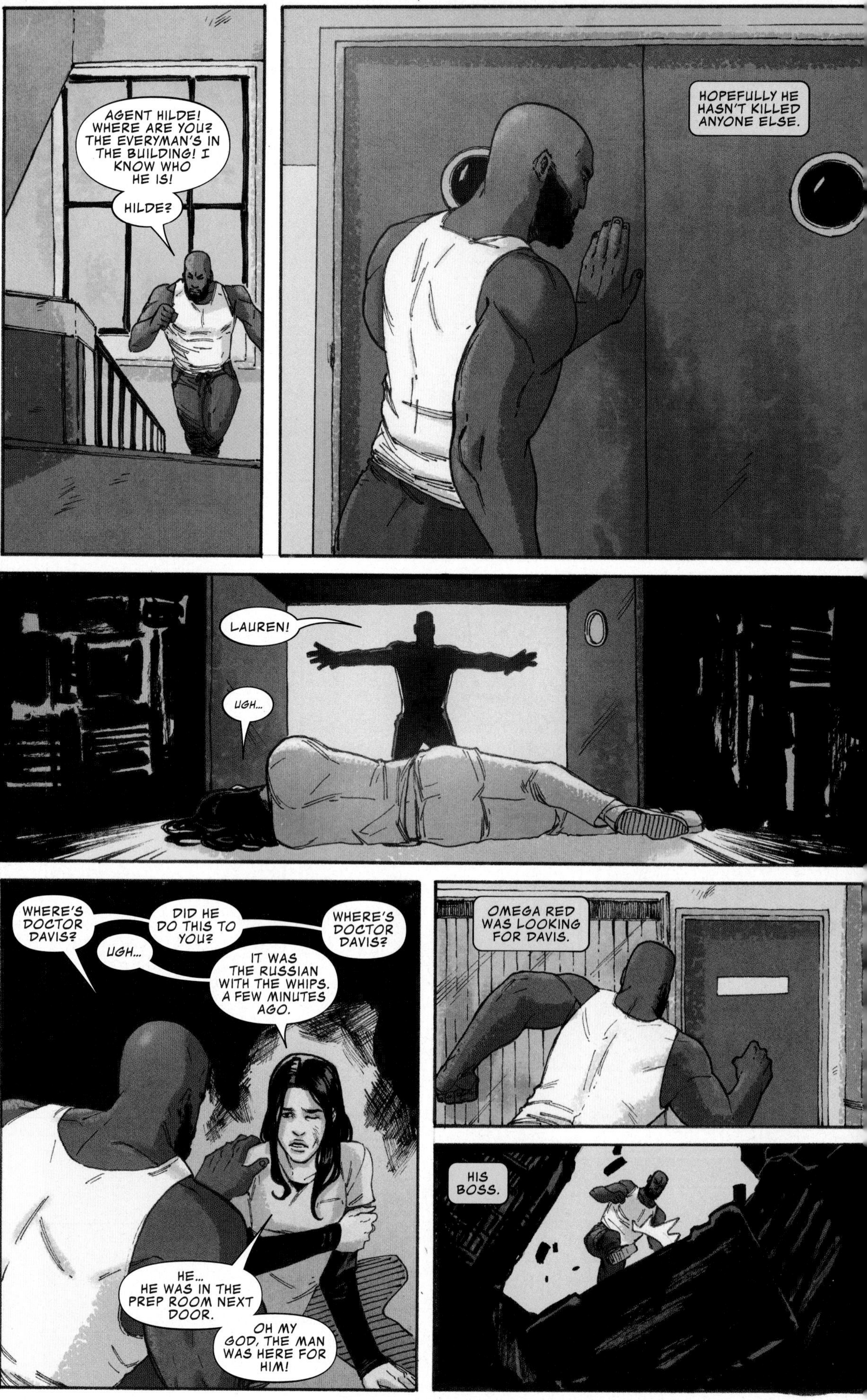
AGENT HILDE! WHERE ARE YOU? THE EVERYMAN'S IN THE BUILDING! I KNOW WHO HE IS!
HILDE?
HOPEFULLY HE HASN'T KILLED ANYONE ELSE.
LAUREN!
UGH...
WHERE'S DOCTOR DAVIS?
DID HE DO THIS TO YOU?
WHERE'S DOCTOR DAVIS?
UGH...
IT WAS THE RUSSIAN WITH THE WHIPS. A FEW MINUTES AGO.
HE... HE WAS IN THE PREP ROOM NEXT DOOR.
OH MY GOD, THE MAN WAS HERE FOR HIM!
OMEGA RED WAS LOOKING FOR DAVIS.
HIS BOSS.

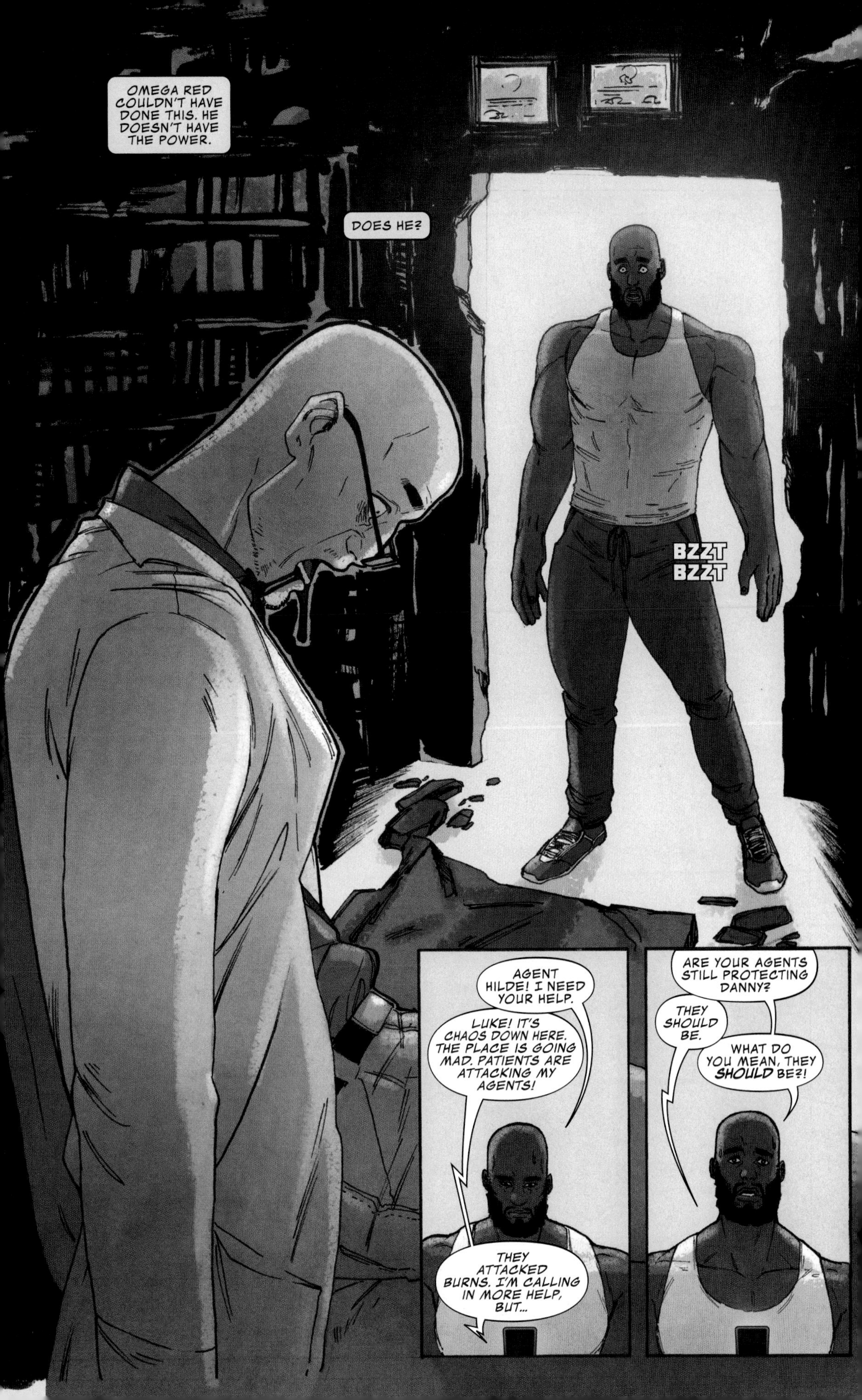
OMEGA RED COULDN'T HAVE DONE THIS. HE DOESN'T HAVE THE POWER.
DOES HE?
BZZT BZZT
AGENT HILDE! I NEED YOUR HELP.
LUKE! IT'S CHAOS DOWN HERE. THE PLACE IS GOING MAD. PATIENTS ARE ATTACKING MY AGENTS!
THEY ATTACKED BURNS. I'M CALLING IN MORE HELP, BUT...
ARE YOUR AGENTS STILL PROTECTING DANNY?
THEY SHOULD BE.
WHAT DO YOU MEAN, THEY SHOULD BE?!

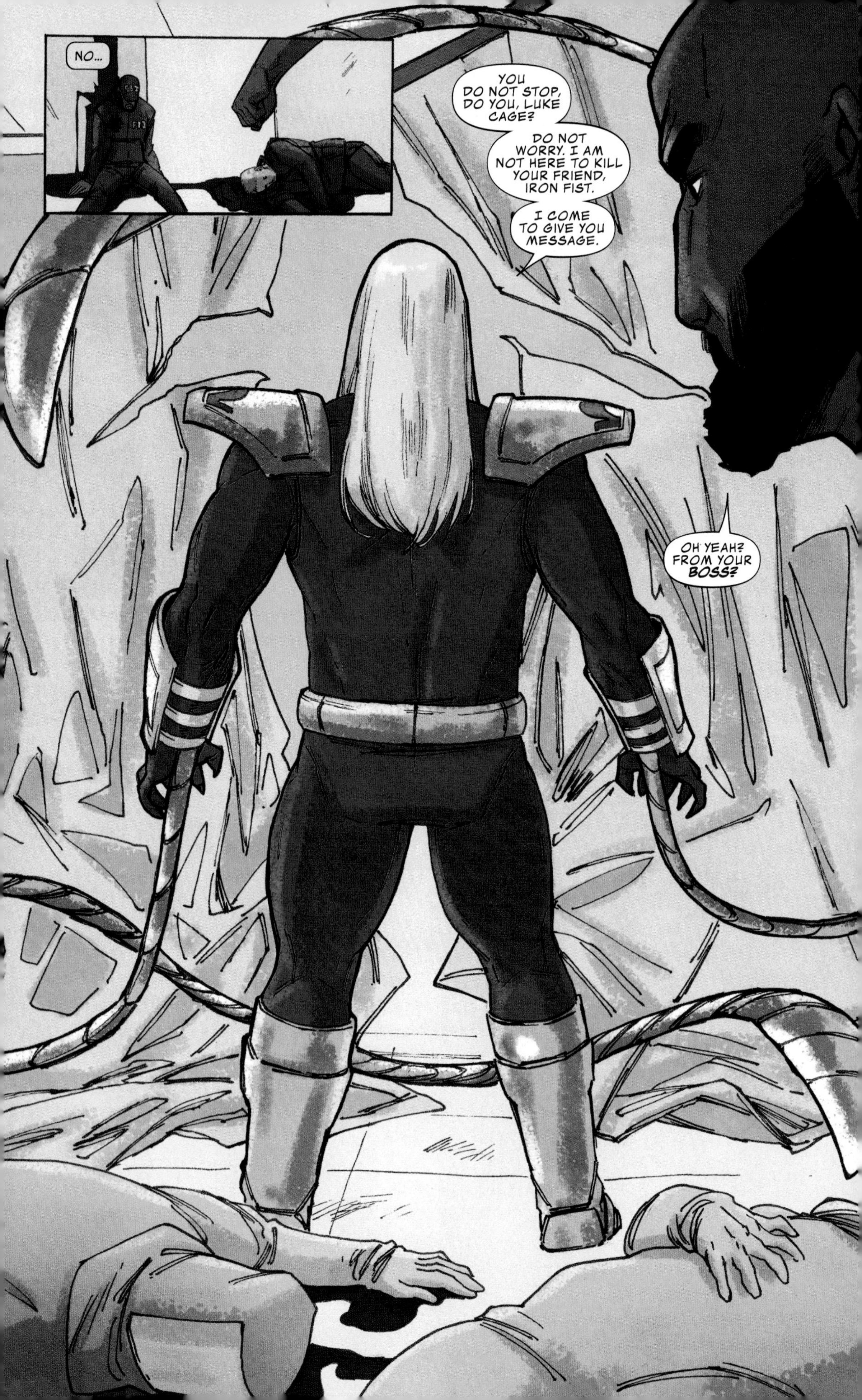
NO...
YOU DO NOT STOP, DO YOU, LUKE CAGE?
DO NOT WORRY. I AM NOT HERE TO KILL YOUR FRIEND, IRON FIST.
I COME TO GIVE YOU MESSAGE.
OH YEAH? FROM YOUR BOSS?

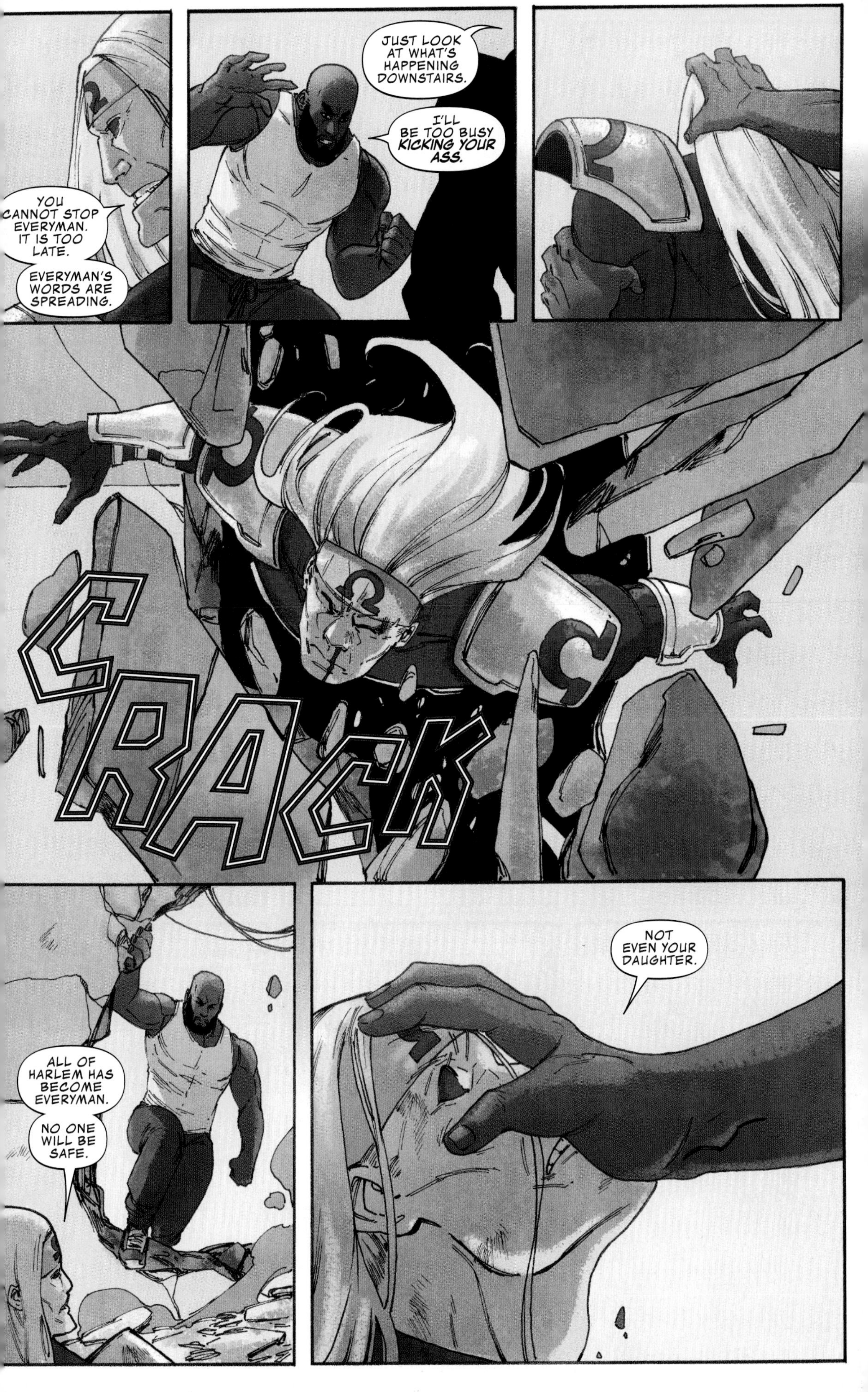
YOU CANNOT STOP EVERYMAN. IT IS TOO LATE.
EVERYMAN'S WORDS ARE SPREADING.
JUST LOOK AT WHAT'S HAPPENING DOWNSTAIRS.
I'LL BE TOO BUSY KICKING YOUR ASS.
CRACK
ALL OF HARLEM HAS BECOME EVERYMAN.
NO ONE WILL BE SAFE.
NOT EVEN YOUR DAUGHTER.

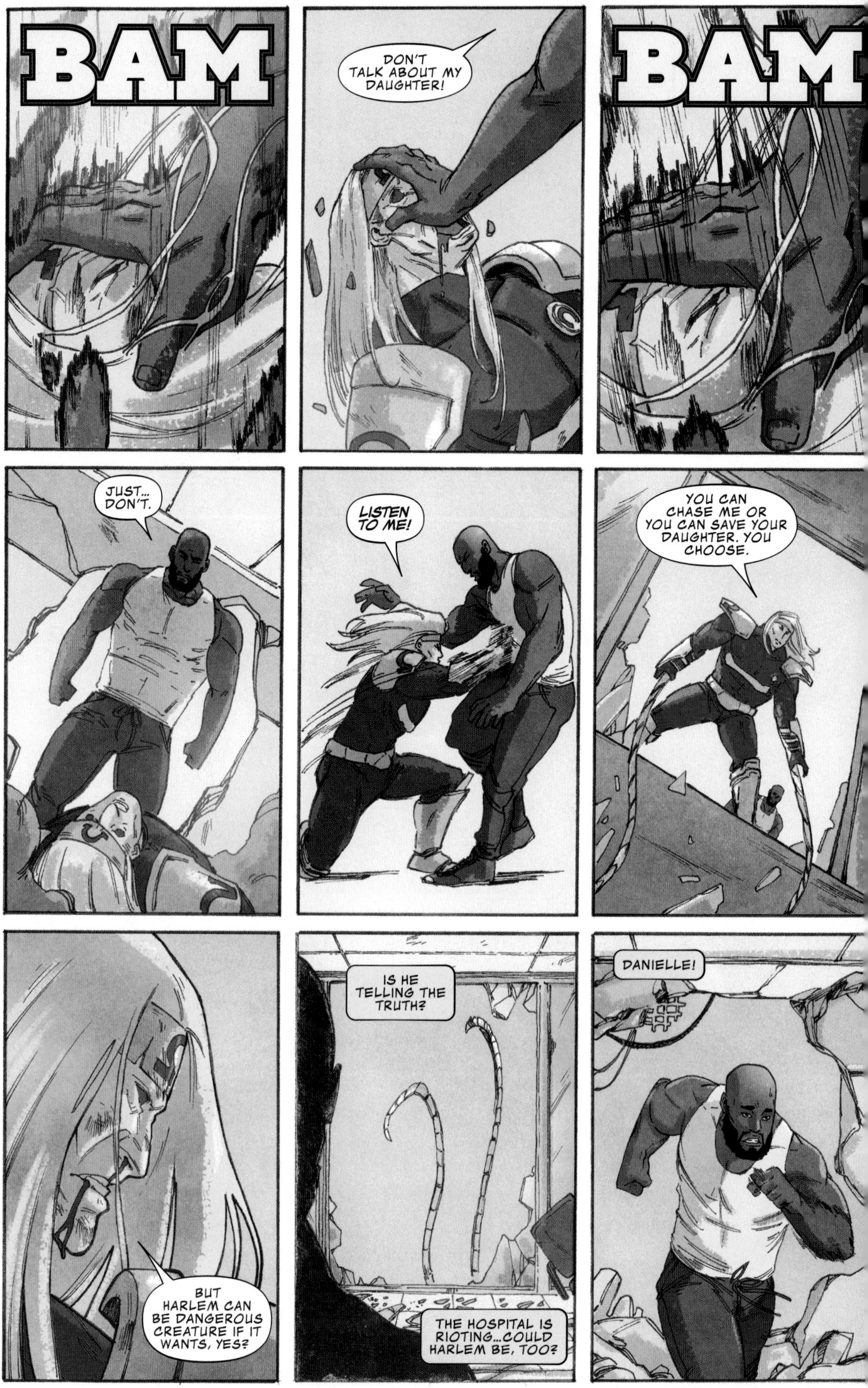
BAM
DON'T TALK ABOUT MY DAUGHTER!
BAM
JUST... DON'T.
LISTEN TO ME!
YOU CAN CHASE ME OR YOU CAN SAVE YOUR DAUGHTER. YOU CHOOSE.
BUT HARLEM CAN BE DANGEROUS CREATURE IF IT WANTS, YES?
IS HE TELLING THE TRUTH?
THE HOSPITAL IS RIOTING...COULD HARLEM BE, TOO?
DANIELLE!

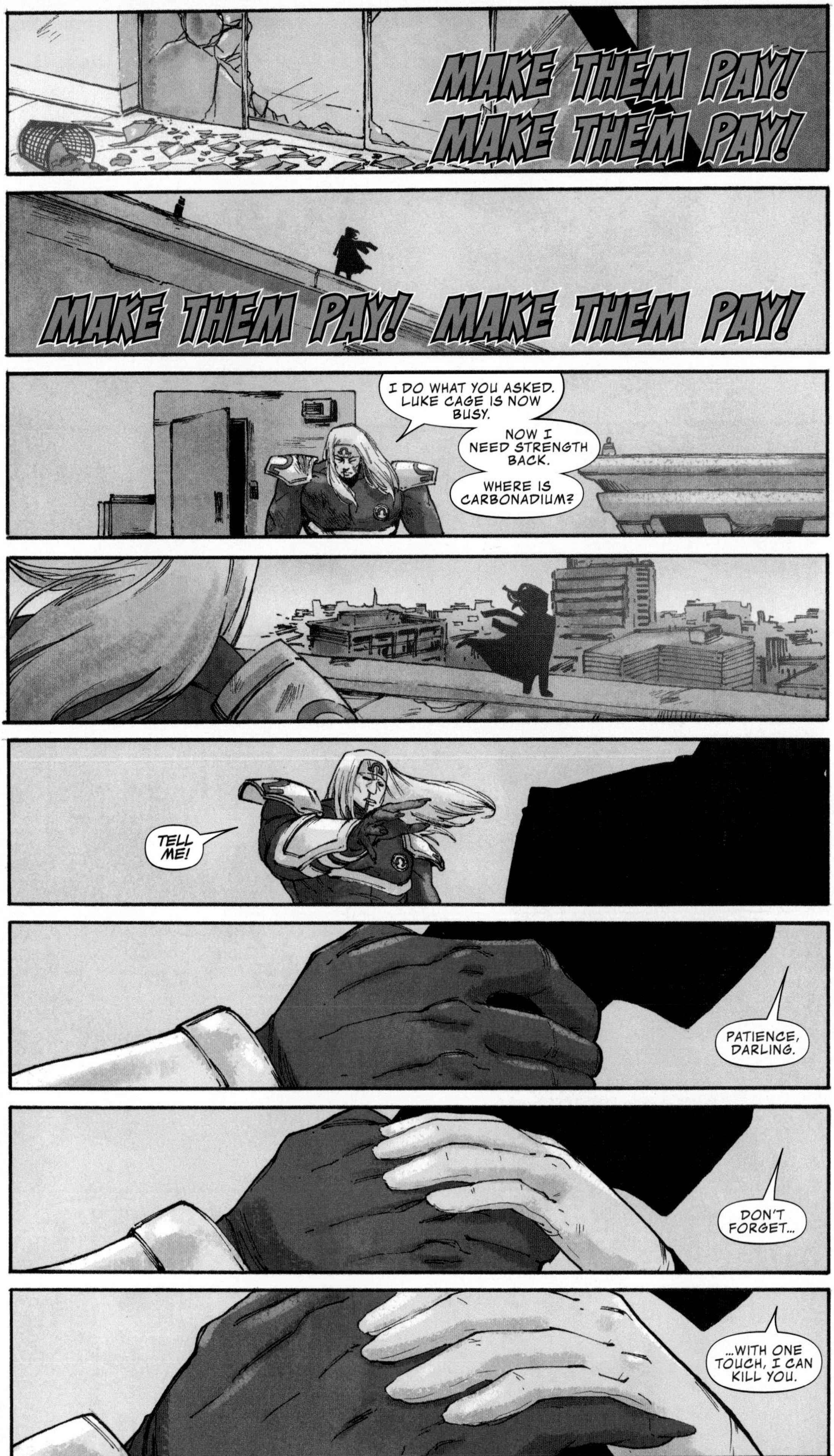
MAKE THEM PAY! MAKE THEM PAY!
MAKE THEM PAY! MAKE THEM PAY!
I DO WHAT YOU ASKED. LUKE CAGE IS NOW BUSY.
NOW I NEED STRENGTH BACK.
WHERE IS CARBONADIUM?
TELL ME!
PATIENCE, DARLING.
DON'T FORGET...
...WITH ONE TOUCH, I CAN KILL YOU.

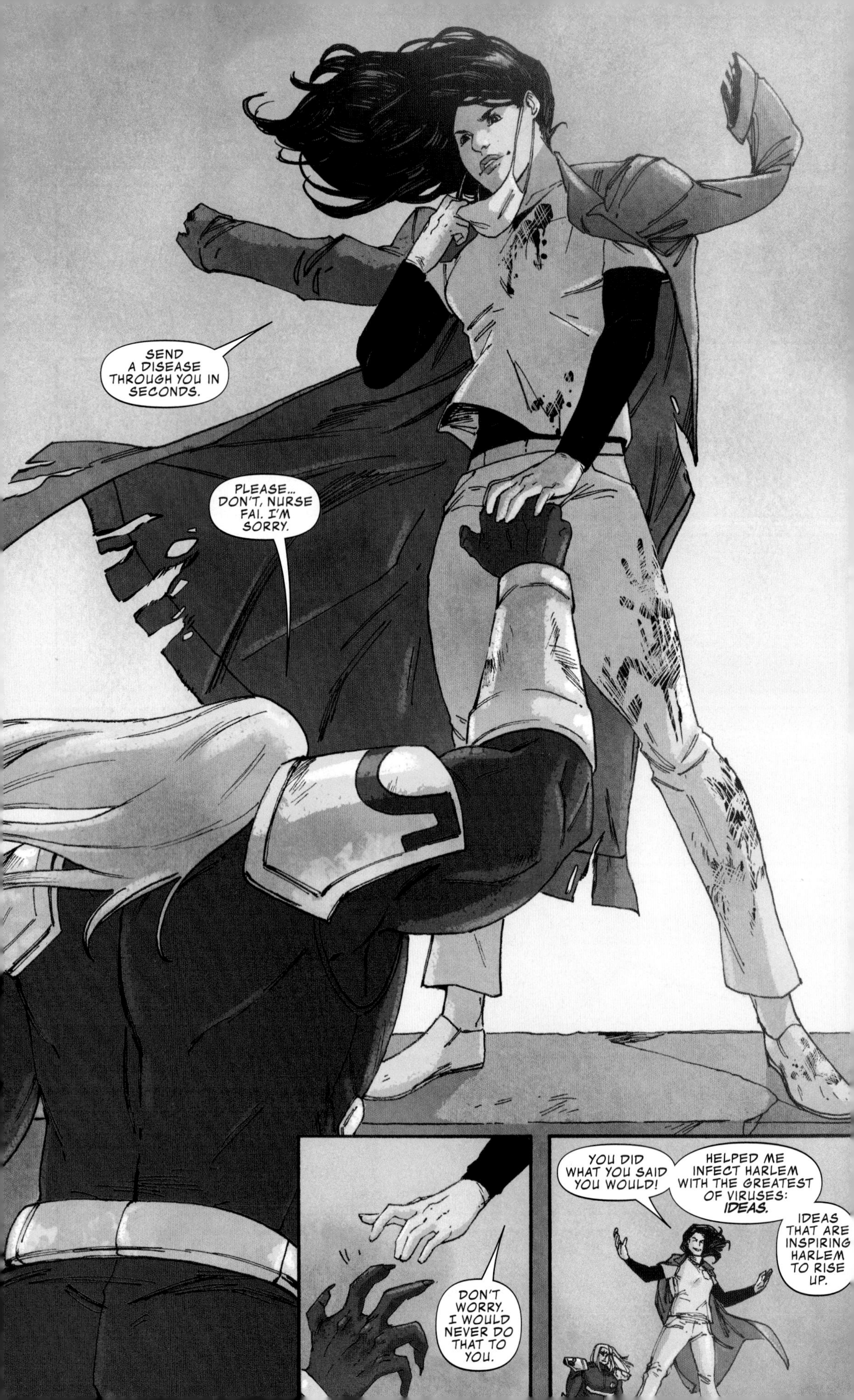
SEND A DISEASE THROUGH YOU IN SECONDS.
PLEASE... DON'T, NURSE FAI. I'M SORRY.
DON'T WORRY. I WOULD NEVER DO THAT TO YOU.
YOU DID WHAT YOU SAID YOU WOULD!
HELPED ME INFECT HARLEM WITH THE GREATEST OF VIRUSES: ***IDEAS.***
IDEAS THAT ARE INSPIRING HARLEM TO RISE UP.

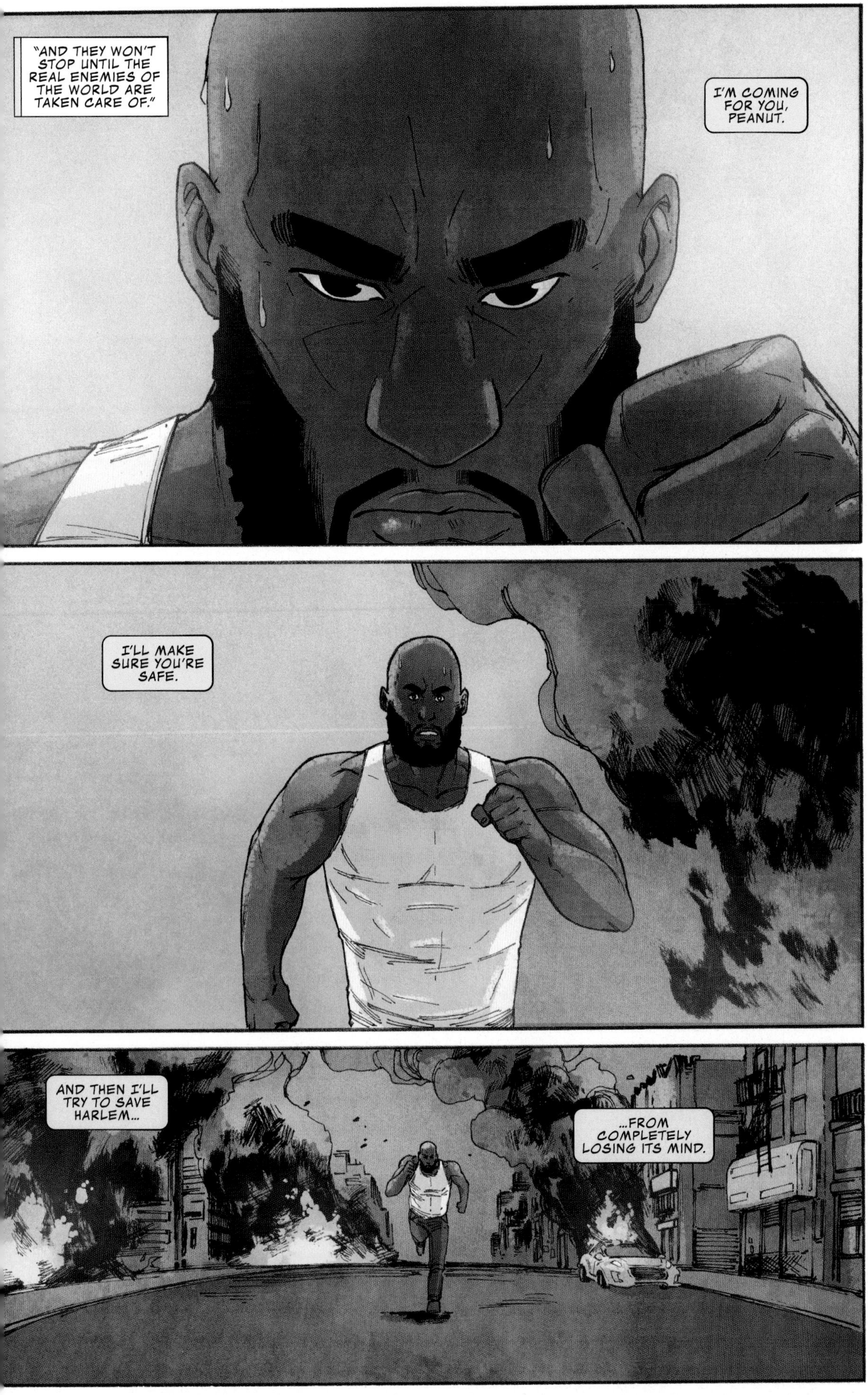
"AND THEY WON'T STOP UNTIL THE REAL ENEMIES OF THE WORLD ARE TAKEN CARE OF."
I'M COMING FOR YOU, PEANUT.
I'LL MAKE SURE YOU'RE SAFE.
AND THEN I'LL TRY TO SAVE HARLEM...
...FROM COMPLETELY LOSING ITS MIND.

EVERYMAN:
CHAPTER 5

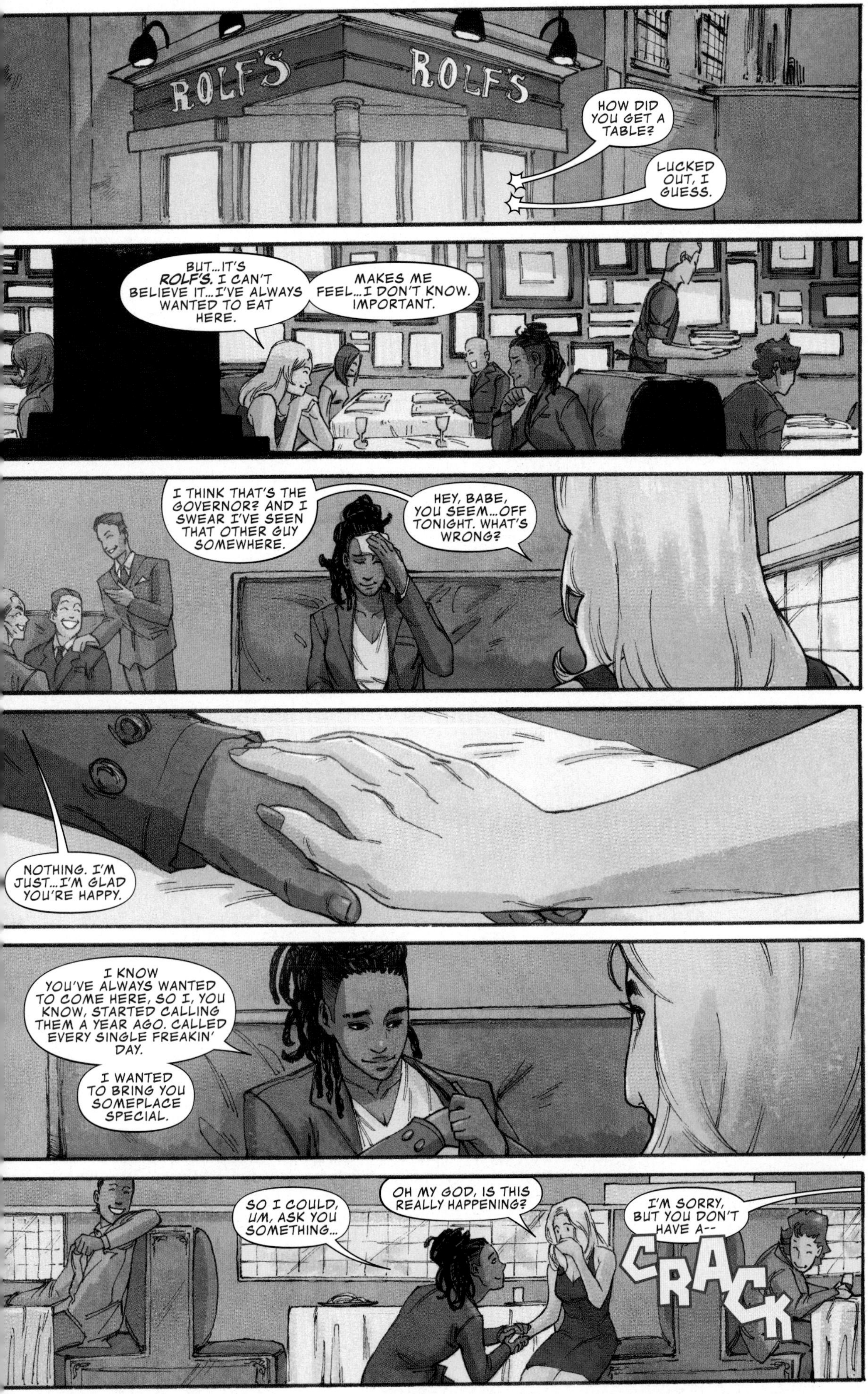
ROLF'S
ROLF'S
HOW DID YOU GET A TABLE?
LUCKED OUT, I GUESS.
BUT...IT'S ROLF'S. I CAN'T BELIEVE IT...I'VE ALWAYS WANTED TO EAT HERE.
MAKES ME FEEL...I DON'T KNOW. IMPORTANT.
I THINK THAT'S THE GOVERNOR? AND I SWEAR I'VE SEEN THAT OTHER GUY SOMEWHERE.
HEY, BABE, YOU SEEM...OFF TONIGHT. WHAT'S WRONG?
NOTHING. I'M JUST...I'M GLAD YOU'RE HAPPY.
I KNOW YOU'VE ALWAYS WANTED TO COME HERE, SO I, YOU KNOW, STARTED CALLING THEM A YEAR AGO. CALLED EVERY SINGLE FREAKIN' DAY.
I WANTED TO BRING YOU SOMEPLACE SPECIAL.
SO I COULD, UM, ASK YOU SOMETHING...
OH MY GOD, IS THIS REALLY HAPPENING?
I'M SORRY, BUT YOU DON'T HAVE A--
CRACK

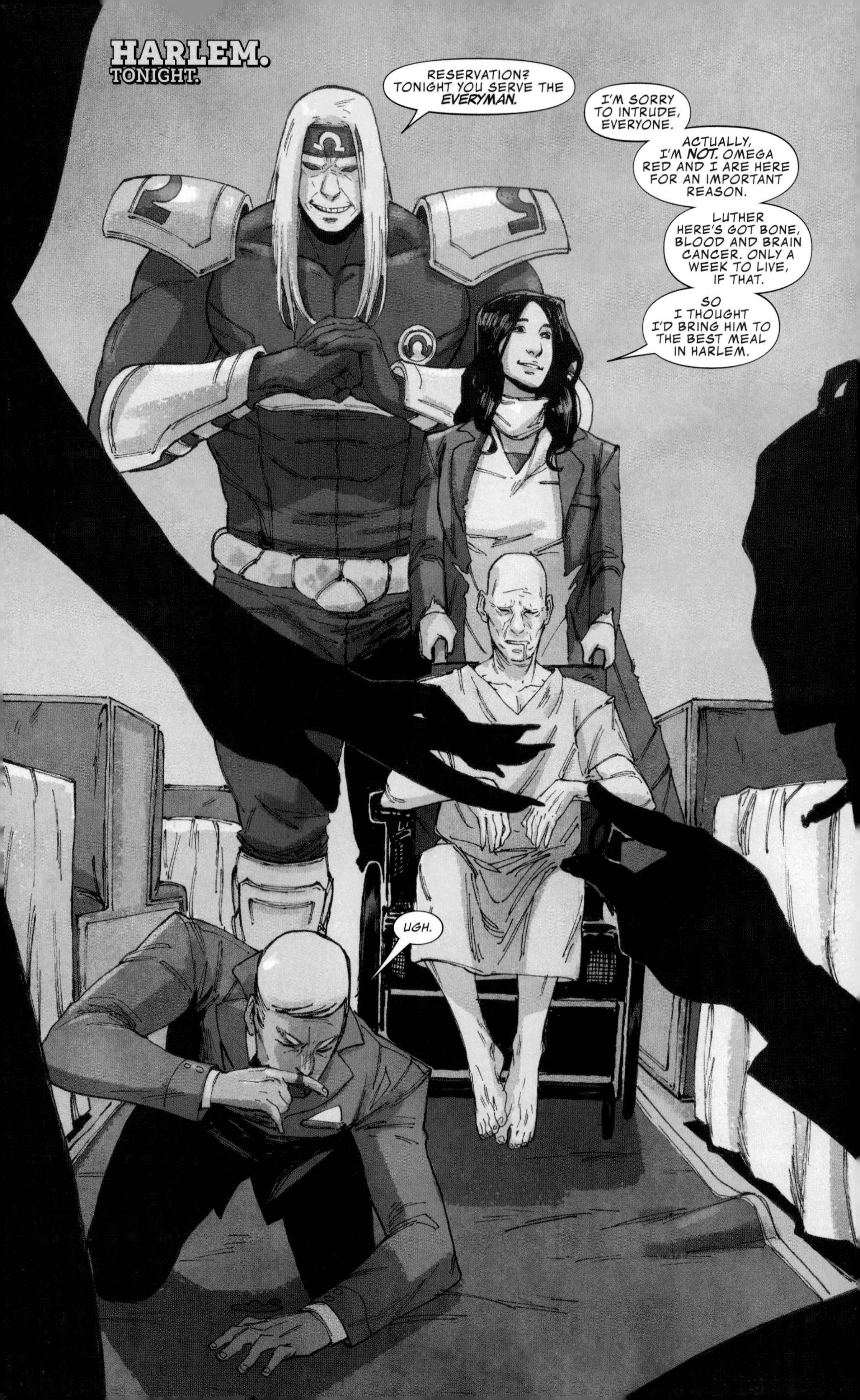
HARLEM.
TONIGHT.
RESERVATION? TONIGHT YOU SERVE THE EVERYMAN.
I'M SORRY TO INTRUDE, EVERYONE.
ACTUALLY, I'M NOT. OMEGA RED AND I ARE HERE FOR AN IMPORTANT REASON.
LUTHER HERE'S GOT BONE, BLOOD AND BRAIN CANCER. ONLY A WEEK TO LIVE, IF THAT.
SO I THOUGHT I'D BRING HIM TO THE BEST MEAL IN HARLEM.
UGH.

I WOULDN'T KNOW THAT FIRSTHAND. I'VE NEVER BEEN HERE.

BUT MY FATHER HELPED BUILD THIS PLACE 30 YEARS AGO. WORKED CONSTRUCTION.

HE ALWAYS WORKED TWO JOBS, AND THIS WAS ONE OF THEM.

HE WORKED LIKE A *DOG.*

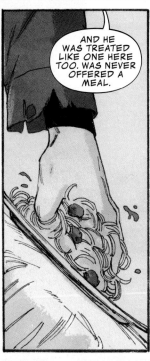

AND HE WAS TREATED LIKE ONE HERE TOO. WAS NEVER OFFERED A MEAL.

NOT GOOD ENOUGH FOR A PLATE OF...IS THIS SPAGHETTI? SPAGHETTINI? I'VE NEVER LEARNED THE DIFFERENCE.

I'M CALLING THE COPS!

YOU DO THAT. I THINK THEY'VE GOT BIGGER FISH TO FRY TONIGHT.

SMASH

SHHHHH, LITTLE MAN...

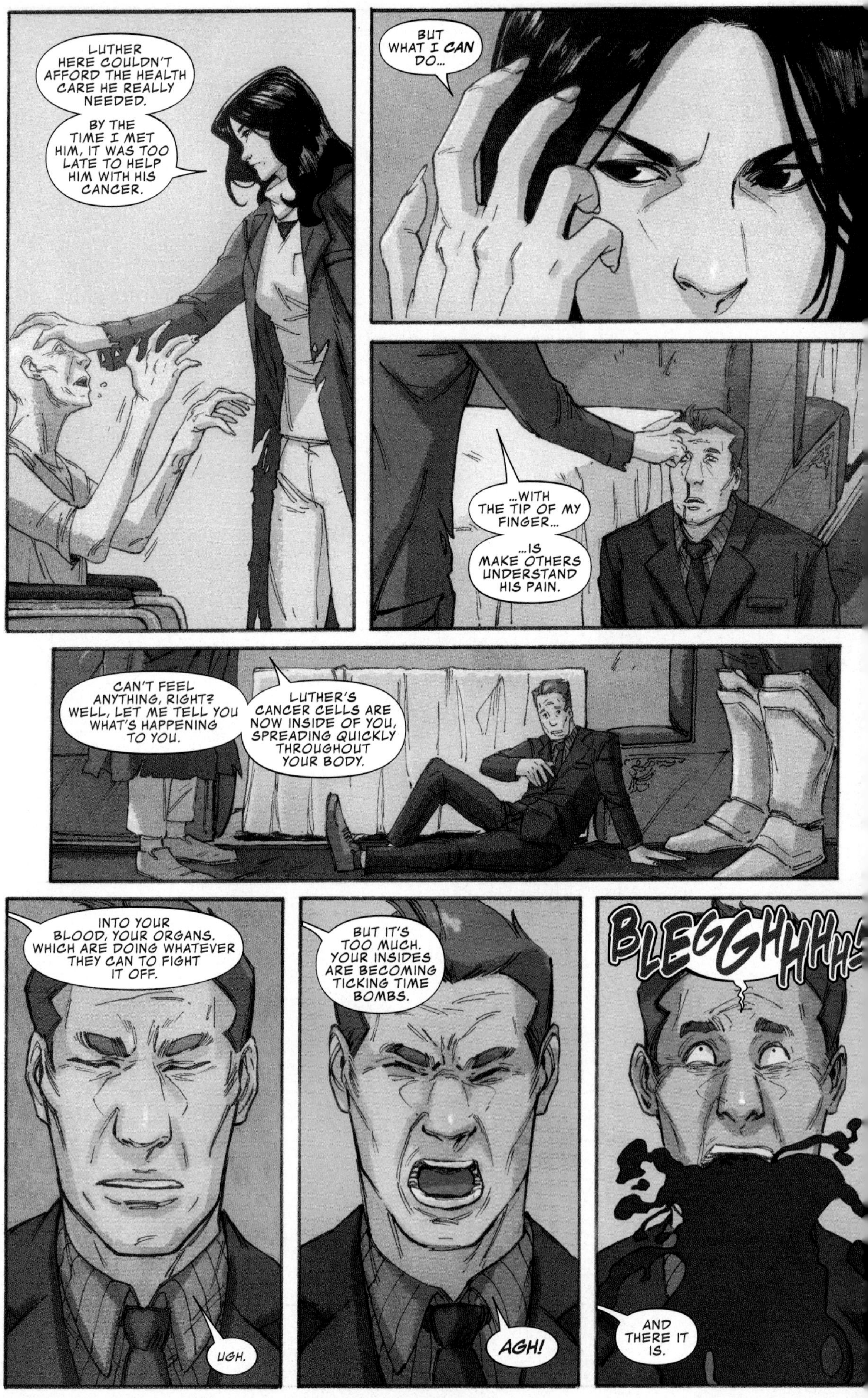
LUTHER HERE COULDN'T AFFORD THE HEALTH CARE HE REALLY NEEDED.
BY THE TIME I MET HIM, IT WAS TOO LATE TO HELP HIM WITH HIS CANCER.
BUT WHAT I CAN DO...
...WITH THE TIP OF MY FINGER...
...IS MAKE OTHERS UNDERSTAND HIS PAIN.
CAN'T FEEL ANYTHING, RIGHT? WELL, LET ME TELL YOU WHAT'S HAPPENING TO YOU.
LUTHER'S CANCER CELLS ARE NOW INSIDE OF YOU, SPREADING QUICKLY THROUGHOUT YOUR BODY.
INTO YOUR BLOOD, YOUR ORGANS. WHICH ARE DOING WHATEVER THEY CAN TO FIGHT IT OFF.
UGH.
BUT IT'S TOO MUCH. YOUR INSIDES ARE BECOMING TICKING TIME BOMBS.
AGH!
AND THERE IT IS.

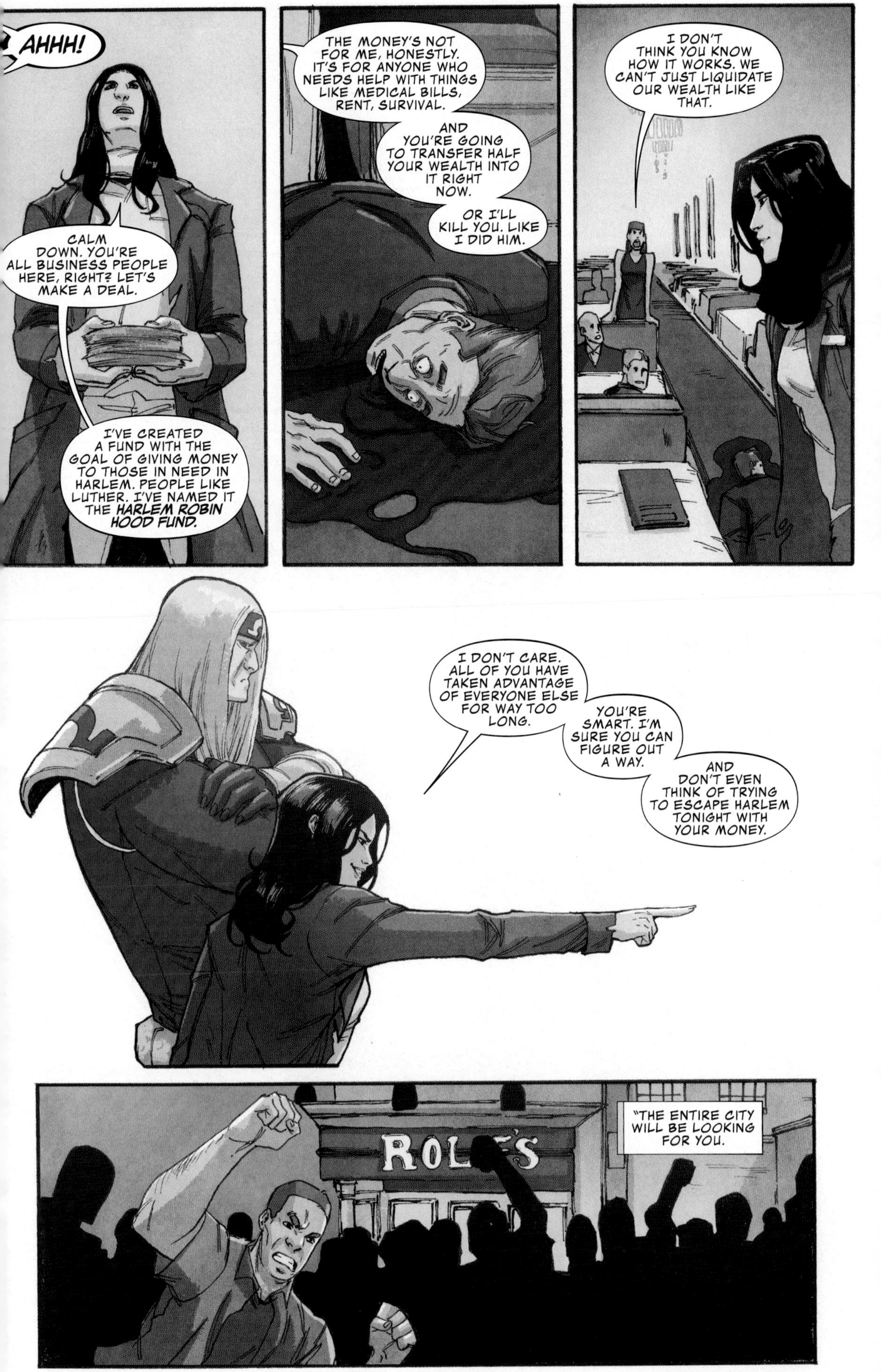
AHHH!
CALM DOWN. YOU'RE ALL BUSINESS PEOPLE HERE, RIGHT? LET'S MAKE A DEAL.
I'VE CREATED A FUND WITH THE GOAL OF GIVING MONEY TO THOSE IN NEED IN HARLEM. PEOPLE LIKE LUTHER. I'VE NAMED IT THE ***HARLEM ROBIN HOOD FUND.***
THE MONEY'S NOT FOR ME, HONESTLY. IT'S FOR ANYONE WHO NEEDS HELP WITH THINGS LIKE MEDICAL BILLS, RENT, SURVIVAL.
AND YOU'RE GOING TO TRANSFER HALF YOUR WEALTH INTO IT RIGHT NOW.
OR I'LL KILL YOU. LIKE I DID HIM.
I DON'T THINK YOU KNOW HOW IT WORKS. WE CAN'T JUST LIQUIDATE OUR WEALTH LIKE THAT.
I DON'T CARE. ALL OF YOU HAVE TAKEN ADVANTAGE OF EVERYONE ELSE FOR WAY TOO LONG.
YOU'RE SMART. I'M SURE YOU CAN FIGURE OUT A WAY.
AND DON'T EVEN THINK OF TRYING TO ESCAPE HARLEM TONIGHT WITH YOUR MONEY.
"THE ENTIRE CITY WILL BE LOOKING FOR YOU.

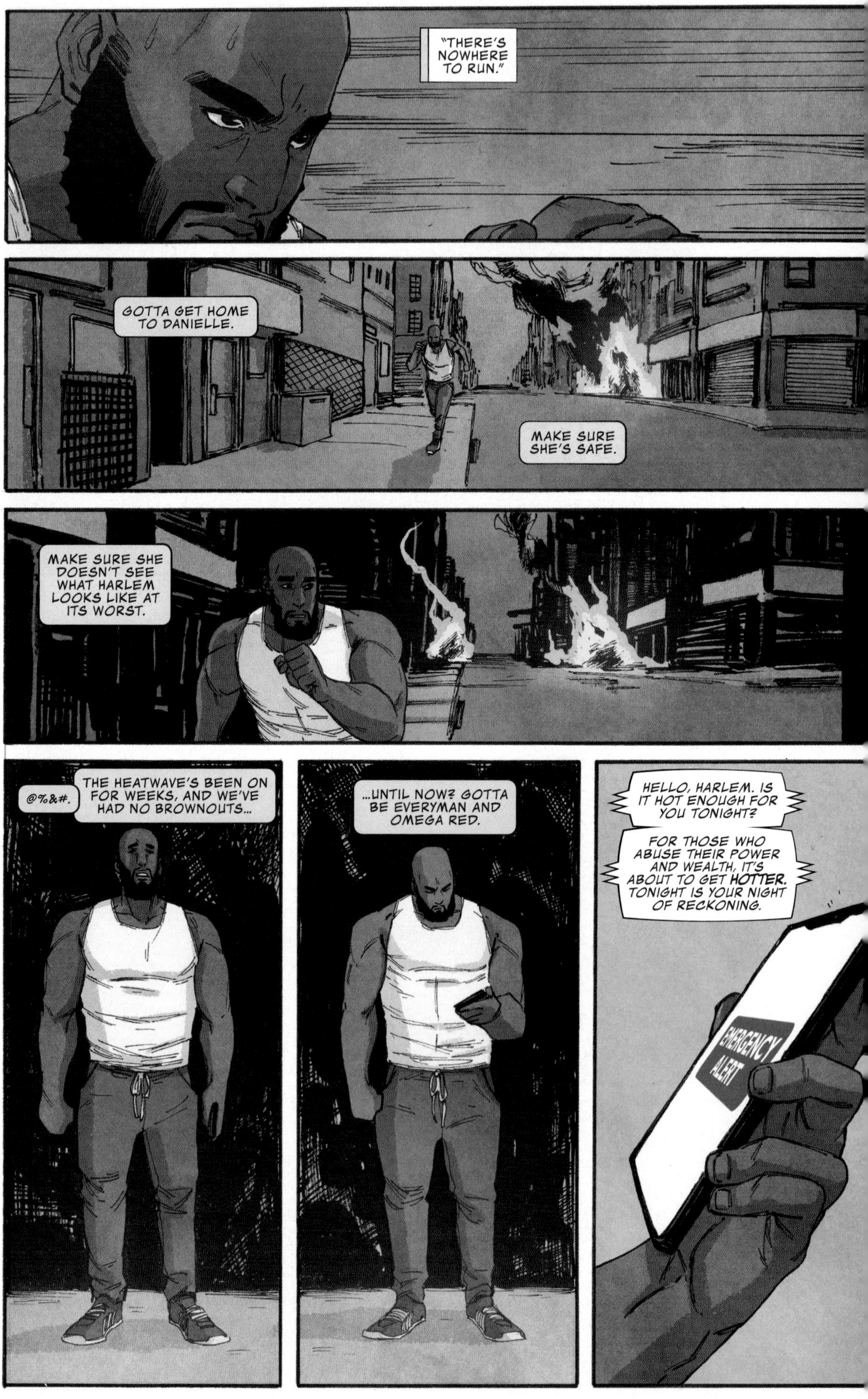
"THERE'S NOWHERE TO RUN."
GOTTA GET HOME TO DANIELLE.
MAKE SURE SHE'S SAFE.
MAKE SURE SHE DOESN'T SEE WHAT HARLEM LOOKS LIKE AT ITS WORST.
@%&#.
THE HEATWAVE'S BEEN ON FOR WEEKS, AND WE'VE HAD NO BROWNOUTS...
...UNTIL NOW? GOTTA BE EVERYMAN AND OMEGA RED.
HELLO, HARLEM. IS IT HOT ENOUGH FOR YOU TONIGHT?
FOR THOSE WHO ABUSE THEIR POWER AND WEALTH, IT'S ABOUT TO GET HOTTER. TONIGHT IS YOUR NIGHT OF RECKONING.
EMERGENCY ALERT

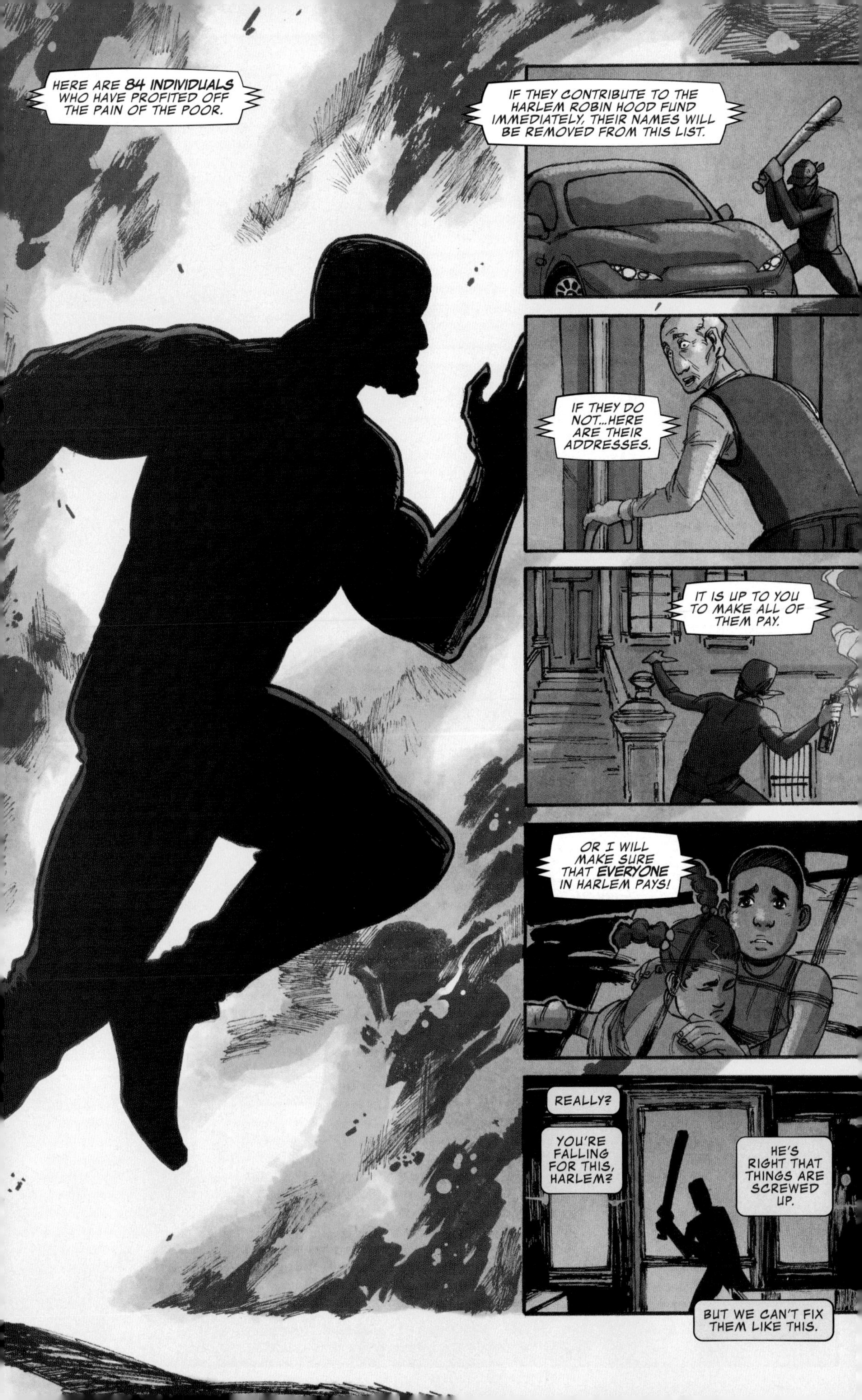
HERE ARE 84 INDIVIDUALS WHO HAVE PROFITED OFF THE PAIN OF THE POOR.
IF THEY CONTRIBUTE TO THE HARLEM ROBIN HOOD FUND IMMEDIATELY, THEIR NAMES WILL BE REMOVED FROM THIS LIST.
IF THEY DO NOT...HERE ARE THEIR ADDRESSES.
IT IS UP TO YOU TO MAKE ALL OF THEM PAY.
OR I WILL MAKE SURE THAT EVERYONE IN HARLEM PAYS!
REALLY?
YOU'RE FALLING FOR THIS, HARLEM?
HE'S RIGHT THAT THINGS ARE SCREWED UP.
BUT WE CAN'T FIX THEM LIKE THIS.

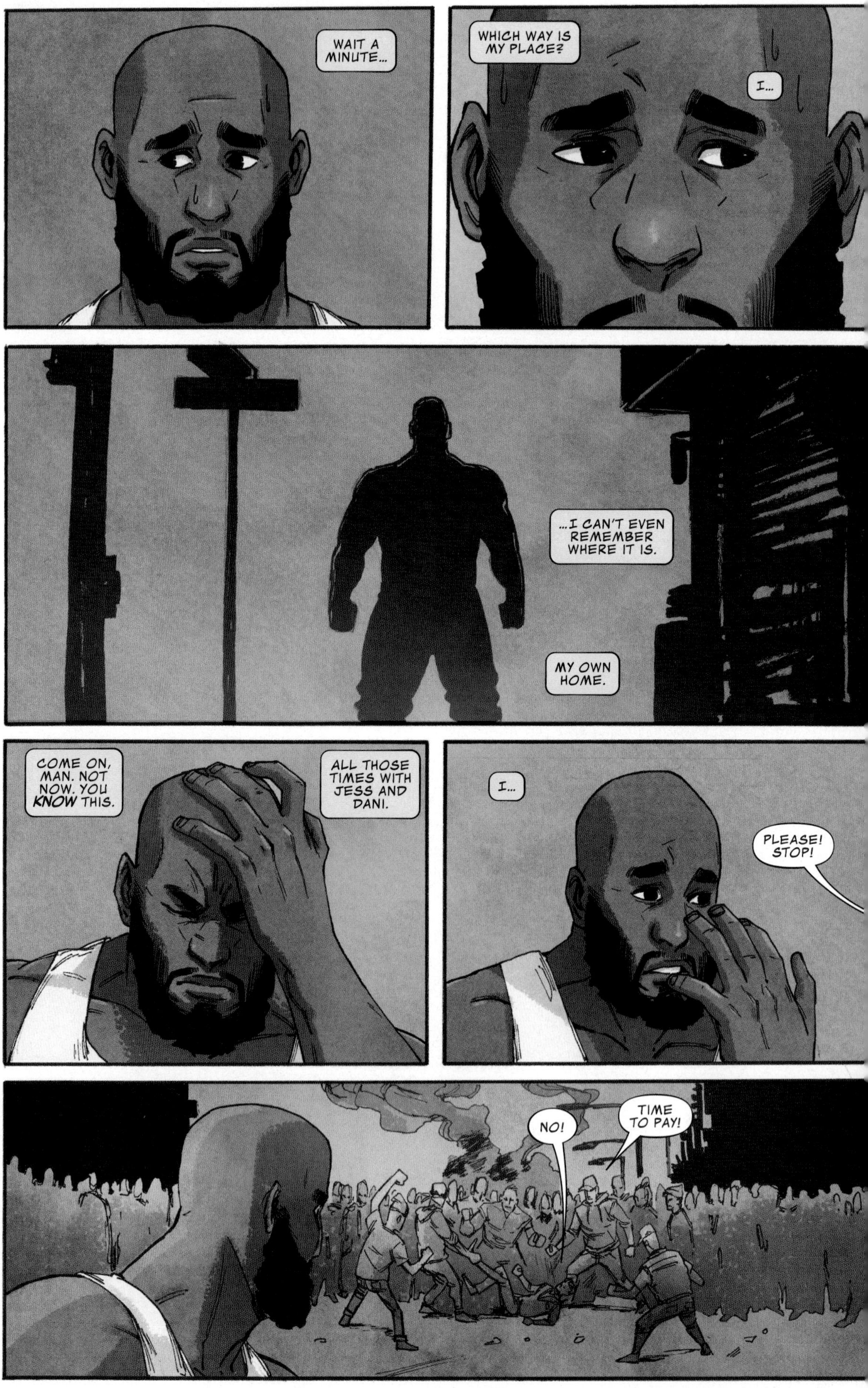
WAIT A MINUTE...
WHICH WAY IS MY PLACE?
I...
...I CAN'T EVEN REMEMBER WHERE IT IS.
MY OWN HOME.
COME ON, MAN. NOT NOW. YOU KNOW THIS.
ALL THOSE TIMES WITH JESS AND DANI.
I...
PLEASE! STOP!
NO!
TIME TO PAY!

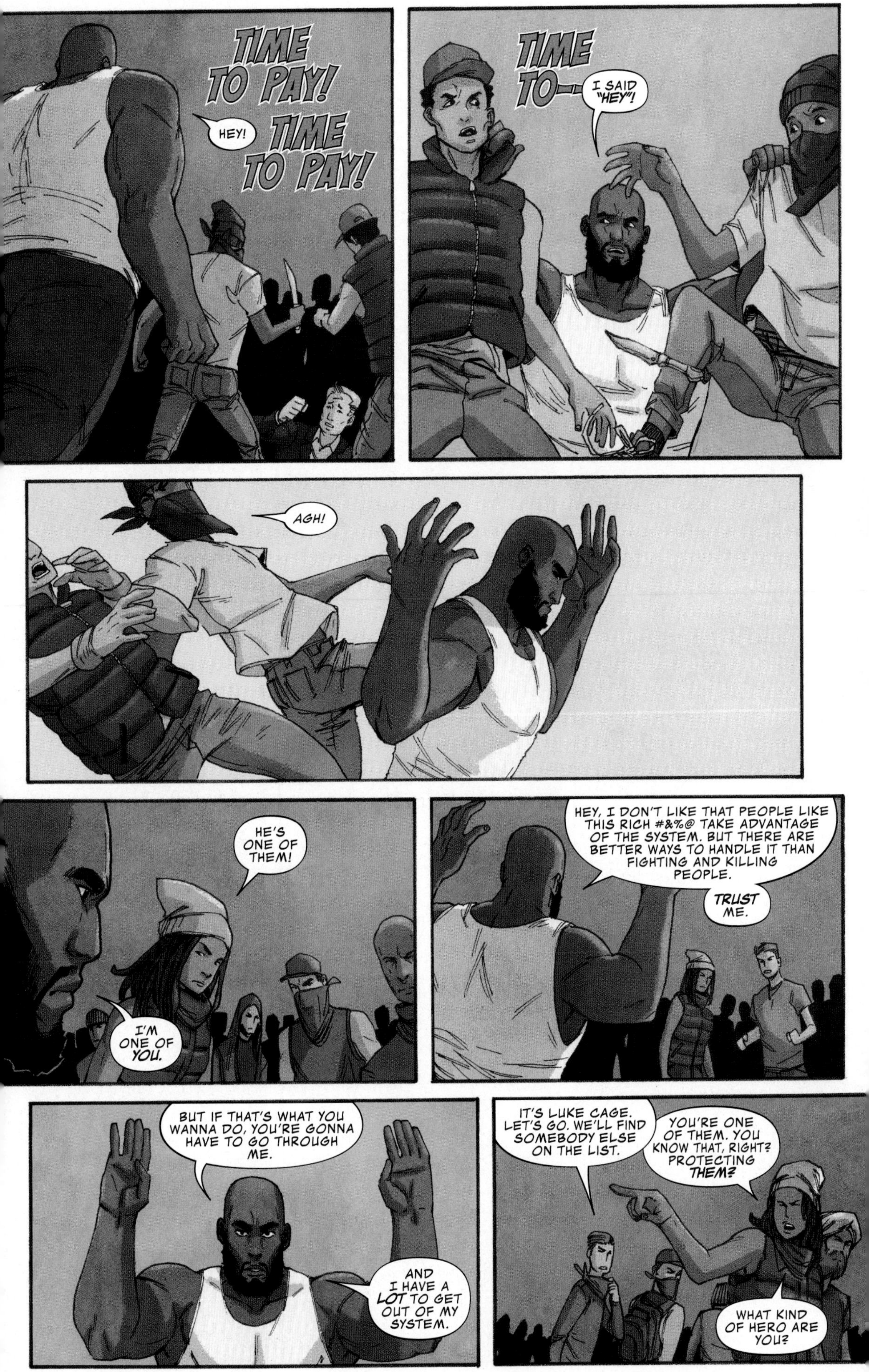
TIME TO PAY!
HEY!
TIME TO PAY!
TIME TO--
I SAID "HEY"!
AGH!
HE'S ONE OF THEM!
I'M ONE OF YOU.
HEY, I DON'T LIKE THAT PEOPLE LIKE THIS RICH #&%@ TAKE ADVANTAGE OF THE SYSTEM. BUT THERE ARE BETTER WAYS TO HANDLE IT THAN FIGHTING AND KILLING PEOPLE.
TRUST ME.
BUT IF THAT'S WHAT YOU WANNA DO, YOU'RE GONNA HAVE TO GO THROUGH ME.
AND I HAVE A LOT TO GET OUT OF MY SYSTEM.
IT'S LUKE CAGE. LET'S GO. WE'LL FIND SOMEBODY ELSE ON THE LIST.
YOU'RE ONE OF THEM. YOU KNOW THAT, RIGHT? PROTECTING THEM?
WHAT KIND OF HERO ARE YOU?

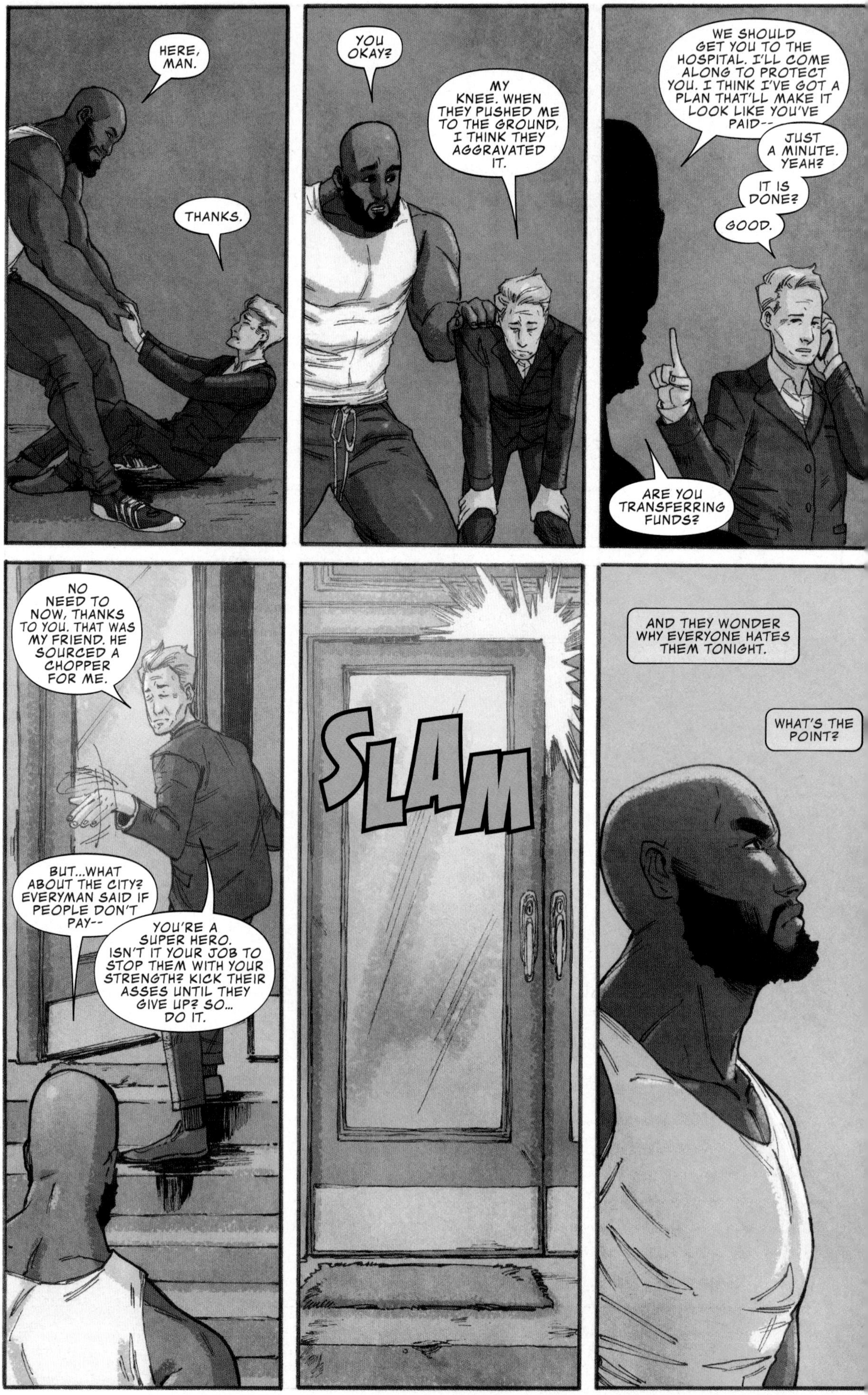
HERE, MAN.
THANKS.
YOU OKAY?
MY KNEE. WHEN THEY PUSHED ME TO THE GROUND, I THINK THEY AGGRAVATED IT.
WE SHOULD GET YOU TO THE HOSPITAL. I'LL COME ALONG TO PROTECT YOU. I THINK I'VE GOT A PLAN THAT'LL MAKE IT LOOK LIKE YOU'VE PAID--
JUST A MINUTE. YEAH?
IT IS DONE?
GOOD.
ARE YOU TRANSFERRING FUNDS?
NO NEED TO NOW, THANKS TO YOU. THAT WAS MY FRIEND. HE SOURCED A CHOPPER FOR ME.
BUT...WHAT ABOUT THE CITY? EVERYMAN SAID IF PEOPLE DON'T PAY--
YOU'RE A SUPER HERO. ISN'T IT YOUR JOB TO STOP THEM WITH YOUR STRENGTH? KICK THEIR ASSES UNTIL THEY GIVE UP? SO... DO IT.
SLAM
AND THEY WONDER WHY EVERYONE HATES THEM TONIGHT.
WHAT'S THE POINT?

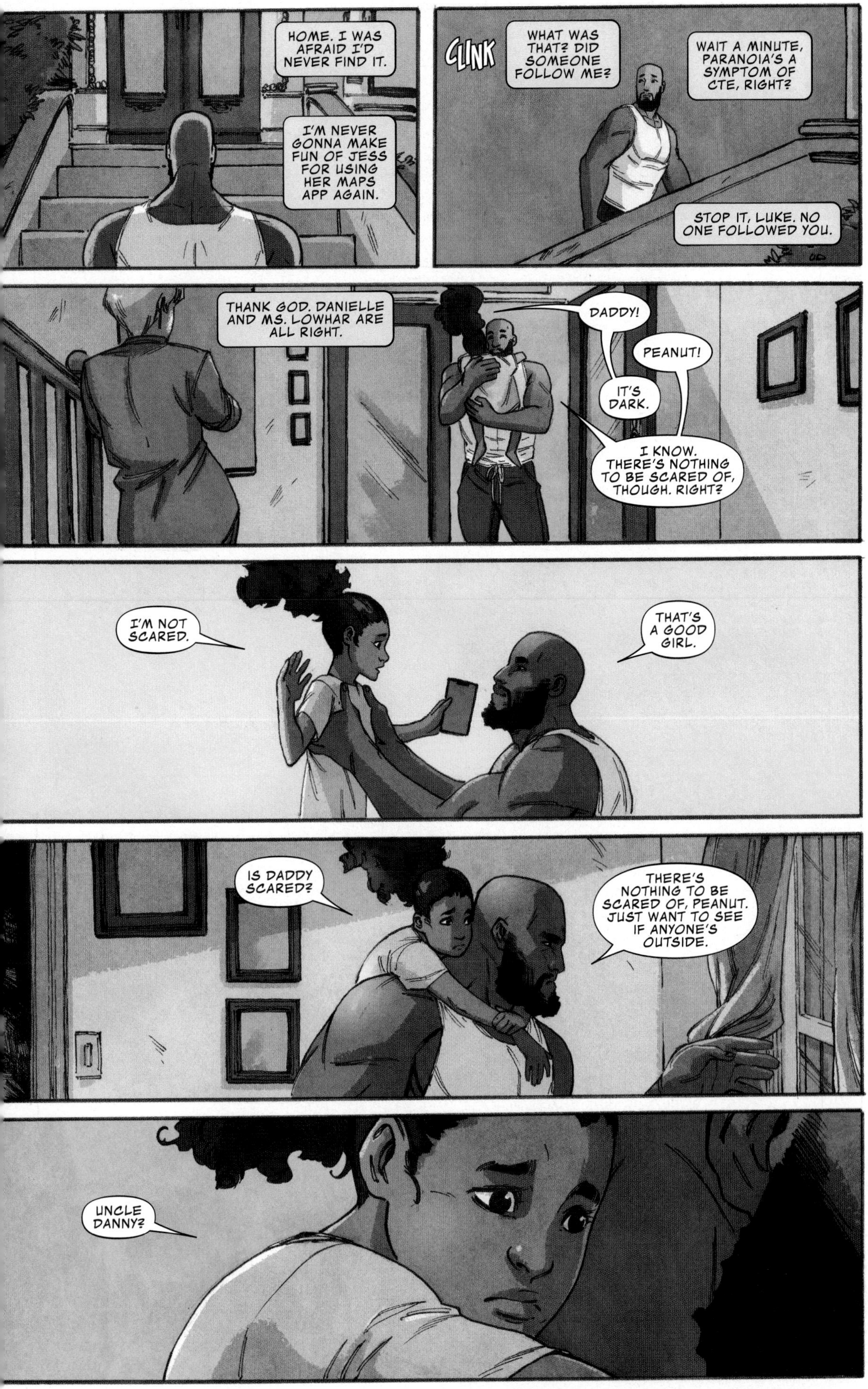
HOME. I WAS AFRAID I'D NEVER FIND IT.
I'M NEVER GONNA MAKE FUN OF JESS FOR USING HER MAPS APP AGAIN.
CLINK
WHAT WAS THAT? DID SOMEONE FOLLOW ME?
WAIT A MINUTE, PARANOIA'S A SYMPTOM OF CTE, RIGHT?
STOP IT, LUKE. NO ONE FOLLOWED YOU.
THANK GOD. DANIELLE AND MS. LOWHAR ARE ALL RIGHT.
DADDY!
PEANUT!
IT'S DARK.
I KNOW. THERE'S NOTHING TO BE SCARED OF, THOUGH. RIGHT?
I'M NOT SCARED.
THAT'S A GOOD GIRL.
IS DADDY SCARED?
THERE'S NOTHING TO BE SCARED OF, PEANUT. JUST WANT TO SEE IF ANYONE'S OUTSIDE.
UNCLE DANNY?

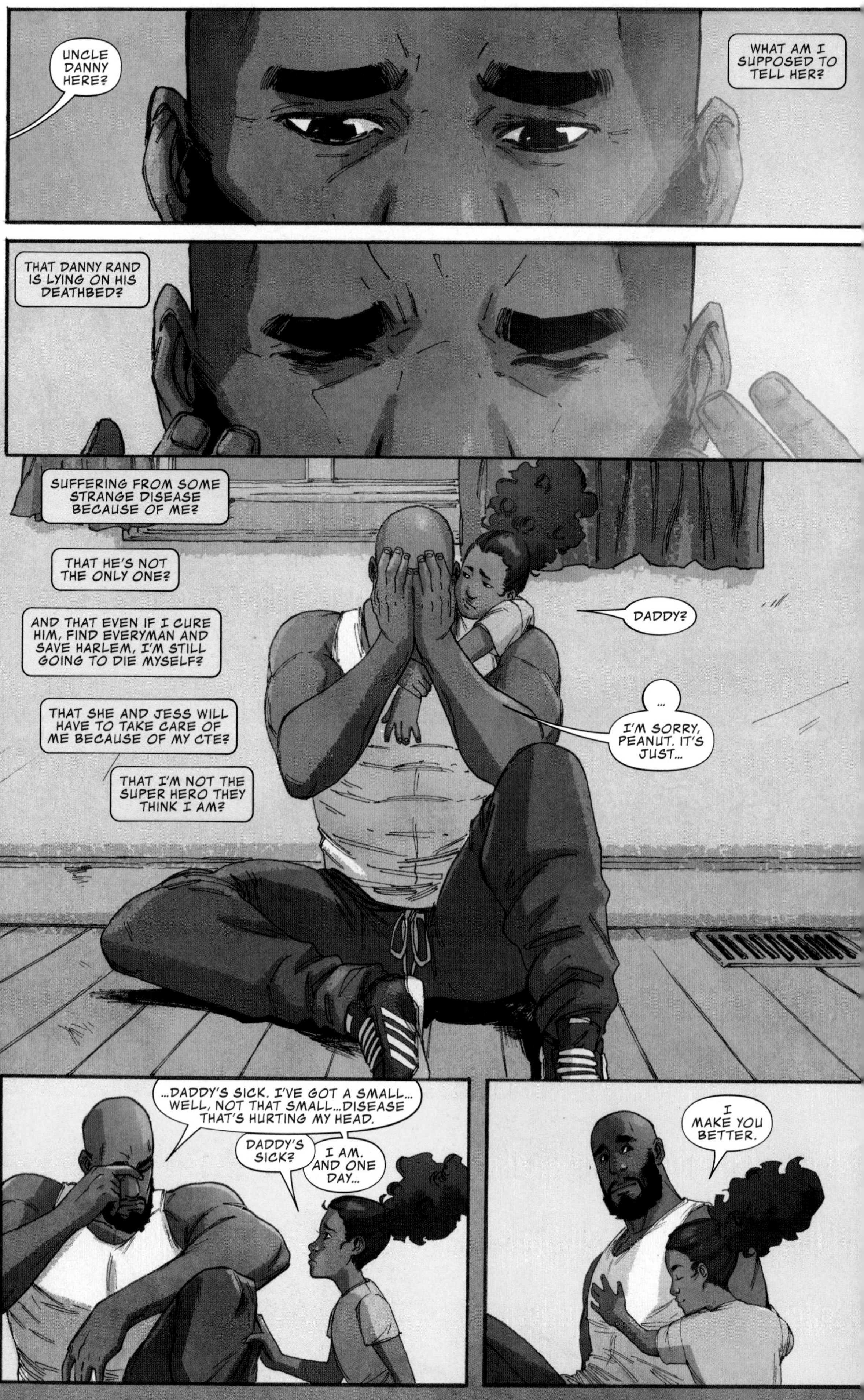
UNCLE DANNY HERE?
WHAT AM I SUPPOSED TO TELL HER?
THAT DANNY RAND IS LYING ON HIS DEATHBED?
SUFFERING FROM SOME STRANGE DISEASE BECAUSE OF ME?
THAT HE'S NOT THE ONLY ONE?
AND THAT EVEN IF I CURE HIM, FIND EVERYMAN AND SAVE HARLEM, I'M STILL GOING TO DIE MYSELF?
THAT SHE AND JESS WILL HAVE TO TAKE CARE OF ME BECAUSE OF MY CTE?
THAT I'M NOT THE SUPER HERO THEY THINK I AM?
DADDY?
...
I'M SORRY, PEANUT. IT'S JUST...
...DADDY'S SICK. I'VE GOT A SMALL... WELL, NOT THAT SMALL...DISEASE THAT'S HURTING MY HEAD.
DADDY'S SICK?
I AM. AND ONE DAY...
I MAKE YOU BETTER.

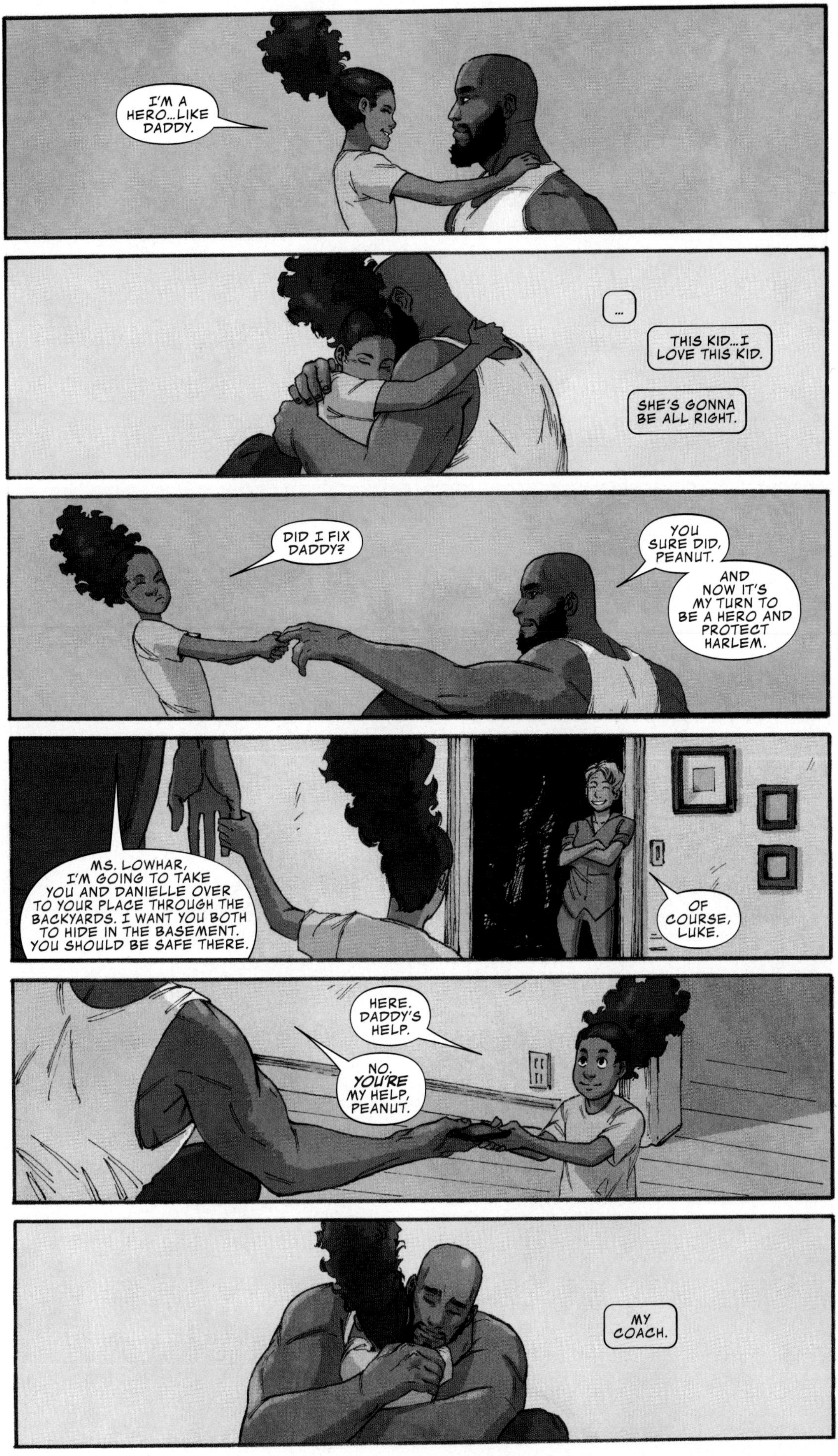
I'M A HERO...LIKE DADDY.
...
THIS KID...I LOVE THIS KID.
SHE'S GONNA BE ALL RIGHT.
DID I FIX DADDY?
YOU SURE DID, PEANUT.
AND NOW IT'S MY TURN TO BE A HERO AND PROTECT HARLEM.
MS. LOWHAR, I'M GOING TO TAKE YOU AND DANIELLE OVER TO YOUR PLACE THROUGH THE BACKYARDS. I WANT YOU BOTH TO HIDE IN THE BASEMENT. YOU SHOULD BE SAFE THERE.
OF COURSE, LUKE.
HERE. DADDY'S HELP.
NO. *YOU'RE* MY HELP, PEANUT.
MY COACH.

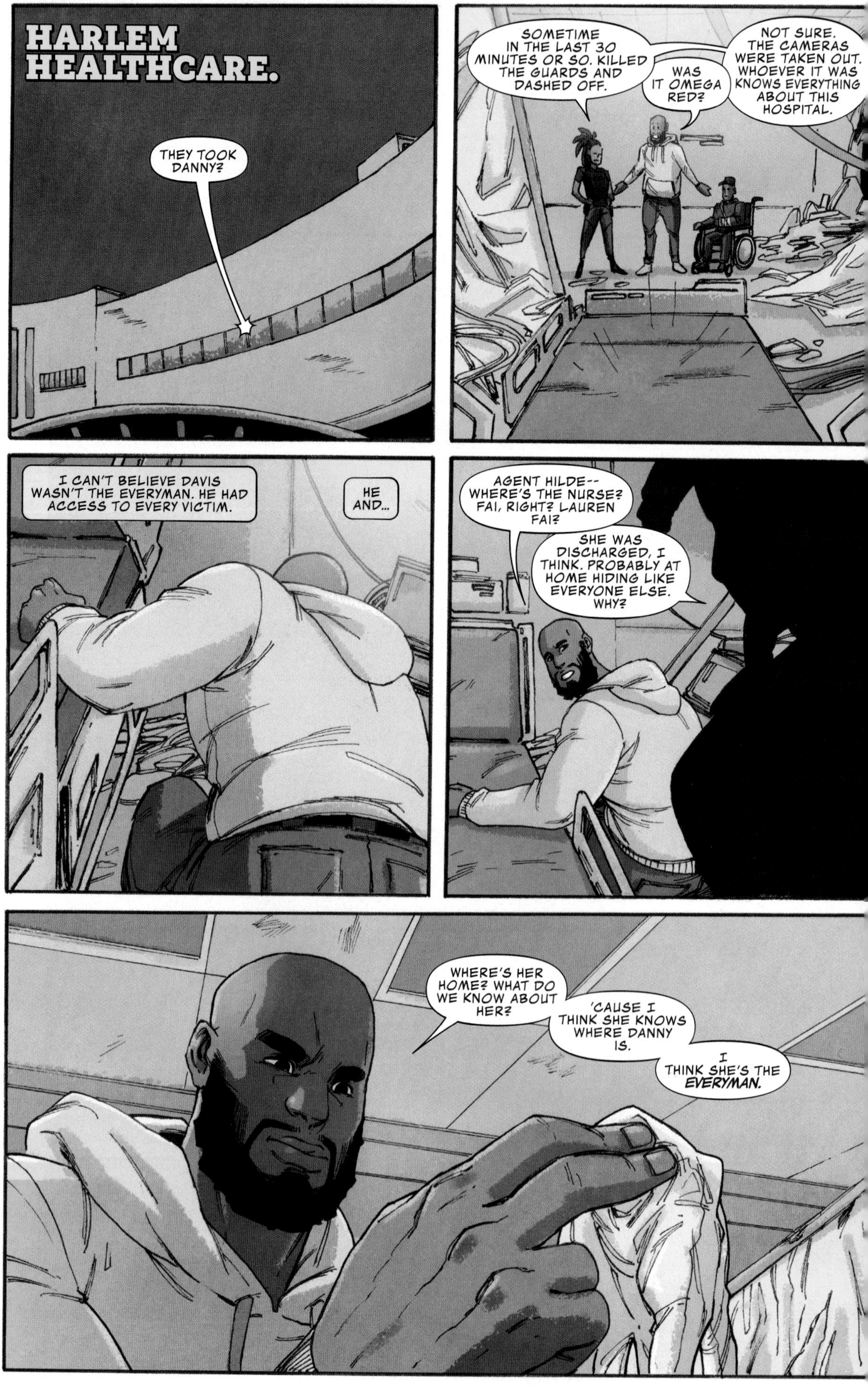

HARLEM HEALTHCARE.
THEY TOOK DANNY?
SOMETIME IN THE LAST 30 MINUTES OR SO. KILLED THE GUARDS AND DASHED OFF.
WAS IT OMEGA RED?
NOT SURE. THE CAMERAS WERE TAKEN OUT. WHOEVER IT WAS KNOWS EVERYTHING ABOUT THIS HOSPITAL.
I CAN'T BELIEVE DAVIS WASN'T THE EVERYMAN. HE HAD ACCESS TO EVERY VICTIM.
HE AND...
AGENT HILDE-- WHERE'S THE NURSE? FAI, RIGHT? LAUREN FAI?
SHE WAS DISCHARGED, I THINK. PROBABLY AT HOME HIDING LIKE EVERYONE ELSE. WHY?
WHERE'S HER HOME? WHAT DO WE KNOW ABOUT HER?
'CAUSE I THINK SHE KNOWS WHERE DANNY IS.
I THINK SHE'S THE EVERYMAN.

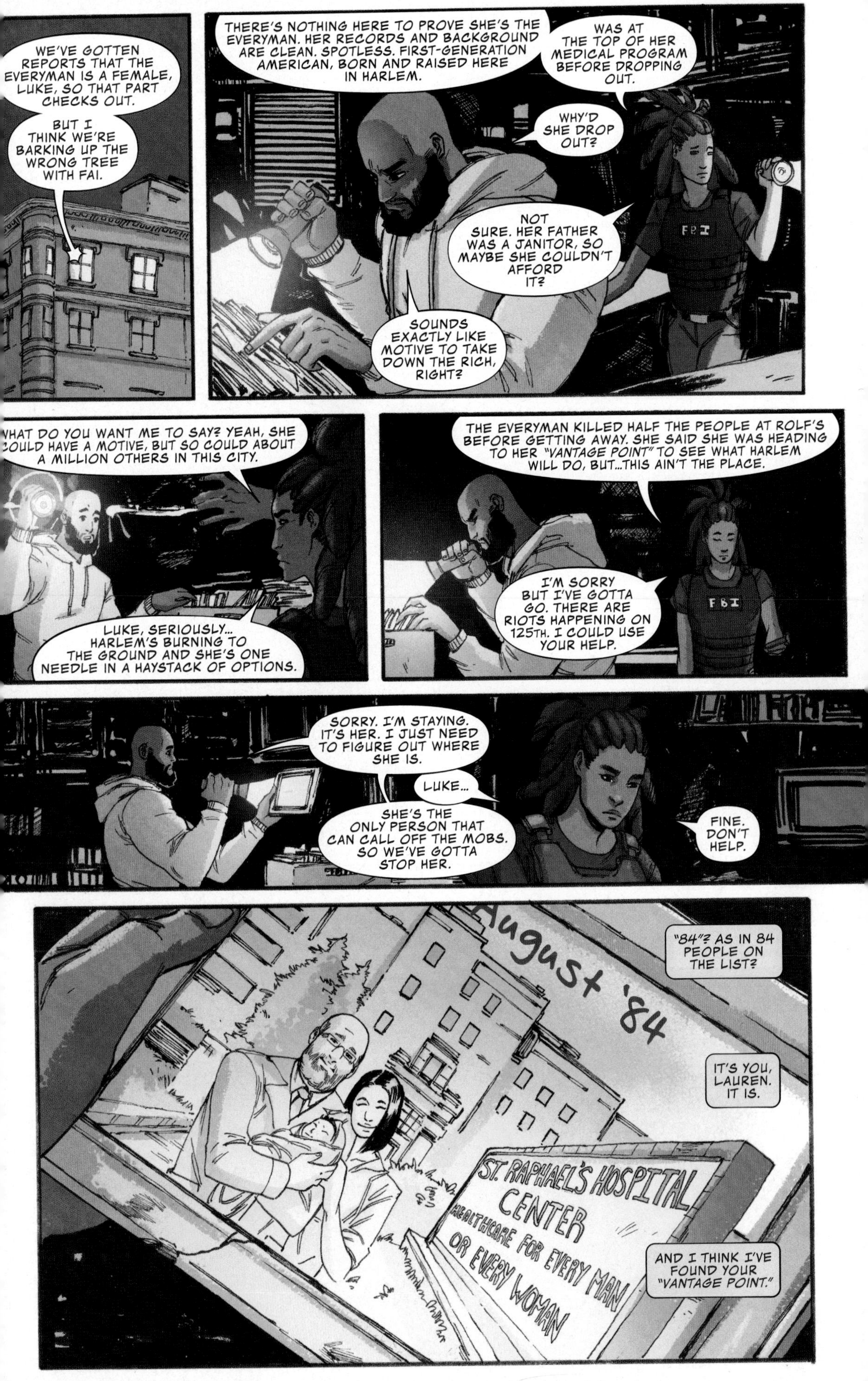
WE'VE GOTTEN REPORTS THAT THE EVERYMAN IS A FEMALE, LUKE, SO THAT PART CHECKS OUT.
BUT I THINK WE'RE BARKING UP THE WRONG TREE WITH FAI.
THERE'S NOTHING HERE TO PROVE SHE'S THE EVERYMAN. HER RECORDS AND BACKGROUND ARE CLEAN. SPOTLESS. FIRST-GENERATION AMERICAN, BORN AND RAISED HERE IN HARLEM.
WAS AT THE TOP OF HER MEDICAL PROGRAM BEFORE DROPPING OUT.
WHY'D SHE DROP OUT?
NOT SURE. HER FATHER WAS A JANITOR, SO MAYBE SHE COULDN'T AFFORD IT?
SOUNDS EXACTLY LIKE MOTIVE TO TAKE DOWN THE RICH, RIGHT?
WHAT DO YOU WANT ME TO SAY? YEAH, SHE COULD HAVE A MOTIVE, BUT SO COULD ABOUT A MILLION OTHERS IN THIS CITY.
LUKE, SERIOUSLY... HARLEM'S BURNING TO THE GROUND AND SHE'S ONE NEEDLE IN A HAYSTACK OF OPTIONS.
THE EVERYMAN KILLED HALF THE PEOPLE AT ROLF'S BEFORE GETTING AWAY. SHE SAID SHE WAS HEADING TO HER "VANTAGE POINT" TO SEE WHAT HARLEM WILL DO, BUT...THIS AIN'T THE PLACE.
I'M SORRY BUT I'VE GOTTA GO. THERE ARE RIOTS HAPPENING ON 125TH. I COULD USE YOUR HELP.
SORRY. I'M STAYING. IT'S HER. I JUST NEED TO FIGURE OUT WHERE SHE IS.
LUKE...
SHE'S THE ONLY PERSON THAT CAN CALL OFF THE MOBS. SO WE'VE GOTTA STOP HER.
FINE. DON'T HELP.
August '84
ST. RAPHAEL'S HOSPITAL CENTER
HEALTHCARE FOR EVERY MAN OR EVERY WOMAN
"84"? AS IN 84 PEOPLE ON THE LIST?
IT'S YOU, LAUREN. IT IS.
AND I THINK I'VE FOUND YOUR "VANTAGE POINT."

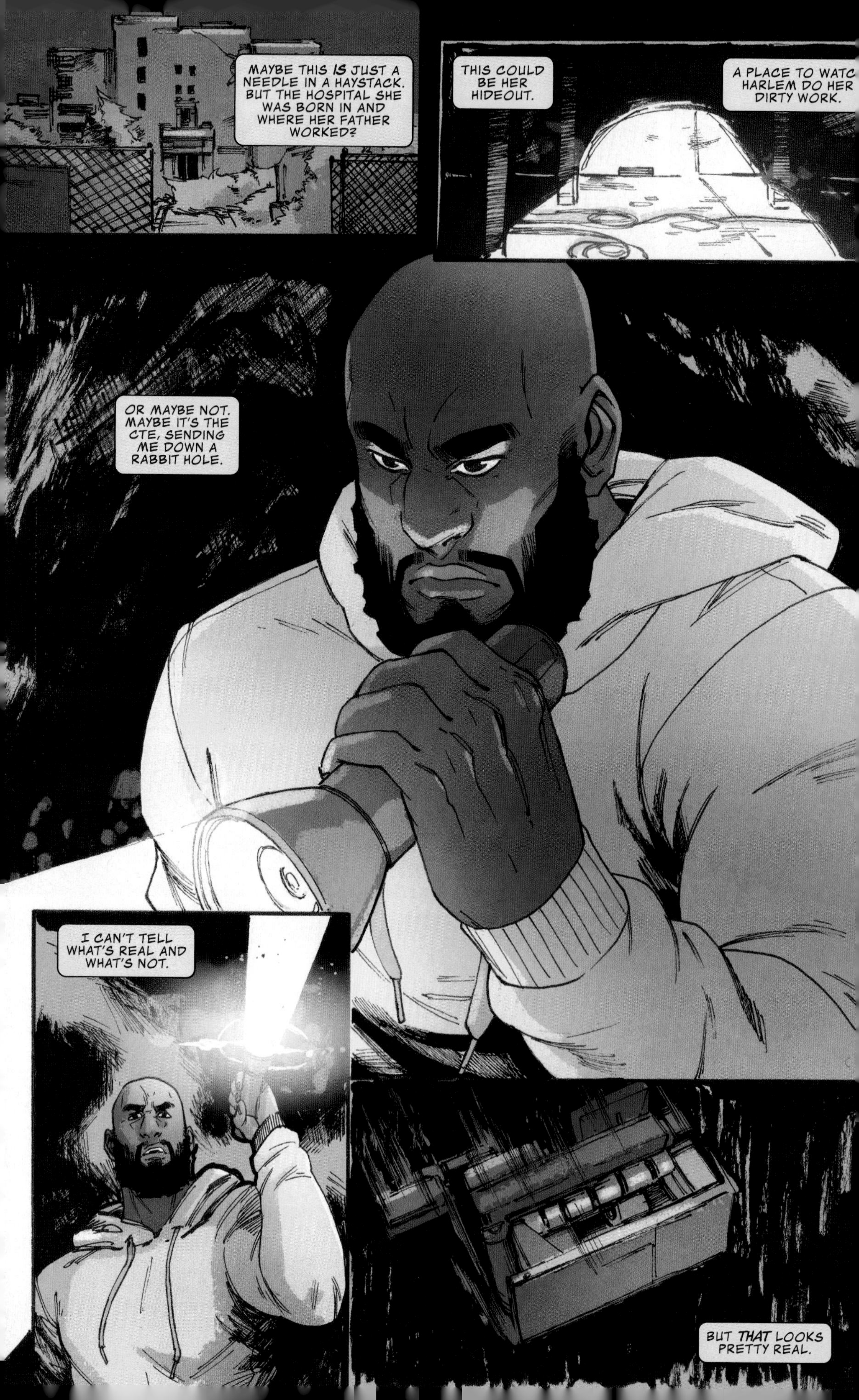
MAYBE THIS IS JUST A NEEDLE IN A HAYSTACK. BUT THE HOSPITAL SHE WAS BORN IN AND WHERE HER FATHER WORKED?
THIS COULD BE HER HIDEOUT.
A PLACE TO WATC HARLEM DO HER DIRTY WORK.
OR MAYBE NOT. MAYBE IT'S THE CTE, SENDING ME DOWN A RABBIT HOLE.
I CAN'T TELL WHAT'S REAL AND WHAT'S NOT.
BUT THAT LOOKS PRETTY REAL.

UGH!

I DO NOT KNOW HOW YOU FIND US. BUT I HAVE HAD ENOUGH OF YOU.

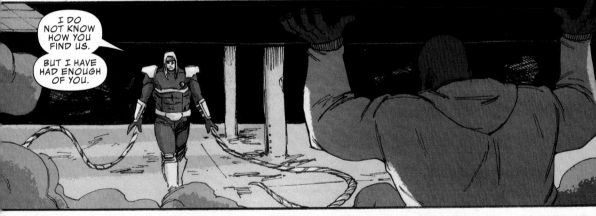

FEELING'S MUTUAL, OMEGA RED.

BOOM

DAMMIT. MY AIM'S OFF. BUT IT MIGHT BE ENOUGH.

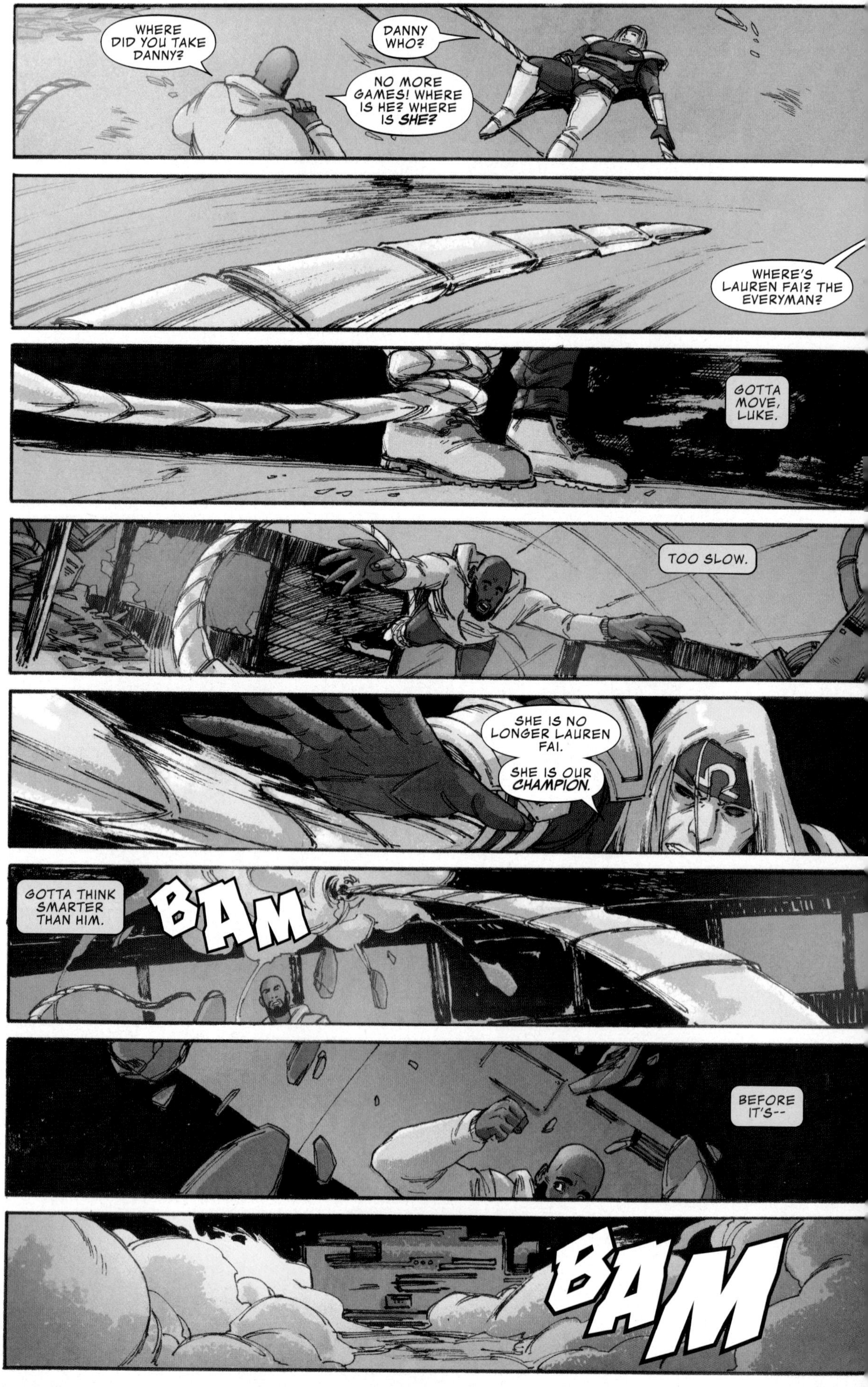
WHERE DID YOU TAKE DANNY?
DANNY WHO?
NO MORE GAMES! WHERE IS HE? WHERE IS SHE?
WHERE'S LAUREN FAI? THE EVERYMAN?
GOTTA MOVE, LUKE.
TOO SLOW.
SHE IS NO LONGER LAUREN FAI.
SHE IS OUR CHAMPION.
GOTTA THINK SMARTER THAN HIM.
BAM
BEFORE IT'S--
BAM

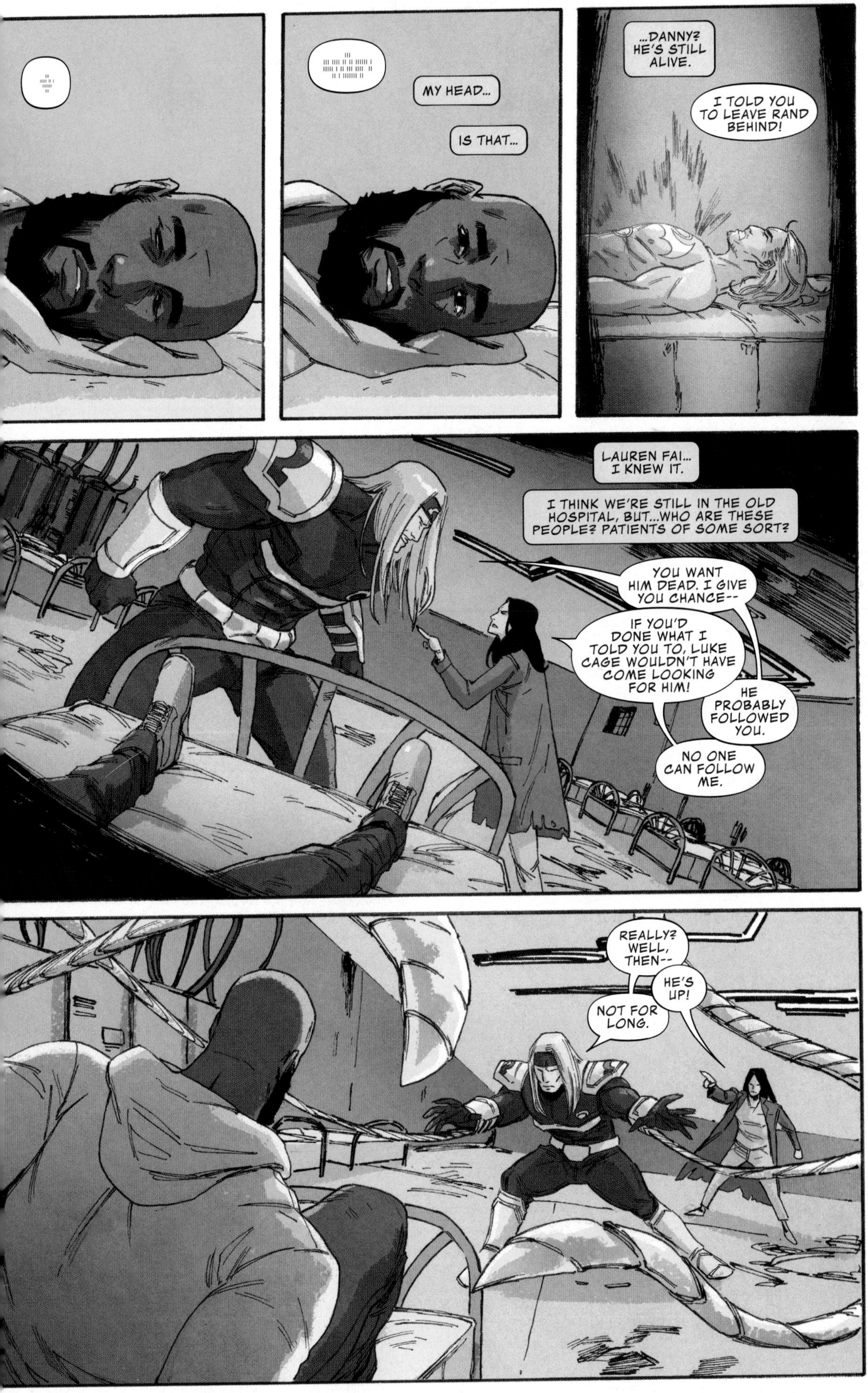
MY HEAD...
IS THAT...
...DANNY? HE'S STILL ALIVE.
I TOLD YOU TO LEAVE RAND BEHIND!
LAUREN FAI... I KNEW IT.
I THINK WE'RE STILL IN THE OLD HOSPITAL, BUT...WHO ARE THESE PEOPLE? PATIENTS OF SOME SORT?
YOU WANT HIM DEAD. I GIVE YOU CHANCE--
IF YOU'D DONE WHAT I TOLD YOU TO, LUKE CAGE WOULDN'T HAVE COME LOOKING FOR HIM!
HE PROBABLY FOLLOWED YOU.
NO ONE CAN FOLLOW ME.
REALLY? WELL, THEN--
HE'S UP!
NOT FOR LONG.

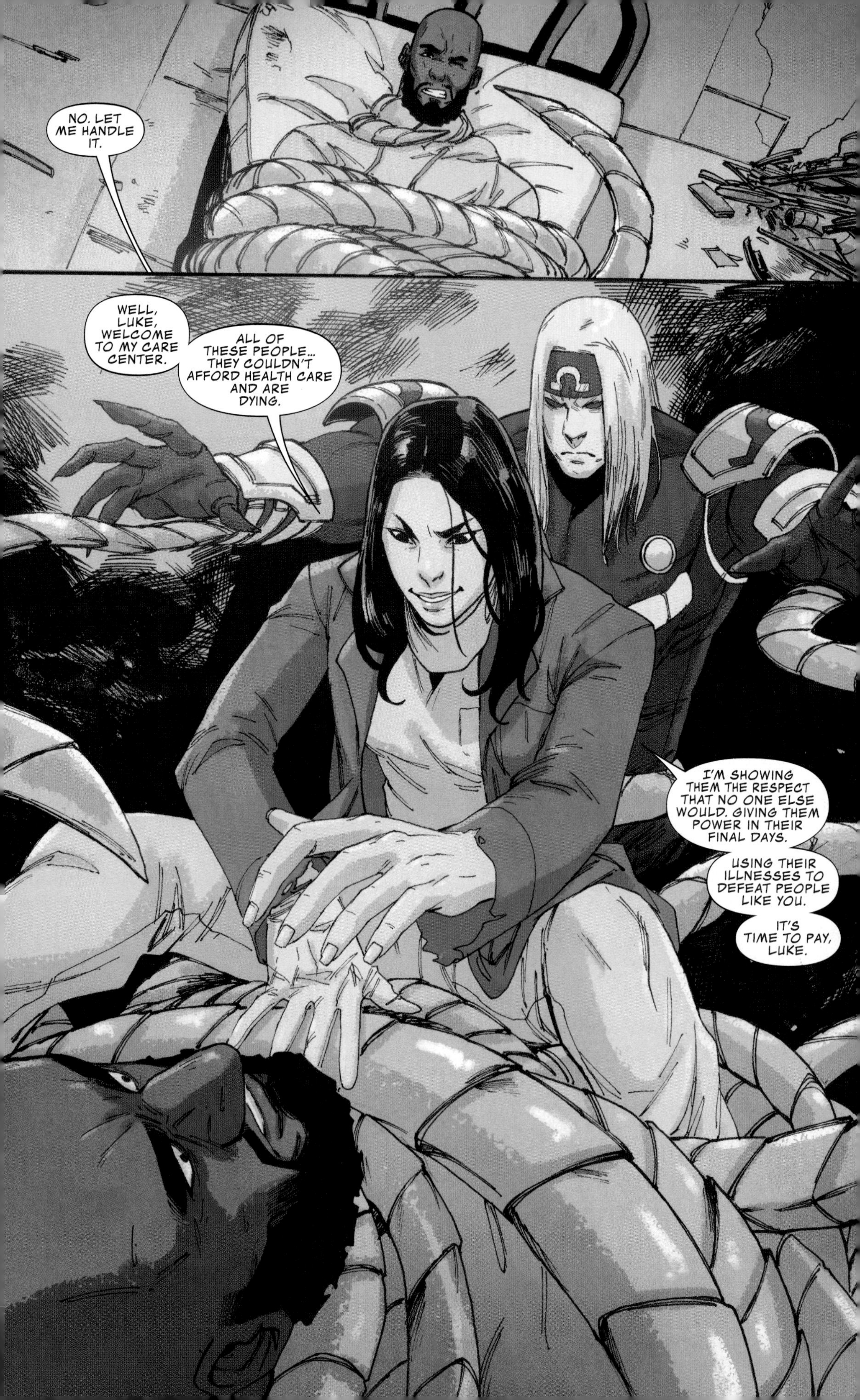
NO. LET ME HANDLE IT.
WELL, LUKE, WELCOME TO MY CARE CENTER.
ALL OF THESE PEOPLE... THEY COULDN'T AFFORD HEALTH CARE AND ARE DYING.
I'M SHOWING THEM THE RESPECT THAT NO ONE ELSE WOULD. GIVING THEM POWER IN THEIR FINAL DAYS.
USING THEIR ILLNESSES TO DEFEAT PEOPLE LIKE YOU.
IT'S TIME TO PAY, LUKE.

EVERYMAN:
CHAPTER 6

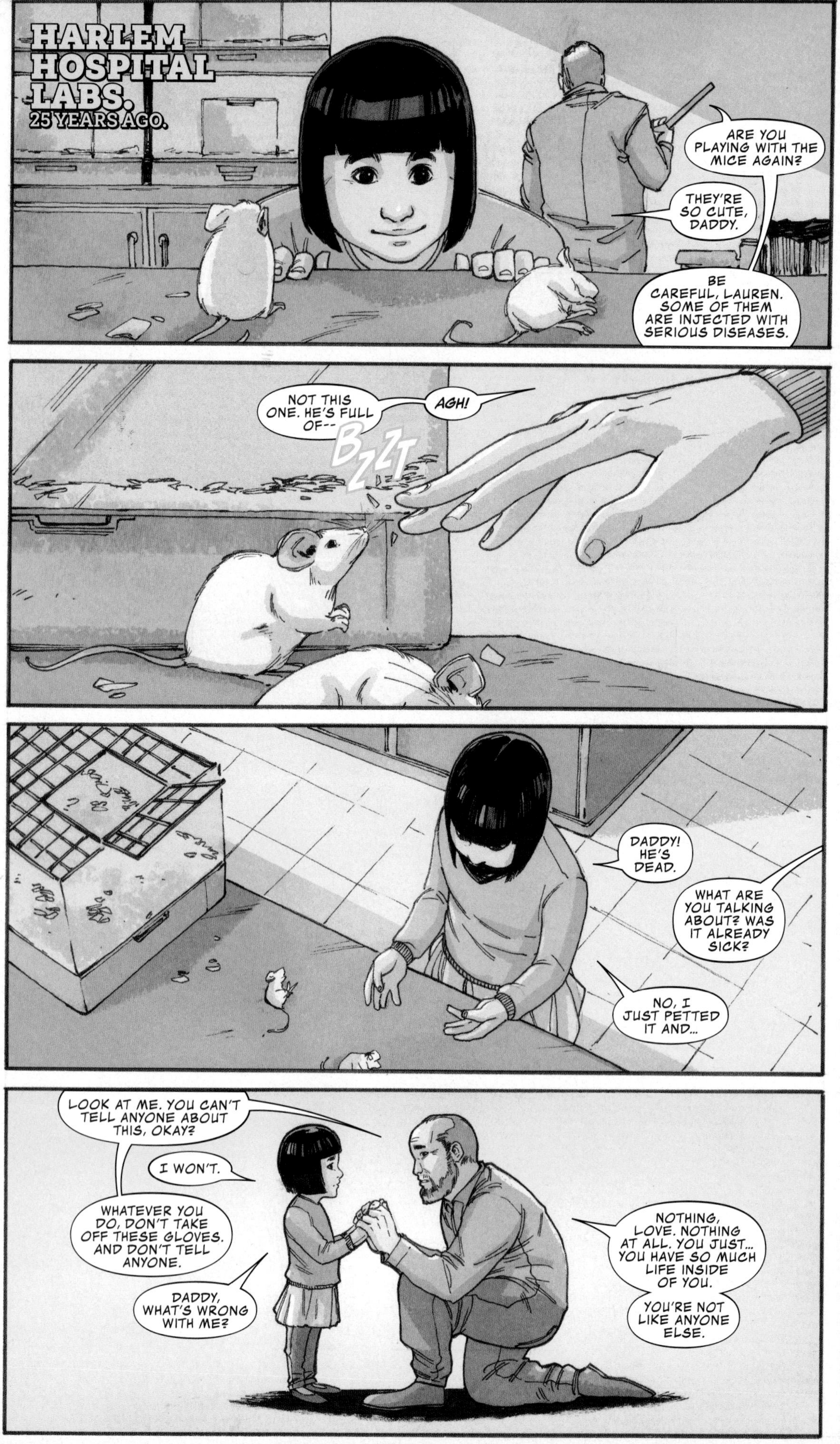
HARLEM HOSPITAL LABS.
25 YEARS AGO.
ARE YOU PLAYING WITH THE MICE AGAIN?
THEY'RE SO CUTE, DADDY.
BE CAREFUL, LAUREN. SOME OF THEM ARE INJECTED WITH SERIOUS DISEASES.
NOT THIS ONE. HE'S FULL OF--
AGH!
BZZT
DADDY! HE'S DEAD.
WHAT ARE YOU TALKING ABOUT? WAS IT ALREADY SICK?
NO, I JUST PETTED IT AND...
LOOK AT ME. YOU CAN'T TELL ANYONE ABOUT THIS, OKAY?
I WON'T.
WHATEVER YOU DO, DON'T TAKE OFF THESE GLOVES. AND DON'T TELL ANYONE.
DADDY, WHAT'S WRONG WITH ME?
NOTHING, LOVE. NOTHING AT ALL. YOU JUST... YOU HAVE SO MUCH LIFE INSIDE OF YOU.
YOU'RE NOT LIKE ANYONE ELSE.

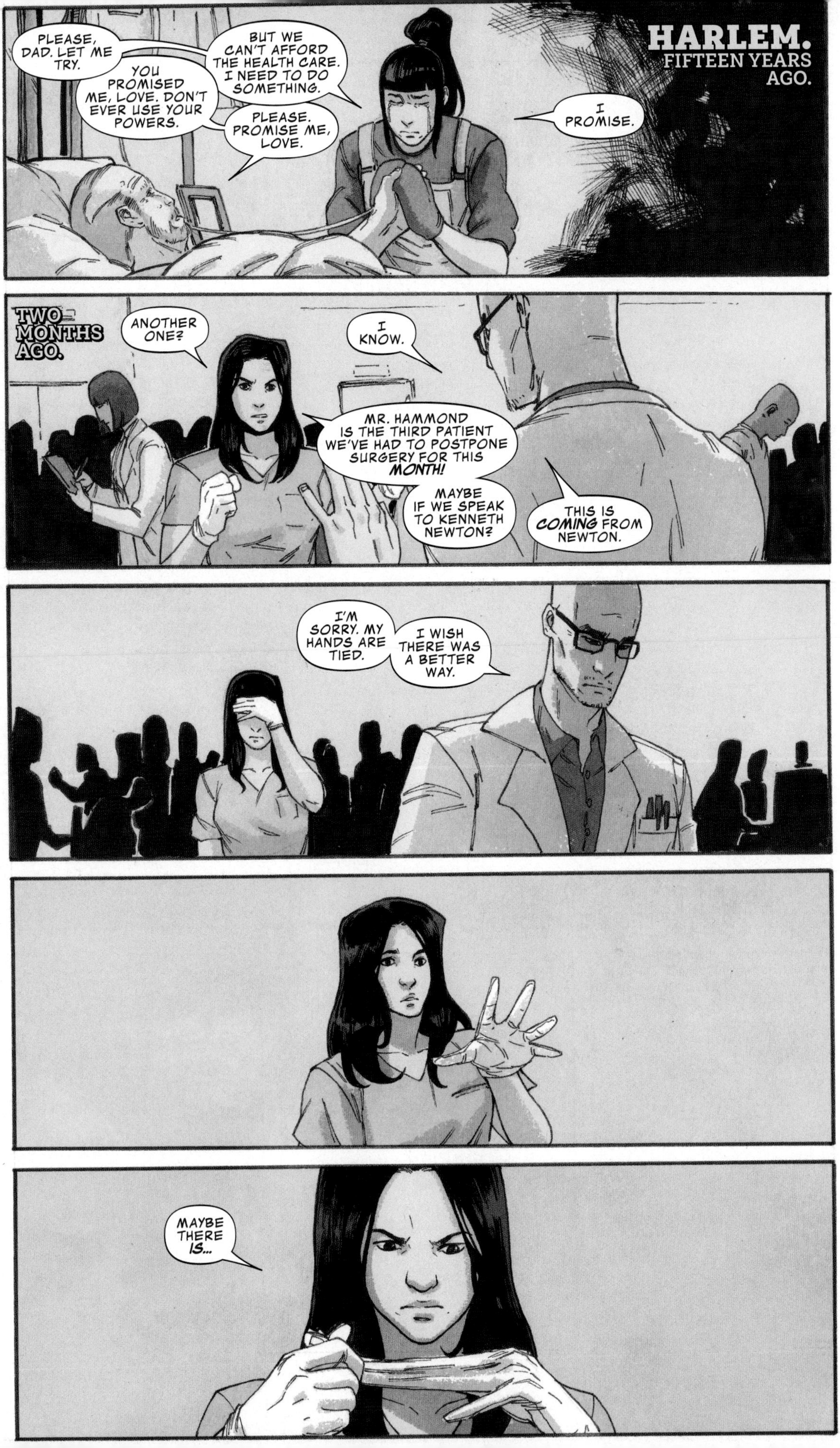
HARLEM. FIFTEEN YEARS AGO.
PLEASE, DAD. LET ME TRY.
YOU PROMISED ME, LOVE. DON'T EVER USE YOUR POWERS.
BUT WE CAN'T AFFORD THE HEALTH CARE. I NEED TO DO SOMETHING.
PLEASE. PROMISE ME, LOVE.
I PROMISE.
TWO MONTHS AGO.
ANOTHER ONE?
I KNOW.
MR. HAMMOND IS THE THIRD PATIENT WE'VE HAD TO POSTPONE SURGERY FOR THIS MONTH!
MAYBE IF WE SPEAK TO KENNETH NEWTON?
THIS IS COMING FROM NEWTON.
I'M SORRY. MY HANDS ARE TIED.
I WISH THERE WAS A BETTER WAY.
MAYBE THERE IS...

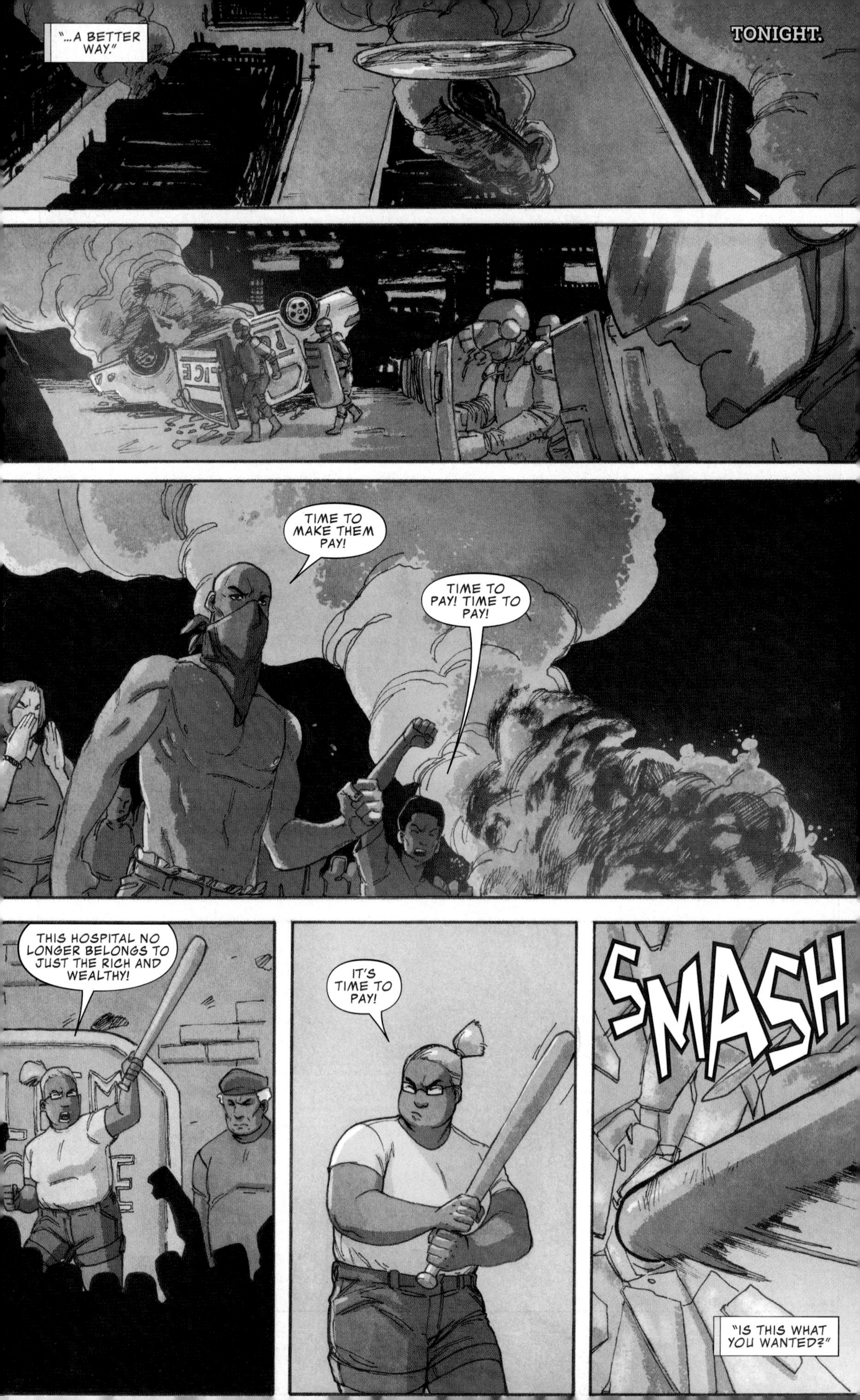
"...A BETTER WAY."
TONIGHT.
TIME TO MAKE THEM PAY!
TIME TO PAY! TIME TO PAY!
THIS HOSPITAL NO LONGER BELONGS TO JUST THE RICH AND WEALTHY!
IT'S TIME TO PAY!
SMASH
"IS THIS WHAT YOU WANTED?"

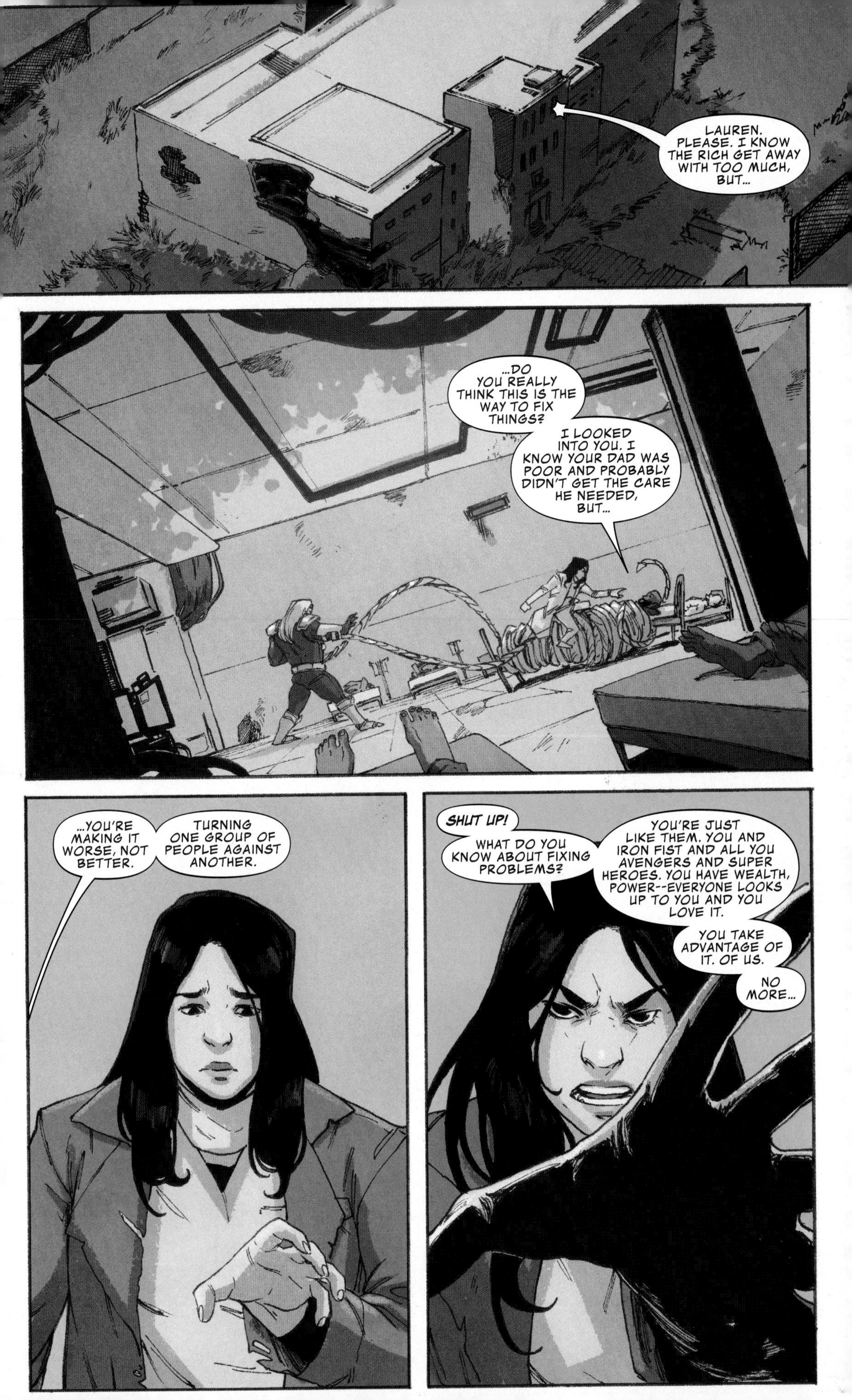
LAUREN. PLEASE. I KNOW THE RICH GET AWAY WITH TOO MUCH, BUT...
...DO YOU REALLY THINK THIS IS THE WAY TO FIX THINGS?
I LOOKED INTO YOU. I KNOW YOUR DAD WAS POOR AND PROBABLY DIDN'T GET THE CARE HE NEEDED, BUT...
...YOU'RE MAKING IT WORSE, NOT BETTER.
TURNING ONE GROUP OF PEOPLE AGAINST ANOTHER.
SHUT UP!
WHAT DO YOU KNOW ABOUT FIXING PROBLEMS?
YOU'RE JUST LIKE THEM. YOU AND IRON FIST AND ALL YOU AVENGERS AND SUPER HEROES. YOU HAVE WEALTH, POWER--EVERYONE LOOKS UP TO YOU AND YOU LOVE IT.
YOU TAKE ADVANTAGE OF IT. OF US.
NO MORE...

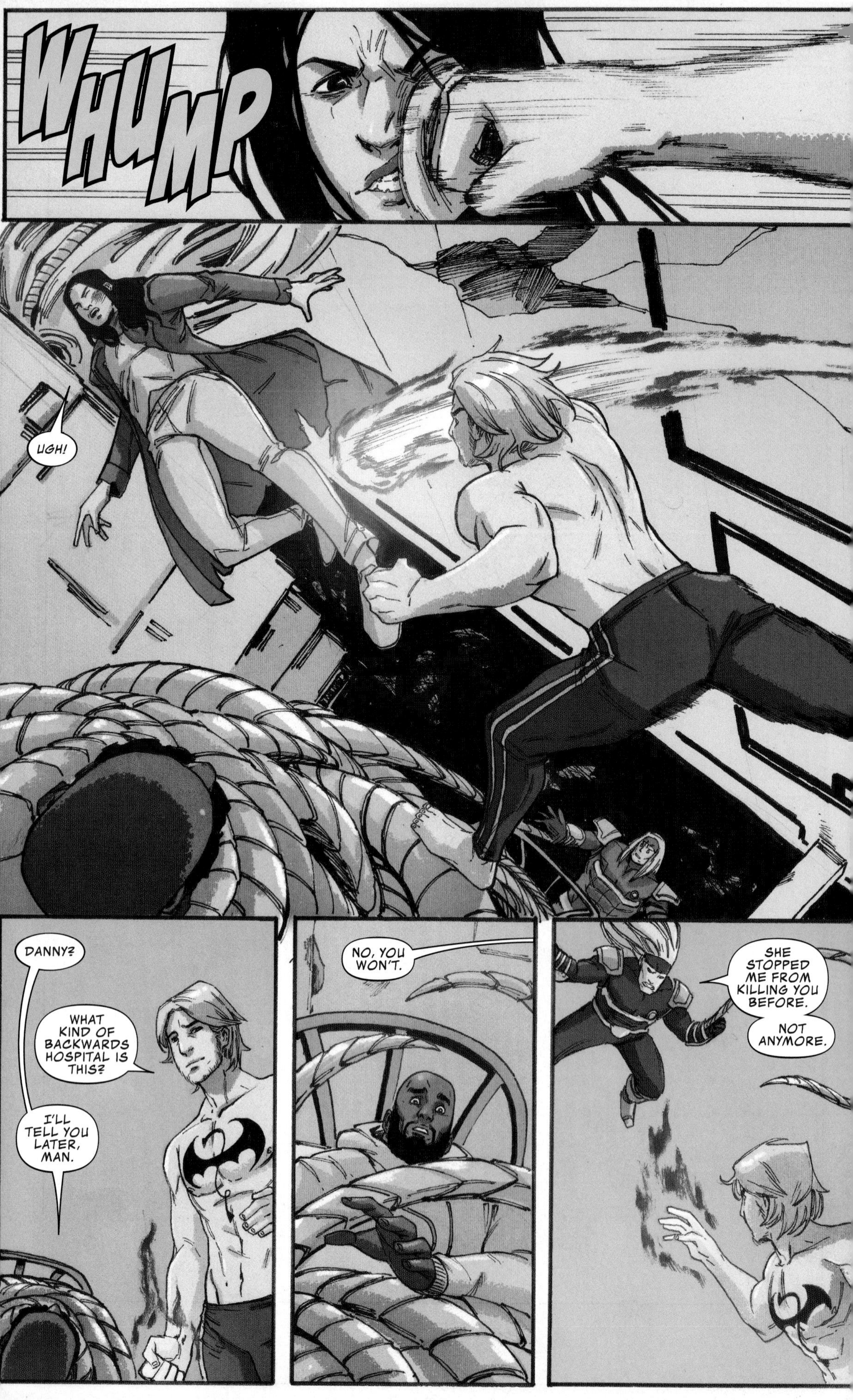
WHUMP
UGH!
DANNY?
WHAT KIND OF BACKWARDS HOSPITAL IS THIS?
I'LL TELL YOU LATER, MAN.
NO, YOU WON'T.
SHE STOPPED ME FROM KILLING YOU BEFORE.
NOT ANYMORE.

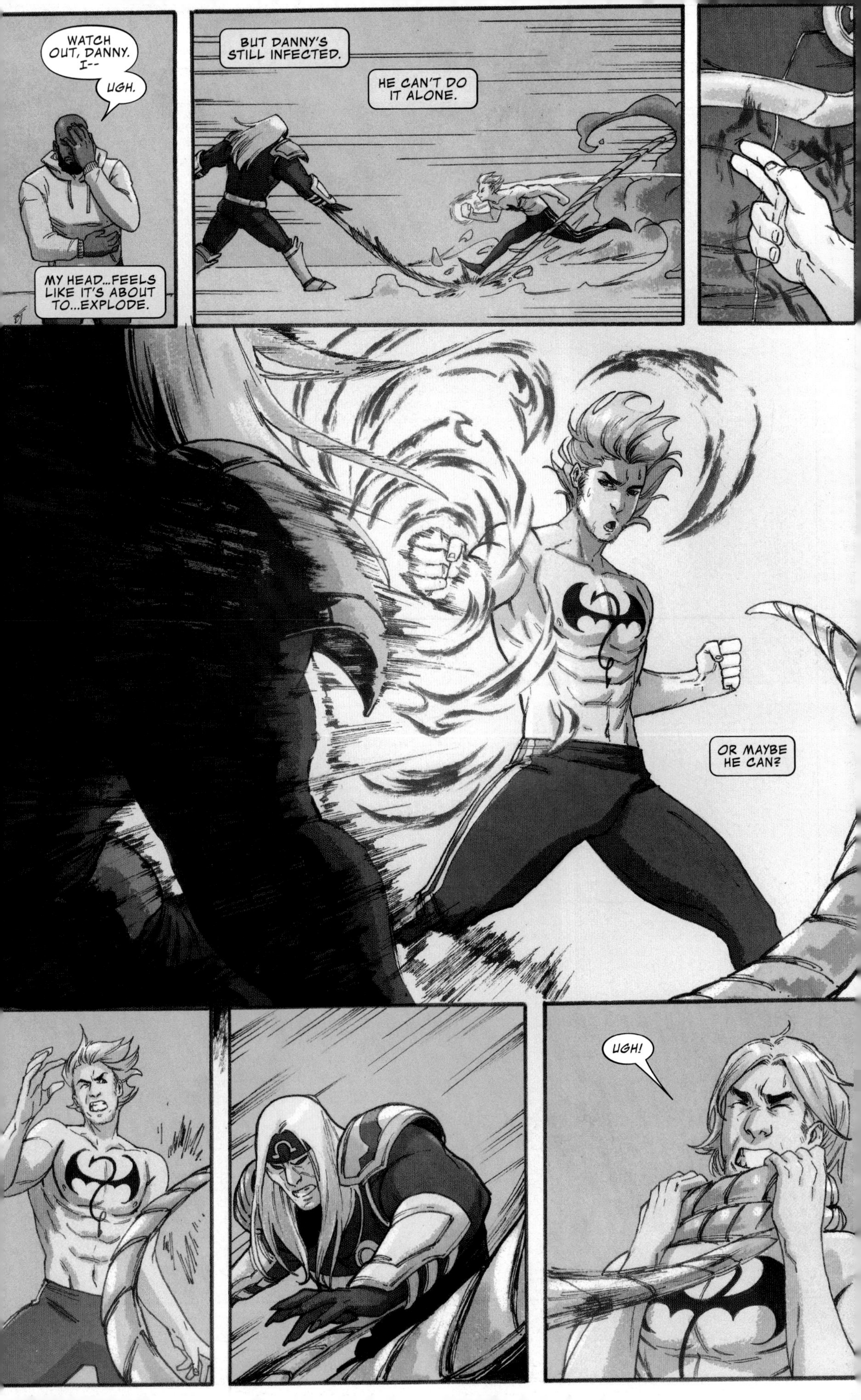
WATCH OUT, DANNY. I--
UGH.
MY HEAD...FEELS LIKE IT'S ABOUT TO...EXPLODE.
BUT DANNY'S STILL INFECTED.
HE CAN'T DO IT ALONE.
OR MAYBE HE CAN?
UGH!

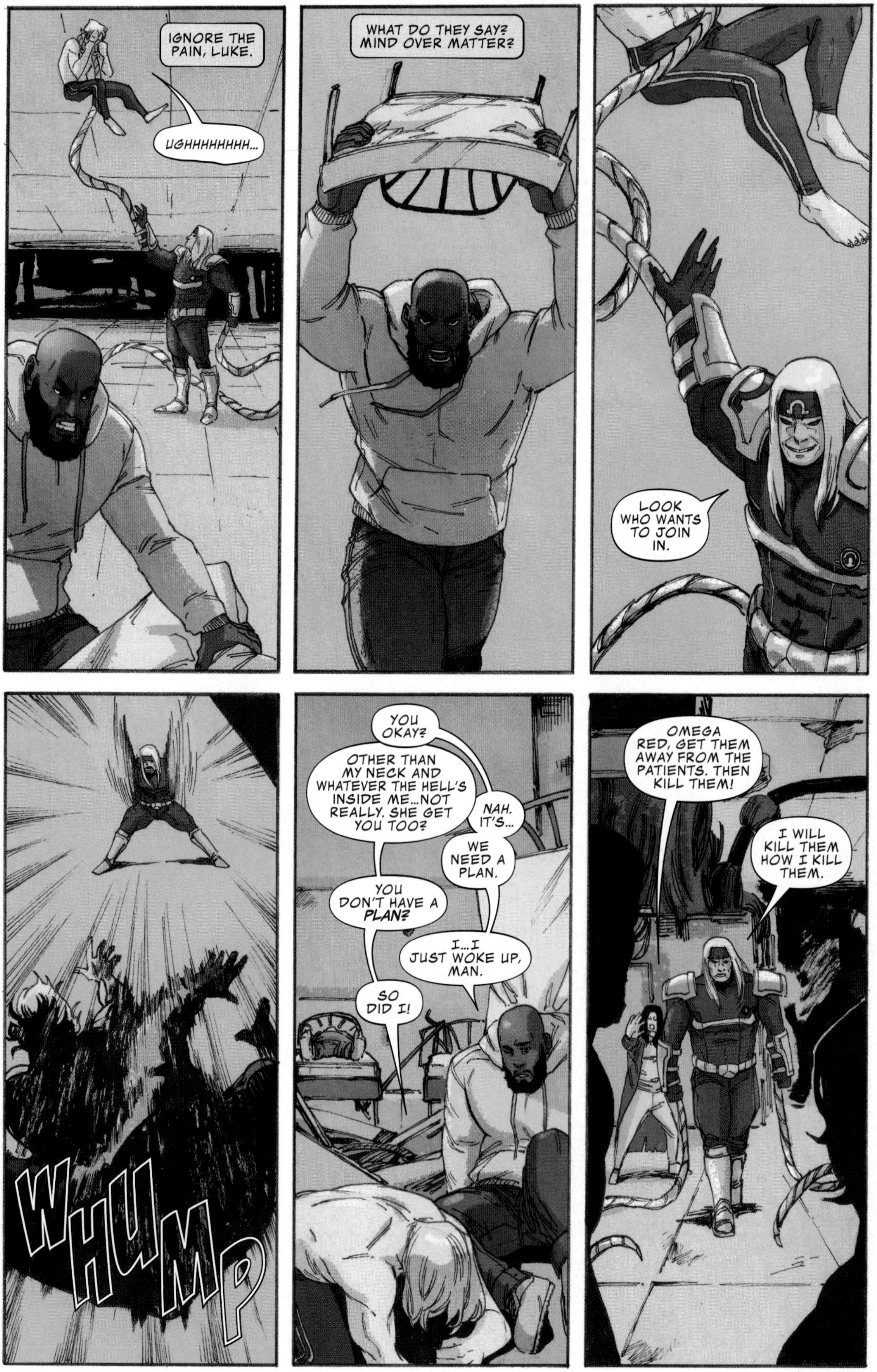
IGNORE THE PAIN, LUKE.
UGHHHHHHHH...
WHAT DO THEY SAY? MIND OVER MATTER?
LOOK WHO WANTS TO JOIN IN.
WHUMP
YOU OKAY?
OTHER THAN MY NECK AND WHATEVER THE HELL'S INSIDE ME...NOT REALLY. SHE GET YOU TOO?
NAH. IT'S...
WE NEED A PLAN.
YOU DON'T HAVE A PLAN?
I...I JUST WOKE UP, MAN.
SO DID I!
OMEGA RED, GET THEM AWAY FROM THE PATIENTS. THEN KILL THEM!
I WILL KILL THEM HOW I KILL THEM.

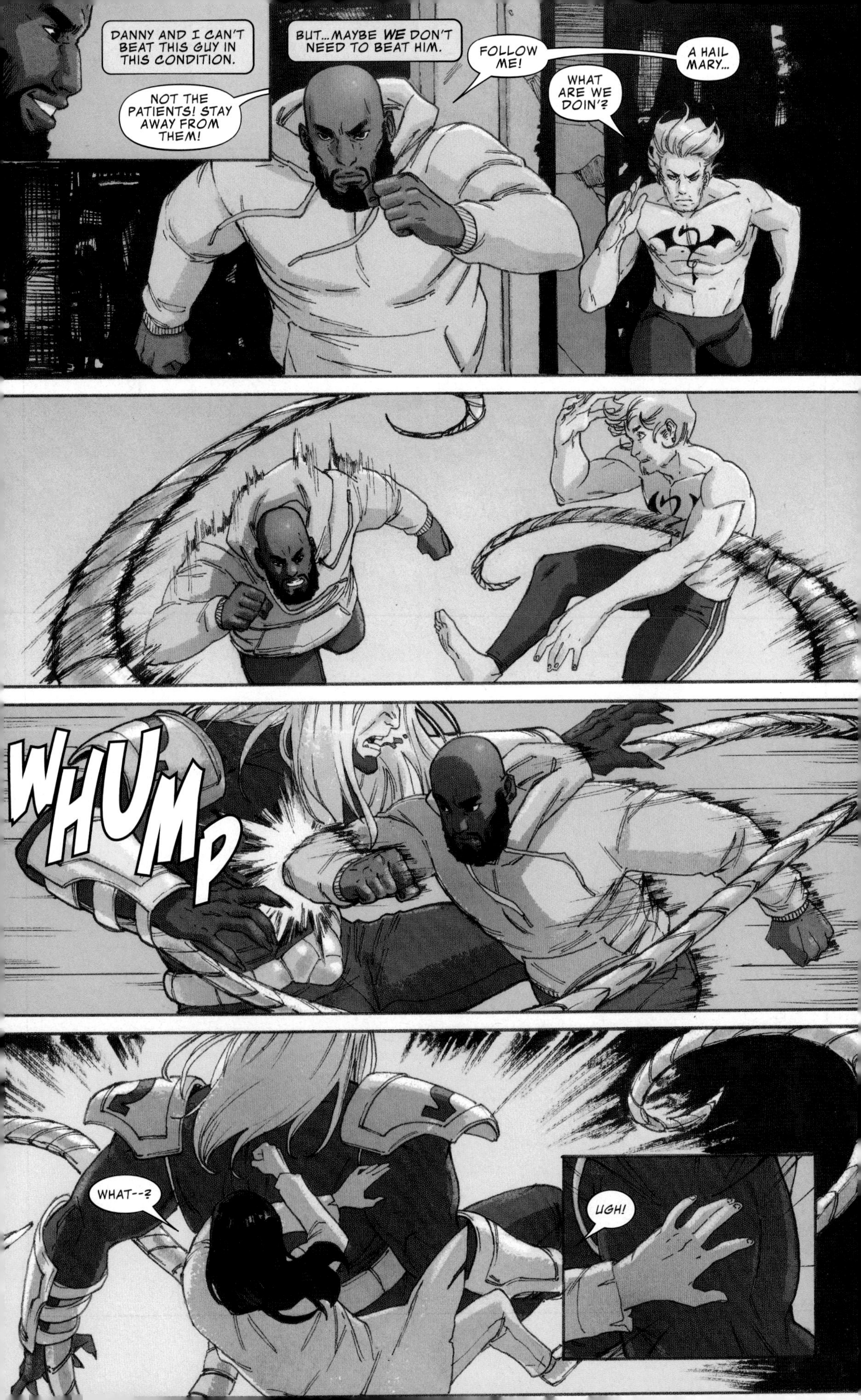
DANNY AND I CAN'T BEAT THIS GUY IN THIS CONDITION.
BUT...MAYBE **WE** DON'T NEED TO BEAT HIM.
NOT THE PATIENTS! STAY AWAY FROM THEM!
FOLLOW ME!
A HAIL MARY...
WHAT ARE WE DOIN'?
WHUMP
WHAT--?
UGH!

YOUR HAND...

I... I DIDN'T MEAN TO...

IT IS NOTHING.

I AM MORE POWERFUL THAN HUMAN.

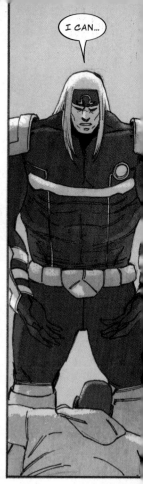

I CAN...

I... UGH.

YOU GAVE ME DISEASE.

YOU MUST FIX ME!

WHAT IS HE TALKING ABOUT?

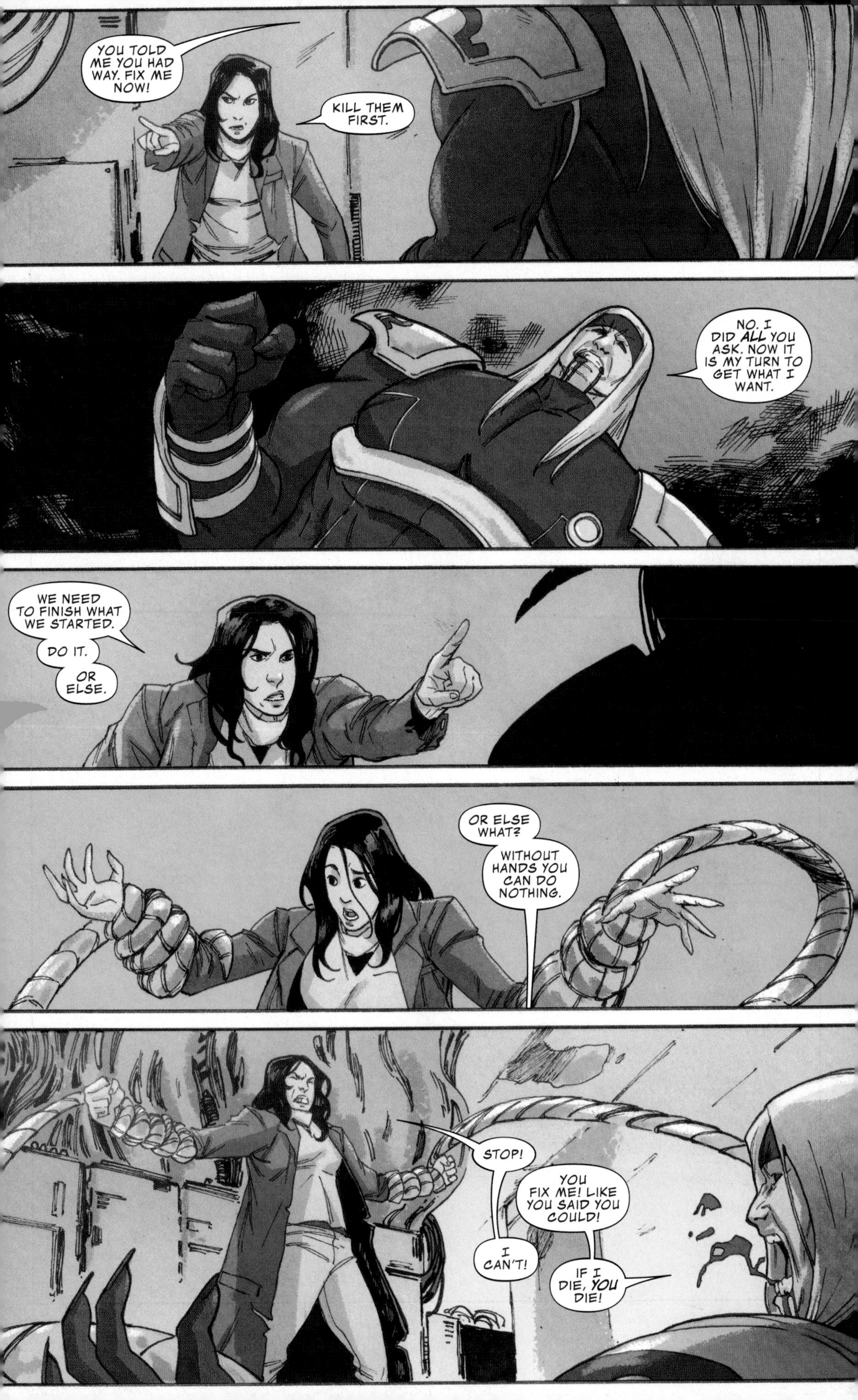
YOU TOLD ME YOU HAD WAY. FIX ME NOW!
KILL THEM FIRST.
NO. I DID ALL YOU ASK. NOW IT IS MY TURN TO GET WHAT I WANT.
WE NEED TO FINISH WHAT WE STARTED.
DO IT.
OR ELSE.
OR ELSE WHAT?
WITHOUT HANDS YOU CAN DO NOTHING.
STOP!
YOU FIX ME! LIKE YOU SAID YOU COULD!
I CAN'T!
IF I DIE, YOU DIE!

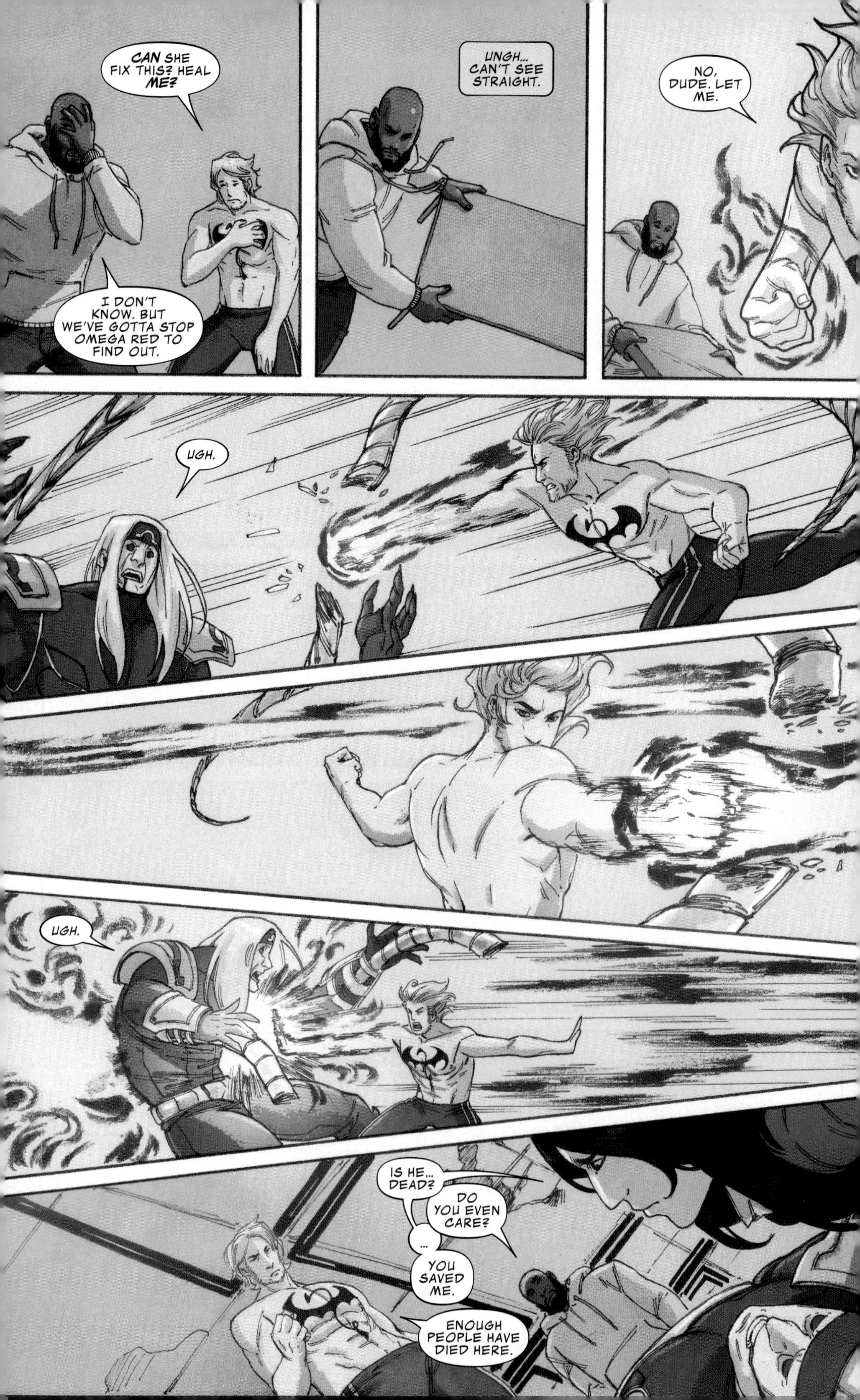
CAN SHE FIX THIS? HEAL ME?
I DON'T KNOW. BUT WE'VE GOTTA STOP OMEGA RED TO FIND OUT.
UNGH... CAN'T SEE STRAIGHT.
NO, DUDE. LET ME.
UGH.
UGH.
IS HE... DEAD?
DO YOU EVEN CARE?
...
YOU SAVED ME.
ENOUGH PEOPLE HAVE DIED HERE.

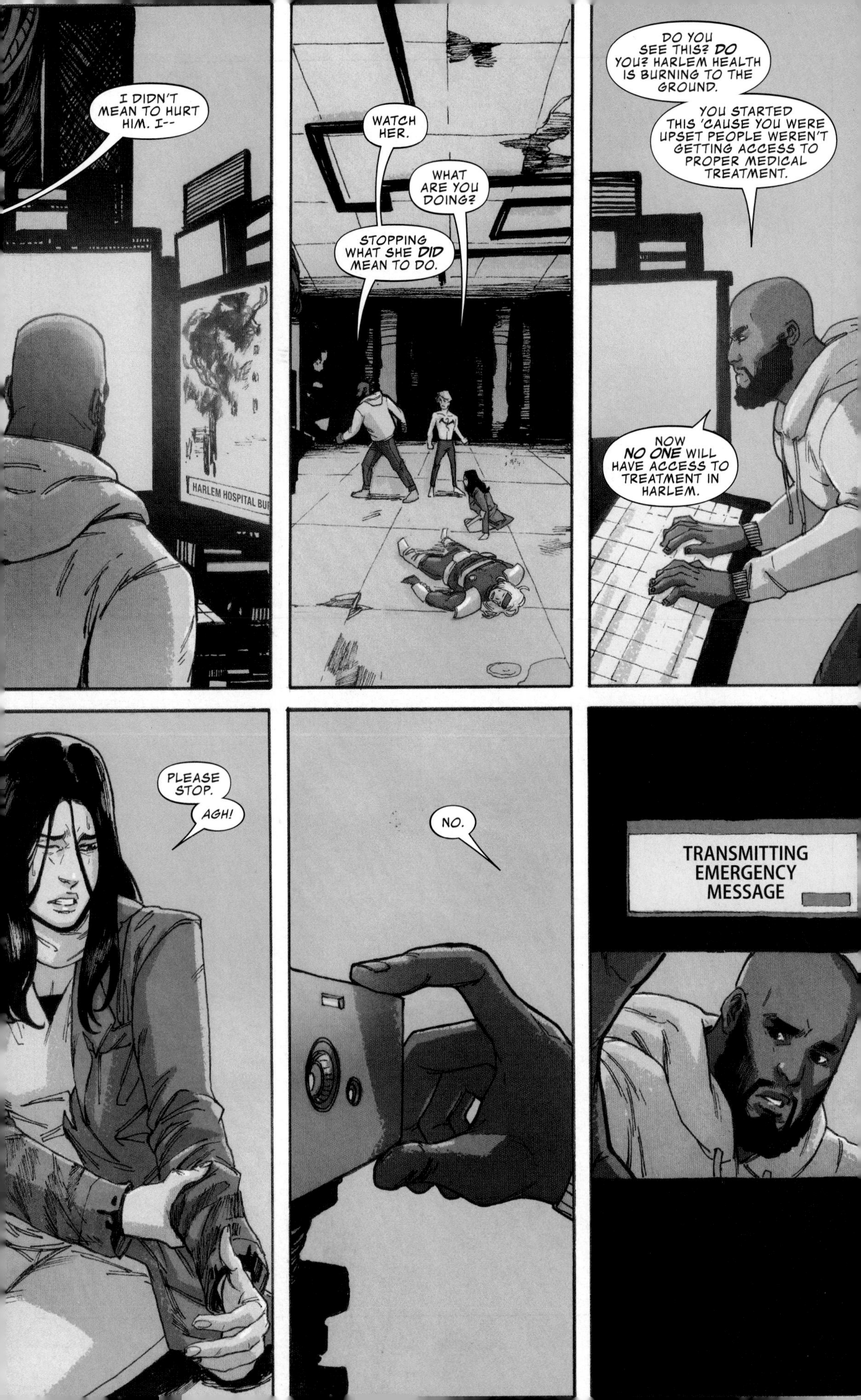
I DIDN'T MEAN TO HURT HIM. I--
HARLEM HOSPITAL BU
WATCH HER.
WHAT ARE YOU DOING?
STOPPING WHAT SHE DID MEAN TO DO.
DO YOU SEE THIS? DO YOU? HARLEM HEALTH IS BURNING TO THE GROUND.
YOU STARTED THIS 'CAUSE YOU WERE UPSET PEOPLE WEREN'T GETTING ACCESS TO PROPER MEDICAL TREATMENT.
NOW NO ONE WILL HAVE ACCESS TO TREATMENT IN HARLEM.
PLEASE STOP.
AGH!
NO.
TRANSMITTING EMERGENCY MESSAGE

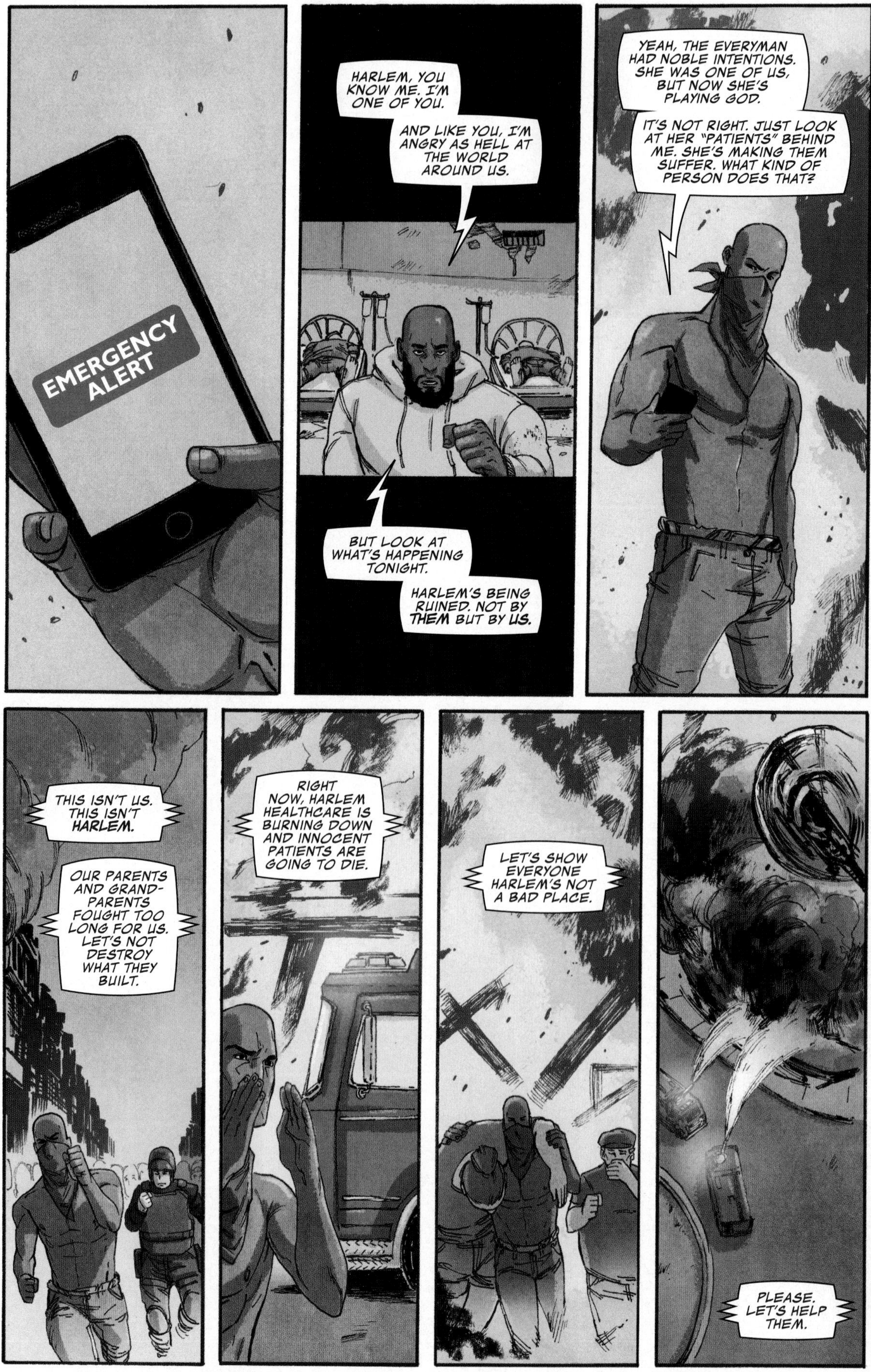
EMERGENCY ALERT
HARLEM, YOU KNOW ME. I'M ONE OF YOU.
AND LIKE YOU, I'M ANGRY AS HELL AT THE WORLD AROUND US.
BUT LOOK AT WHAT'S HAPPENING TONIGHT.
HARLEM'S BEING RUINED. NOT BY THEM BUT BY US.
YEAH, THE EVERYMAN HAD NOBLE INTENTIONS. SHE WAS ONE OF US, BUT NOW SHE'S PLAYING GOD.
IT'S NOT RIGHT. JUST LOOK AT HER "PATIENTS" BEHIND ME. SHE'S MAKING THEM SUFFER. WHAT KIND OF PERSON DOES THAT?
THIS ISN'T US. THIS ISN'T HARLEM.
OUR PARENTS AND GRAND-PARENTS FOUGHT TOO LONG FOR US. LET'S NOT DESTROY WHAT THEY BUILT.
RIGHT NOW, HARLEM HEALTHCARE IS BURNING DOWN AND INNOCENT PATIENTS ARE GOING TO DIE.
LET'S SHOW EVERYONE HARLEM'S NOT A BAD PLACE.
PLEASE. LET'S HELP THEM.

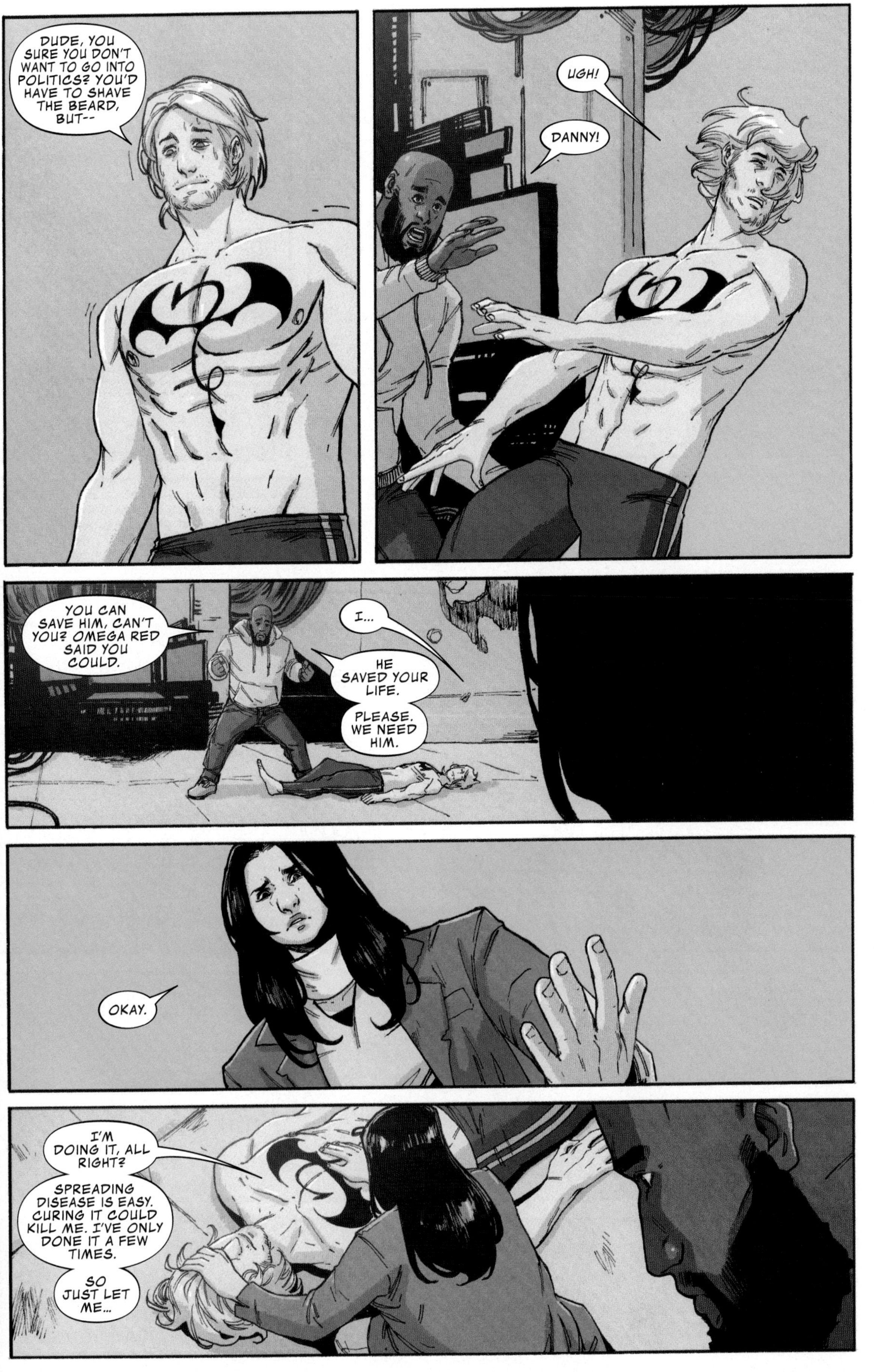
DUDE, YOU SURE YOU DON'T WANT TO GO INTO POLITICS? YOU'D HAVE TO SHAVE THE BEARD, BUT--
UGH!
DANNY!
YOU CAN SAVE HIM, CAN'T YOU? OMEGA RED SAID YOU COULD.
I...
HE SAVED YOUR LIFE.
PLEASE. WE NEED HIM.
OKAY.
I'M DOING IT, ALL RIGHT?
SPREADING DISEASE IS EASY. CURING IT COULD KILL ME. I'VE ONLY DONE IT A FEW TIMES.
SO JUST LET ME...

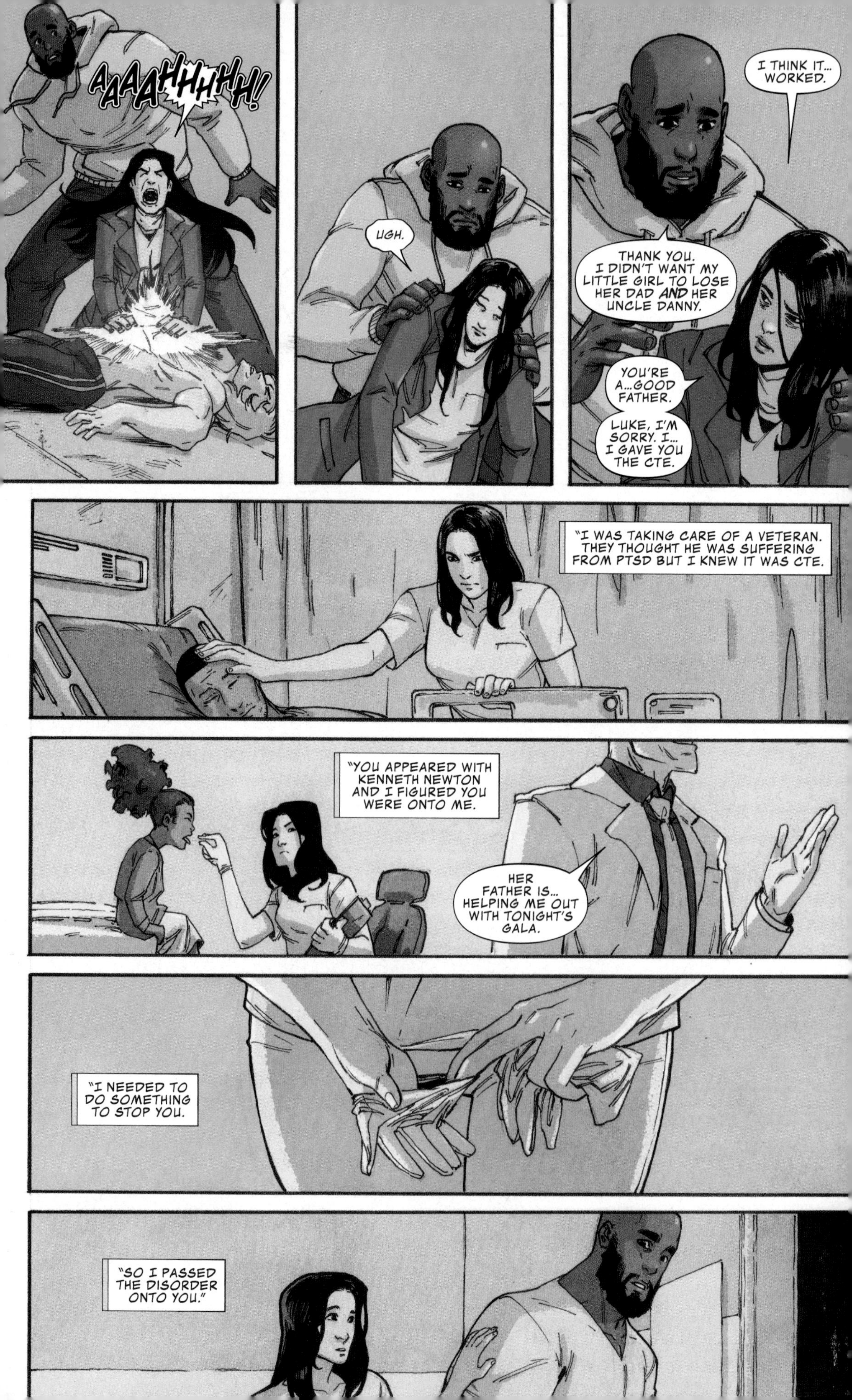

AAAAHHHHH!
UGH.
I THINK IT... WORKED.
THANK YOU. I DIDN'T WANT MY LITTLE GIRL TO LOSE HER DAD AND HER UNCLE DANNY.
YOU'RE A...GOOD FATHER.
LUKE, I'M SORRY. I... I GAVE YOU THE CTE.
"I WAS TAKING CARE OF A VETERAN. THEY THOUGHT HE WAS SUFFERING FROM PTSD BUT I KNEW IT WAS CTE.
"YOU APPEARED WITH KENNETH NEWTON AND I FIGURED YOU WERE ONTO ME.
HER FATHER IS... HELPING ME OUT WITH TONIGHT'S GALA.
"I NEEDED TO DO SOMETHING TO STOP YOU.
"SO I PASSED THE DISORDER ONTO YOU."

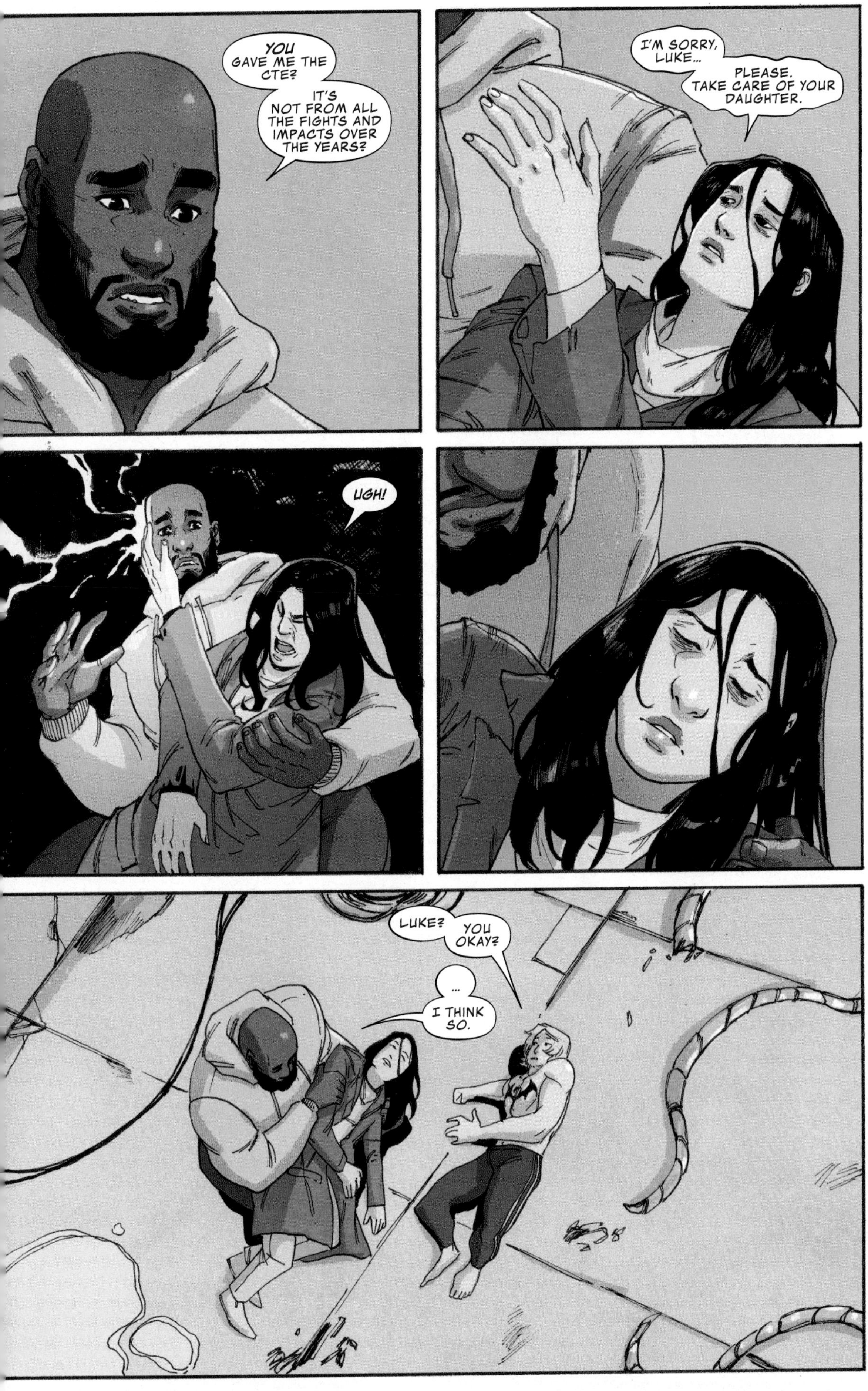
YOU GAVE ME THE CTE?
IT'S NOT FROM ALL THE FIGHTS AND IMPACTS OVER THE YEARS?
I'M SORRY, LUKE...
PLEASE. TAKE CARE OF YOUR DAUGHTER.
UGH!
LUKE?
YOU OKAY?
... I THINK SO.

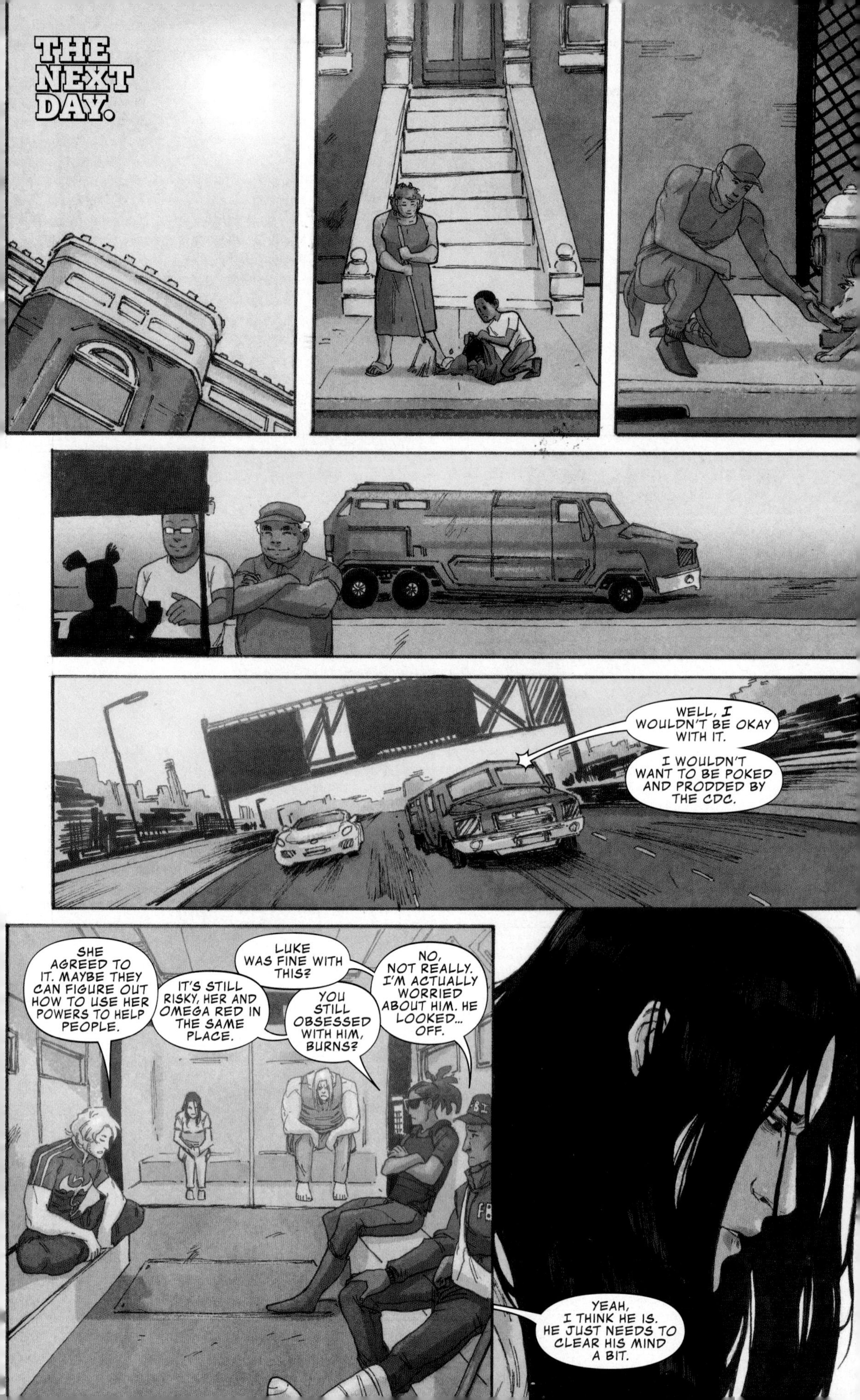
THE NEXT DAY.
WELL, I WOULDN'T BE OKAY WITH IT.
I WOULDN'T WANT TO BE POKED AND PRODDED BY THE CDC.
SHE AGREED TO IT. MAYBE THEY CAN FIGURE OUT HOW TO USE HER POWERS TO HELP PEOPLE.
IT'S STILL RISKY, HER AND OMEGA RED IN THE SAME PLACE.
LUKE WAS FINE WITH THIS?
YOU STILL OBSESSED WITH HIM, BURNS?
NO, NOT REALLY. I'M ACTUALLY WORRIED ABOUT HIM. HE LOOKED... OFF.
YEAH, I THINK HE IS. HE JUST NEEDS TO CLEAR HIS MIND A BIT.

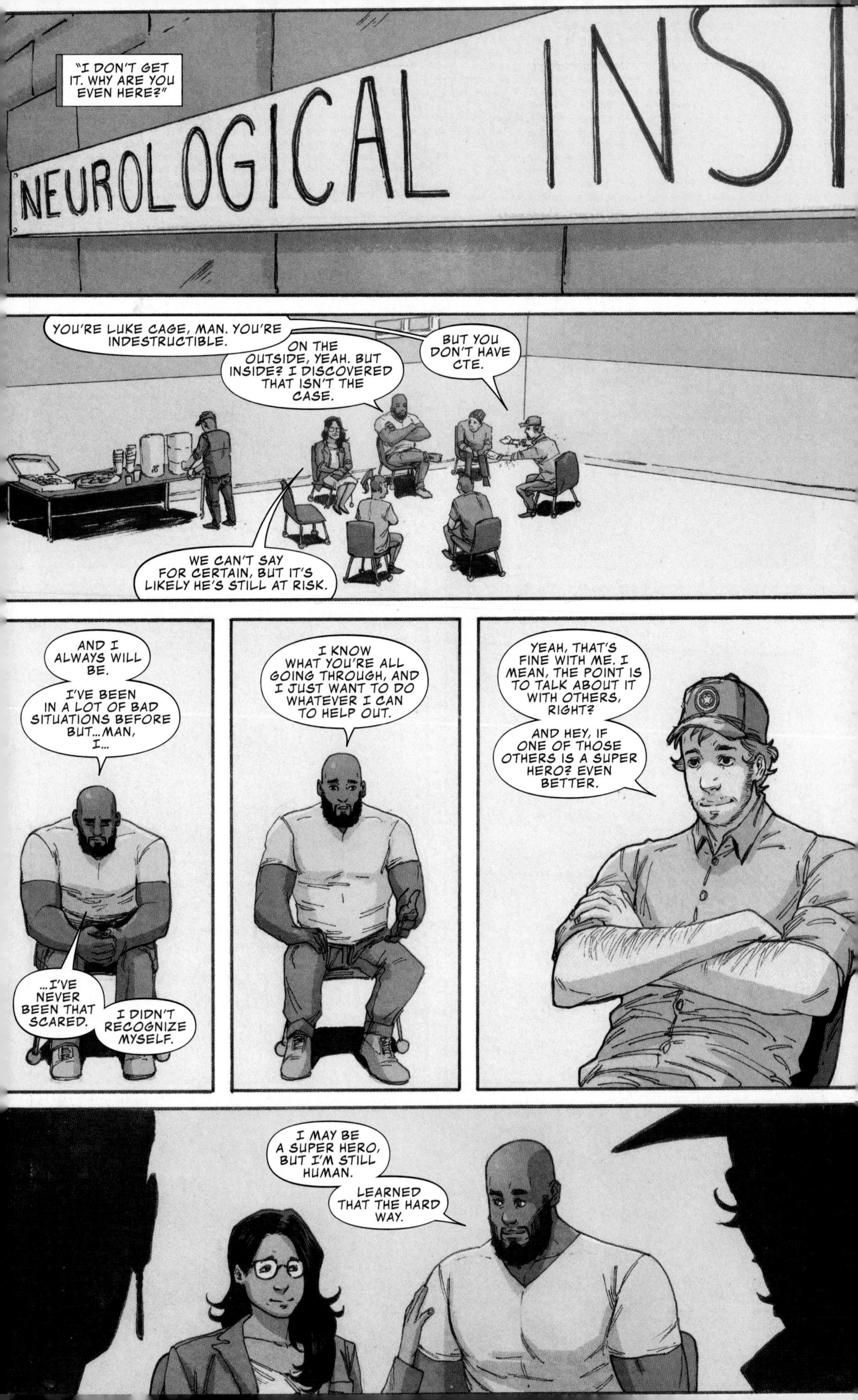
"I DON'T GET IT. WHY ARE YOU EVEN HERE?"
NEUROLOGICAL INSI
YOU'RE LUKE CAGE, MAN. YOU'RE INDESTRUCTIBLE.
ON THE OUTSIDE, YEAH. BUT INSIDE? I DISCOVERED THAT ISN'T THE CASE.
BUT YOU DON'T HAVE CTE.
WE CAN'T SAY FOR CERTAIN, BUT IT'S LIKELY HE'S STILL AT RISK.
AND I ALWAYS WILL BE.
I'VE BEEN IN A LOT OF BAD SITUATIONS BEFORE BUT...MAN, I...
...I'VE NEVER BEEN THAT SCARED.
I DIDN'T RECOGNIZE MYSELF.
I KNOW WHAT YOU'RE ALL GOING THROUGH, AND I JUST WANT TO DO WHATEVER I CAN TO HELP OUT.
YEAH, THAT'S FINE WITH ME. I MEAN, THE POINT IS TO TALK ABOUT IT WITH OTHERS, RIGHT?
AND HEY, IF ONE OF THOSE OTHERS IS A SUPER HERO? EVEN BETTER.
I MAY BE A SUPER HERO, BUT I'M STILL HUMAN.
LEARNED THAT THE HARD WAY.

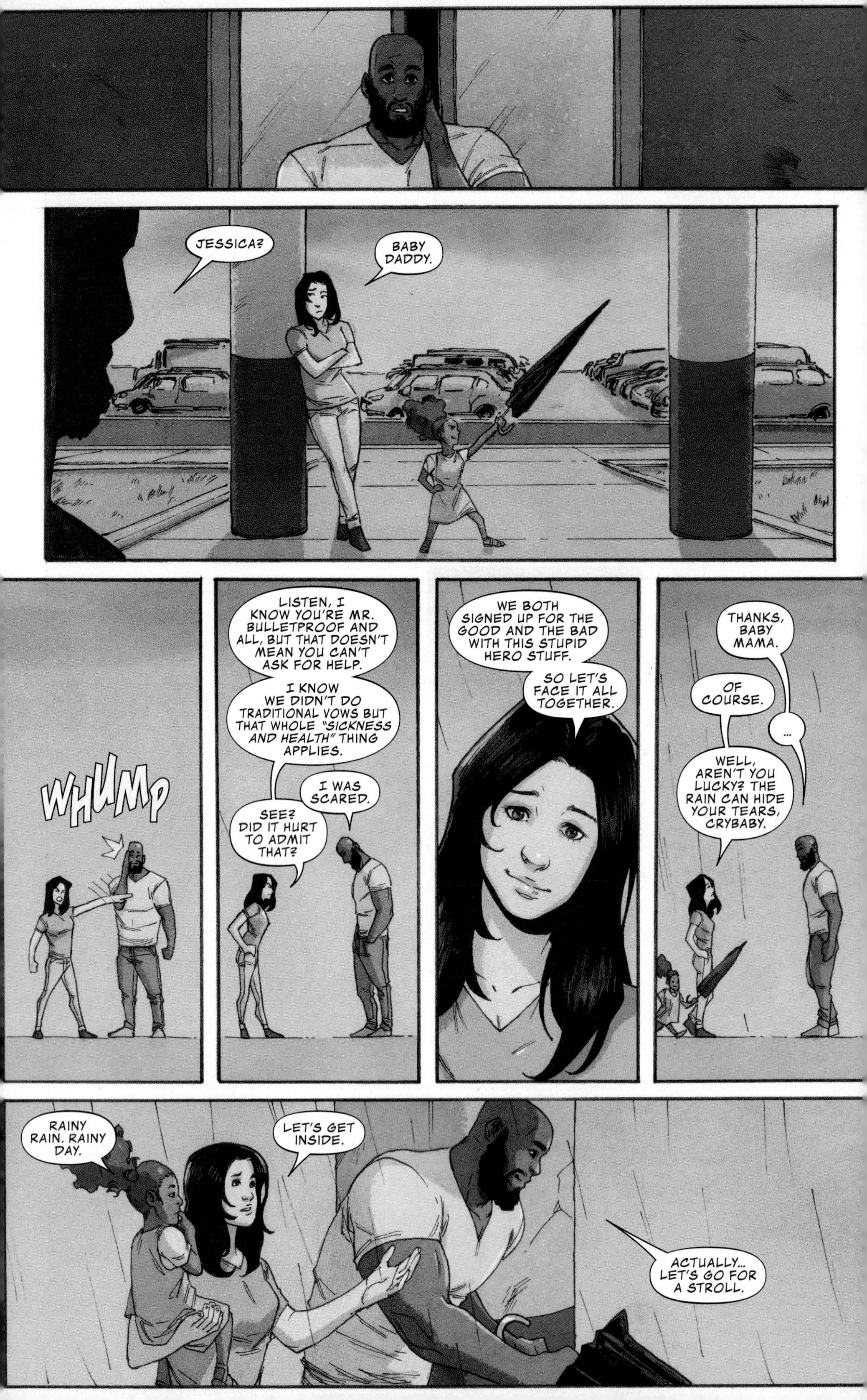
JESSICA?
BABY DADDY.
WHUMP
LISTEN, I KNOW YOU'RE MR. BULLETPROOF AND ALL, BUT THAT DOESN'T MEAN YOU CAN'T ASK FOR HELP.
I KNOW WE DIDN'T DO TRADITIONAL VOWS BUT THAT WHOLE "SICKNESS AND HEALTH" THING APPLIES.
I WAS SCARED.
SEE? DID IT HURT TO ADMIT THAT?
WE BOTH SIGNED UP FOR THE GOOD AND THE BAD WITH THIS STUPID HERO STUFF.
SO LET'S FACE IT ALL TOGETHER.
THANKS, BABY MAMA.
OF COURSE.
...
WELL, AREN'T YOU LUCKY? THE RAIN CAN HIDE YOUR TEARS, CRYBABY.
RAINY RAIN. RAINY DAY.
LET'S GET INSIDE.
ACTUALLY... LET'S GO FOR A STROLL.

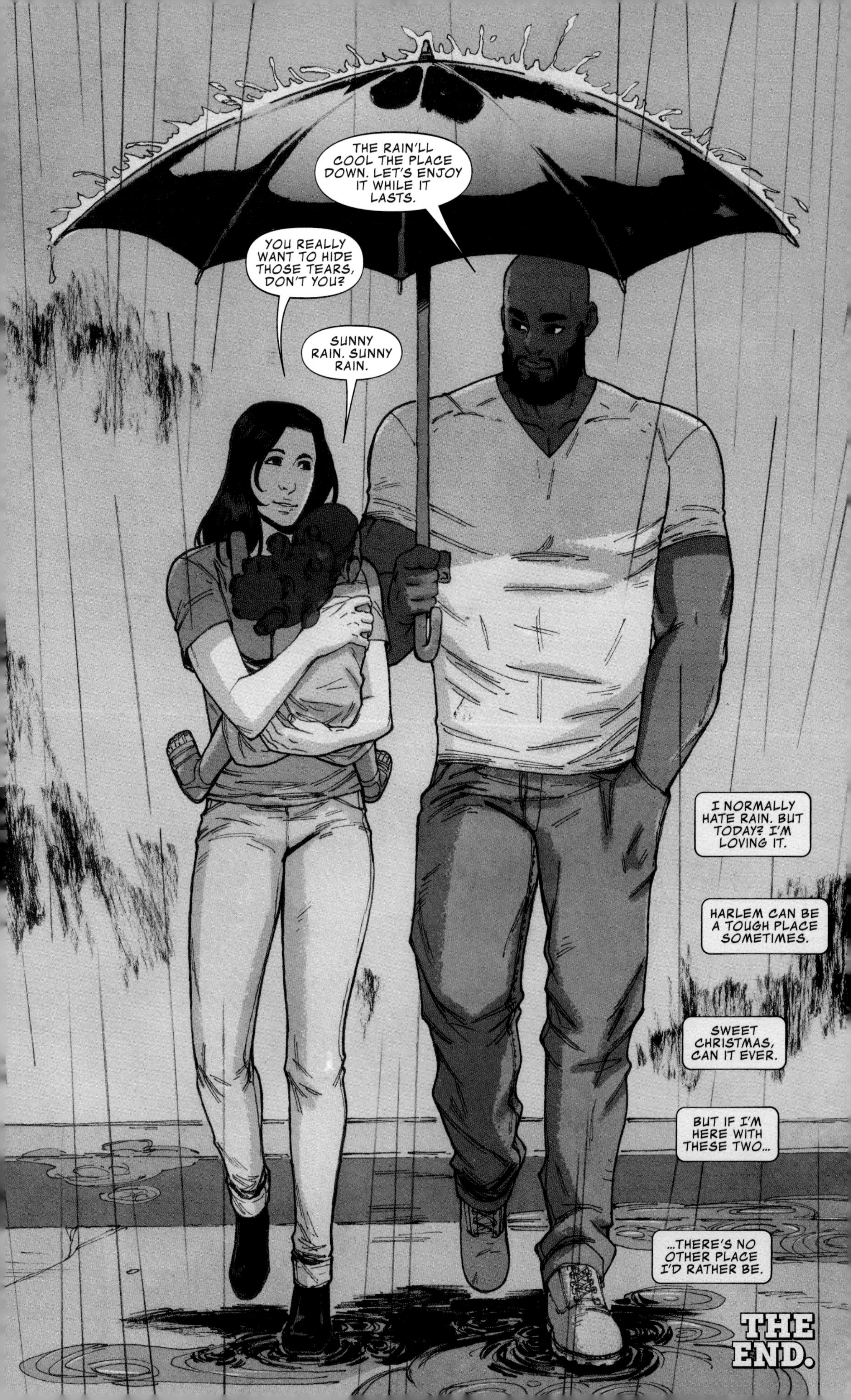
THE RAIN'LL COOL THE PLACE DOWN. LET'S ENJOY IT WHILE IT LASTS.
YOU REALLY WANT TO HIDE THOSE TEARS, DON'T YOU?
SUNNY RAIN. SUNNY RAIN.
I NORMALLY HATE RAIN. BUT TODAY? I'M LOVING IT.
HARLEM CAN BE A TOUGH PLACE SOMETIMES.
SWEET CHRISTMAS, CAN IT EVER.
BUT IF I'M HERE WITH THESE TWO...
...THERE'S NO OTHER PLACE I'D RATHER BE.
THE END.

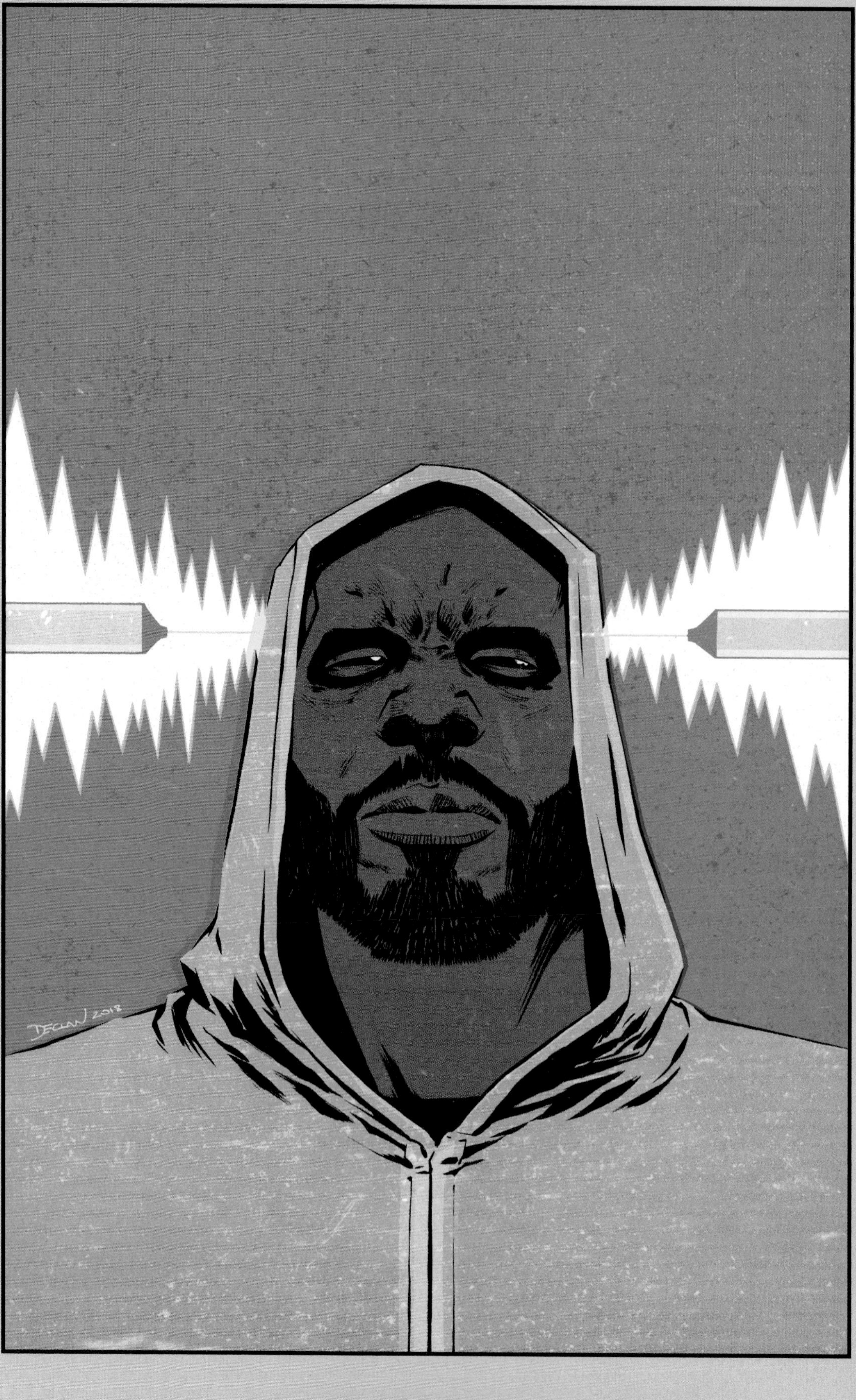
DECLAN 2018

LUKE CAGE: EVERYMAN I COVER

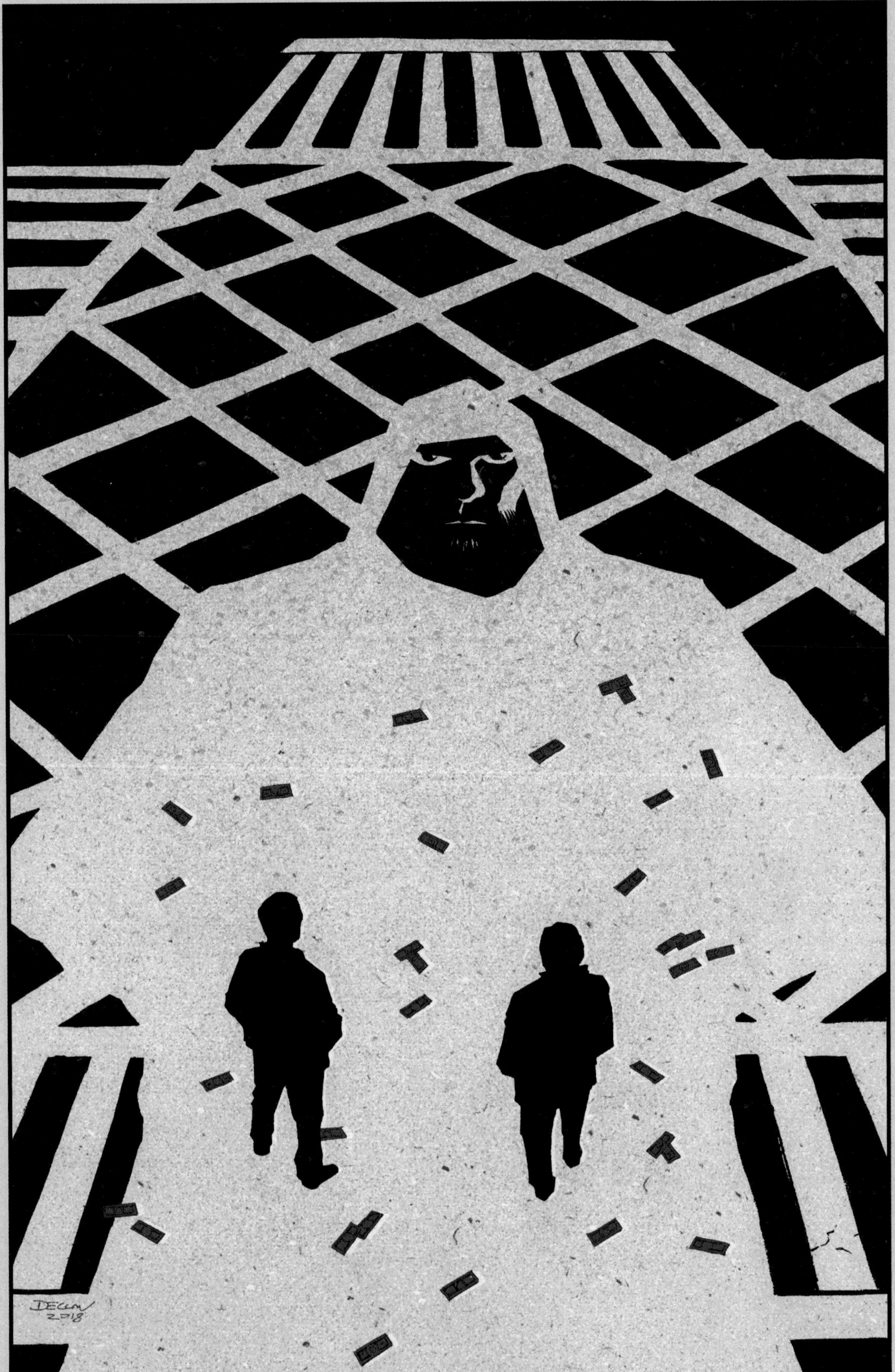
DECLAN
2018

LUKE CAGE: EVERYMAN 2 COVER

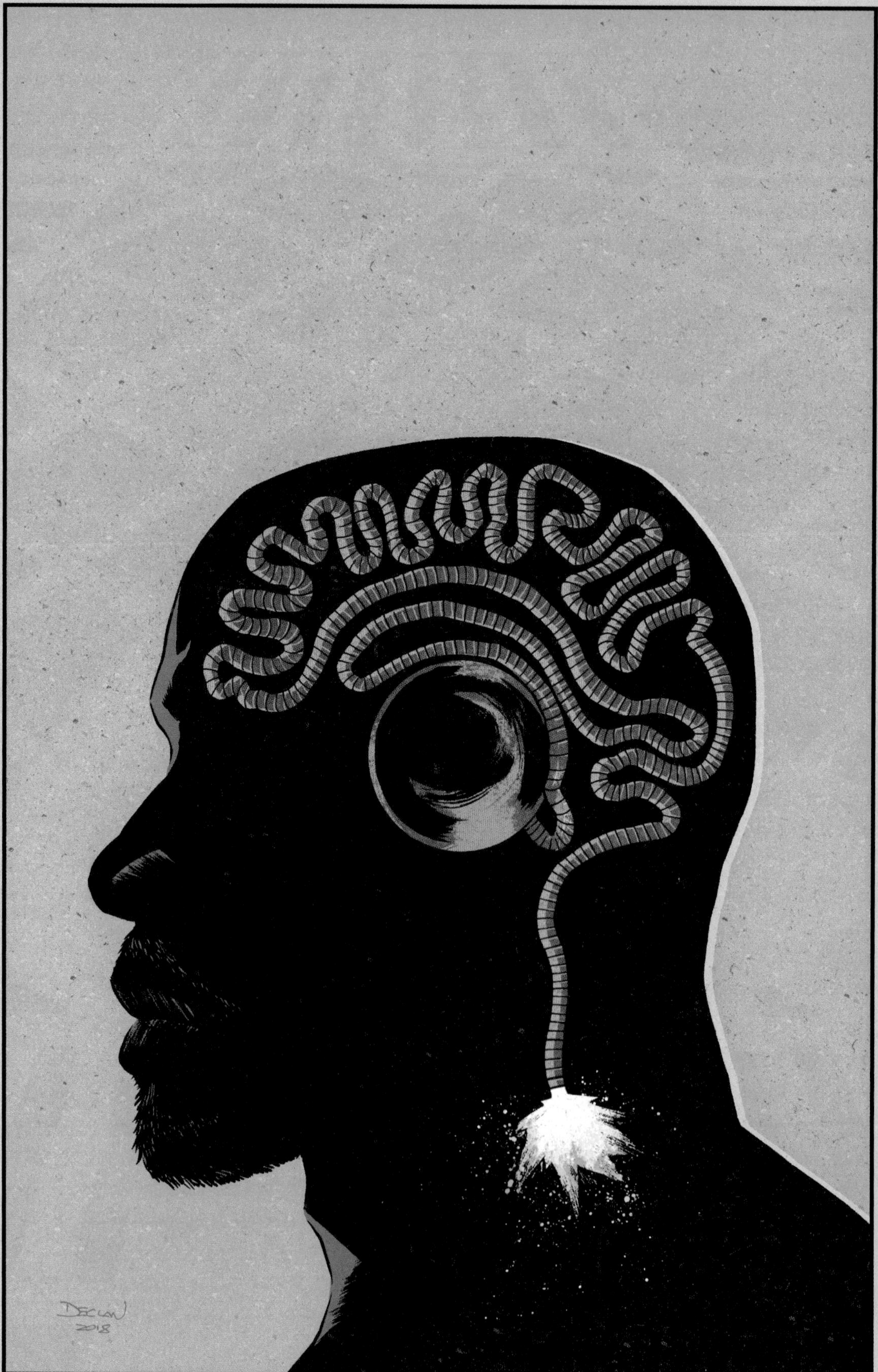
DECLAN
2018

LUKE CAGE: EVERYMAN 3 COVER

LUKE CAGE: EVERYMAN | LETTER FROM ANTHONY DEL COL

As I sit down to write this, I wonder if I'm dreaming. Am I really doing a "Letter from the Writer" for a Marvel super hero comic series (one that I wrote)? And not only that, but a Luke Cage series?

Just checked again. I'm not dreaming.

Wow.

When initial editor Jake Thomas first approached me to ask if I'd be interested in pitching an idea for Luke Cage, I jumped at the chance immediately. And it didn't take me very long to come up with the overall concept.

First off, Luke and Harlem go hand-in-hand. When my wife and I first moved to NYC a few years back, we hopped up to Harlem as soon as we could, and upon stepping off the subway, we thought, "This is Luke Cage territory." So you'll see, as our story goes on, Harlem and the people of it play a big role—perhaps bigger than Luke himself.

Secondly, I'm always interested in characters' weaknesses, and especially super heroes' weaknesses. What can bring down, in this case, a man with bulletproof skin? I realized it would have to be something internal, and that's when the idea of introducing CTE into the Marvel Universe became quite interesting. It's a syndrome that affects soldiers and athletes today (see my Q&A with Dr. Adamson of Stanford) and something that will really challenge Luke over the next four issues.

I'm fortunate to have a great team behind me that's bringing this story to life—artist Jahnoy Lindsay, colorist Ian Herring, letterer Clayton Cowles, cover artists Declan Shalvey & Jordie Bellaire and editors Alanna Smith, the aforementioned Mr. Thomas and Mark Basso.

And finally...thank YOU. For reading this issue and this letter, and for (hopefully) continuing the adventure next month with the next two chapters. Please reach out to me and let me know what you think!

I'm done with this letter now...does it mean it's time to wake up?

Sincerely,
Anthony Del Col
July 2018
Brooklyn, NY

LUKE CAGE: EVERYMAN I Q&A WITH
ANTHONY DEL COL & MAHEEN MAUSOOF ADAMSON, PhD

Anthony: Hello, Dr. Adamson!

When people think of real-life super heroes, they think of people in occupations like law enforcement or firefighting. But I also think of people like you, neuroscientists doing the research into diseases like Chronic Traumatic Encephalopathy (CTE) and doing whatever you can to aid society.

First off, I first became aware of CTE through discussions about football players who have suffered from it, so much so that I initially thought of it as "the football disease." But there are a great deal more people that are affected. Can you tell us briefly what exactly CTE is and who are the people most commonly affected in today's world?

Dr. Adamson: **CTE is a neurodegenerative disease that is associated with changes and deficits in cognition, behavior, mood and motor skills. It is believed to be caused in part by exposure to repetitive head impacts, including concussions, as well as subconcussive trauma. Football players, or anyone engaging in other activities that include repetitive head impacts (soccer, hockey, etc.), can be affected by this.**

Anthony: One of the difficult things about treating CTE is that it can't be diagnosed while someone's alive. I reference this in the first issue of LUKE CAGE, but are there new methods of helping researchers and doctors diagnose those that may be in the early stages?

Dr. Adamson: **At this time, diagnosis of CTE may only be determined by postmortem neuropathological examination. There are ongoing studies, especially in the field of advanced neuroimaging, that hold promise.**

Anthony: What are some of the major symptoms of CTE?

Dr. Adamson: **CTE is believed to be associated with a variety of behavioral, emotional, cognitive and motor function symptoms. Emotional and behavioral symptoms include mood swings, disinhibition, paranoia, irritability, violent outbursts and impulsiveness. Cognitive symptoms include confusion, decreased attention and concentration, memory impairment, executive dysfunction, language impairment and visuospatial difficulties. Motor function symptoms include tremor, mild imbalance, eventual gait or limb ataxia, spasticity and Parkinsonism. As of yet, there have not been any prospective studies linking CTE to specific clinical signs, symptoms or behaviors in living persons.**

Anthony: For years I used to read (in books, articles, etc.) about soldiers returning from the war who were "shell-shocked." Would those soldiers now be presumed to have CTE? What would the difference be?

Dr. Adamson: **It has been suggested that blast exposure may be a risk factor for developing CTE. There are some recent reports from military populations where patients have died with CTE, but these findings have not been validated and are controversial.**

Anthony: Since we are in the pages of a comic book, I would be remiss to not ask a question or two about them. I know that your son is a big fan of comics, but do you have a favorite super hero?

Dr. Adamson: **Hulk.**

Anthony: If you had a super hero power, what would it be, and why?

Dr. Adamson: **I'd want to have super nanovision capabilities that can visualize where the cellular dysfunction is in any living body and target energy to fix it instantaneously without causing a cascade of inflammation.**

Anthony: Maybe I'm a bit of a science geek but I think that's one of the coolest powers anyone could have! Thanks so much for this chat!

LUKE CAGE: EVERYMAN 2 Q&A WITH ANTHONY DEL COL & JAHNOY LINDSAY

Anthony: Jahnoy! I'm really excited to have a chance to do a short Q&A with you. I'd love for it to be a longer one, but we've only got one page. Damn those editors and their page restrictions. [Editor's note: Never work with Anthony again...]

So first off, your work on the series has been amazing. Better than I could have imagined, in fact. It's been great having you bring Luke, Iron Fist, Omega Red, the Everyman, Danielle and others to life. But since you're a fellow Canadian, I'll start with a softball question: What page for this double issue do you like the most?

Jahnoy: **It definitely has to be page 4 (Luke kicking ass through the entire building)! It was a little intimidating at first when I saw it in the script, but I had a lot of fun composing that top-down view.**

Anthony: I really like that page! After having worked with you for a couple issues I figured I'd try to come up with something different for that sequence. This is your second book with Marvel now. Besides LUKE and SHE-HULK (your other book), what is your favorite Marvel character? Which one would you KILL to draw one day?

Jahnoy: **My favourite characters are Ms. Marvel and Storm, so I'd love a chance to draw either of them.**

Anthony: Aww...you ARE Canadian! You put a "u" in favorite! I miss doing that. Speaking of pasts, let's go into yours: When do you first remember falling in love with illustration? And when did you think you could make a living at it?

Jahnoy: **Thinking about it now, I don't remember ever falling in love with illustration, it's just always been apart of my life. And pretty recently, honestly. Despite how long I've been drawing, getting the opportunity to work with Marvel has been pretty validating.**

Anthony: Especially considering how young you are (spoken by an older writer...). And I know it's a cheesy question, but: Who are your favorite artists of all time?

Jahnoy: **Masashi Kishimoto, Takeshi Obata, Akira Toriyama.**

Anthony: I can definitely see the influence of Obata in your work! But no Canadian artists? Well, I guess I should induce one final bit of CanCon into this interview...who's your favorite Canadian of all-time (non-comics)? An actor, politician, athlete, family member, etc.?

Jahnoy: **I'm a bit embarrassed to say, but I think it's Drake. I'm definitely not the biggest fan of his music, but I've got to give credit where it's due: The guy is on an incredible run right now.**

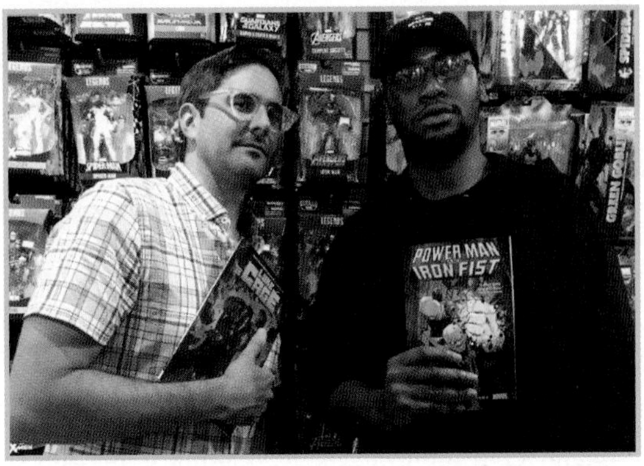
POWER MAN
IRON FIST

Anthony: I can't argue with that statement. The next time we chat I'll tell you about my experiences working in the music industry and seeing him in the offices when he was still "that guy from *Degrassi*." Well, I hope that one day soon you'll be known as the Drake of the comics industry!

LUKE CAGE: EVERYMAN 3 Q&A WITH
ANTHONY DEL COL & IAN HERRING

Anthony: Ian! It was almost ten years ago that you and I found ourselves starting out in the comics industry and working together on *Kill Shakespeare*…and here we are bringing Luke Cage, Iron Fist and others to life in this series. I was so excited when editors Alanna Smith and Jake Thomas suggested you for the series, and it's great to be working with you again!

So I guess I'll begin with an easy, softball-esque question for you: What's the hardest part of the coloring process (other than dealing with quirky writers like myself and Q&As overseen with said quirky writers…)?

Ian: Deadlines. Juggling and hitting them. Even when a book runs like clockwork, they can overlap with another project and there's only so much time in a day.

Anthony: I'd like the reader to note that I actually sent you these questions in the midst of two looming deadlines, so thanks so much for obliging us… You've been at Marvel now for a number of years, and worked on some of its top series. What's the most challenging part of working on Marvel series?

Ian: First issues (of every series) are always the most challenging. A lot of the time, it's working with new writers and new artists, and their own expectations for the book. The first issue sets the tone for the rest of the publication, leaving you to react to the next parts based on the choices you made. Once it's out in the world, you can't bring it back.

Anthony: In LUKE CAGE: EVERYMAN we find ourselves in the middle of a heat wave. How do you like to capture this vibe through your work?

Ian: A lot of this was completed in my old studio that lacked air conditioning during our own heat wave in Toronto. I was laughing and shaking my fist at you for writing that!

Anthony: You're a method colorist…I like it! As a proud Canadian I think I'm legally required to ask the following: You're a fellow Canadian comics creator, working in Toronto (at the acclaimed RAID Studios). What is it about Toronto that breeds such amazing comics talent?

Ian: I like it a lot and chose to move here from a small town. It's a large city with a lot of variety, but I haven't figured out why so many people gravitate here specifically. I think the presence of all the great artists in the city pull in more each year.

Anthony: Of all the comics (or even books) that you've ever read, what is the most influential one? Something that you'd recommend for all colorists (or aspiring colorists) to read?

Ian: I would definitely list both *Beauty* as well as *Miss Don't Touch Me* by Hubert/Kerascoët. I can't look at them enough.

Anthony: If I admit I haven't read those—does that mean that Marvel will never hire me again?

Ian: Not sure about that, but I'll take it personally if you don't order them after reading this.

Anthony: Wow. Our friendship is now on the line! I can respect that. Thanks so much for answering these questions. Now get back to your non-AC studio and get working again— more deadlines to hit!